THE REVOLT AGAINST REASON

THE REVOLT
AGAINST REASON

BY

ARNOLD LUNN

EYRE & SPOTTISWOODE
LONDON

*This book, first published in 1950, is printed in Great Britain
for Eyre & Spottiswoode (Publishers) Ltd., 15 Bedford Street,
London, W.C.2, by Hunt, Barnard & Co. Ltd., Aylesbury, Bucks.*

TO

DOUGLAS JERROLD

CONTENTS

INTRODUCTION

WHEN my publishers asked me to revise and enlarge *The Flight from Reason*, I re-read the book and realised that my knowledge of the subject in 1929 might well have suggested to *The Times* reviewer a comparison with David's smooth pebbles. I felt that I made good use of the pebbles and that my thesis was sound, but twenty years of concentrated reading on these subjects, though they have not modified my conclusions, have enabled me, I hope, to state them in greater detail and with greater force. Some passages from the old book are included in *The Revolt against Reason*, but the new material in this book is greater in volume than the whole of the first edition of *The Flight from Reason*. This is to all intents and purposes a new book on an old theme.

Twenty years ago when I wrote *The Flight from Reason* the attack upon reason was still camouflaged, and the behaviourists, existentialists and logical positivists had not yet crowded the old-fashioned Victorian rationalists off the centre of the stage. These later manifestations of irrationalism have one thing in common, the tacit abandonment of all attempt at reasoned refutation of Christianity. The Victorian atheists were made of sturdier stuff. They appealed to reason because they were confident of their ability to refute Christianity by reason and to defend their own position by rational arguments. The modern atheist has no such confidence. He is uneasily aware of the fact that the tide is turning against him, and that the old-fashioned scientific materialism of the nineteenth century is rejected by most of the leading scientists of modern times. Whether materialism is still defensible may be a question of opinion. That it is not in point of fact defended is a question of fact, for the essence of a valid defence is a clear statement of the strongest arguments of your opponent as a preliminary to their refutation. By this test materialism fails, for modern atheists make no attempt to meet the argument which deprives the materialists of any claim to consideration, the argument that if materialism be true, our thoughts are the mere by-product of material processes uninfluenced by reason. Hence, if materialism be right, our thoughts are determined by irrational processes and therefore the thoughts which lead to the conclusions that materialism is right have no relation to reason.

The same argument invalidates Freudianism, behaviourism and logical positivism. All that the prophets of these cults have achieved is to provide their disciples with reasons for rejecting all philosophies, including Marxism, behaviourism, Freudianism and logical positivism.

The reluctance of modern materialists to face this basic criticism of all modern forms of materialism explains the revolution in their methods. Their predecessors did not shrink from controversy but the failure of nerve which demoralised the modern secularists finds expression in the haste with which they scuttle out of the controversial arena and instead of arguing, invent pretexts for *not* arguing. Logical positivism is a case in point, for the attraction of this panacea is that the logical positivists have been very busy inventing good reasons why they should not be called upon to offer good reasons in support of their particular brand of scepticism. If propositions can be classified as "meaningful" or "meaningless" according to an arbitrary criterion, it is easy to relegate to the "meaningless" category those propositions which you are incapable of refuting. Mr. H. G. Wells was, I think, among the first to insist that every separate thing is "unique", and that there are no categories at all, a thesis which is very welcome to the modern nihilist.

In the beginning was the Logos and the Logos was with God and the Logos was God. "Word" is an inadequate translation of "logos", by which St. John meant something not unlike that divine intelligence which the later Greek philosophers worshipped. The revolt against the Logos finds expression not only in the revolt against reason, but also in the revolt against beauty in morals and in art, for truth, beauty and holiness are all aspects of the divine, and the repudiation of one aspect of the divine inevitably leads to the repudiation of the other aspects. It is reason alone which can guarantee the integrity of an objective code of morals, which fallen man is always tempted to adapt and remould in accordance with his subjective desires. It is therefore no accident that Martin Luther, who initiated the modern revolt against reason should have been so ambiguous in his moral teaching. Whether the anti-rationalism of Hitler is derived from Luther is a question of opinion, but it is certain that the anti-rationalism of nazism and communism leads inevitably to Belsen and Dachau, and to the slave camps of Soviet Russia. There is an obvious relationship between the principle that whatever assists a country such as Germany is moral, and the principle that whatever is in the interests of the proletariat is moral. In most cases the rejection of an objective code of morality is the true cause of atrocities so infamous that their cumulative effect has been to destroy one great heresy of the nineteenth century, the belief in the perfectibility of man and the inevitability of human progress. Again, it is no accident, as I have tried to show in the appropriate chapter, that Mr. Herbert Read, the apostle of surrealism, should have stressed its Marxist affinities, for both surrealism and marxism are by-products of anti-rationalism. Anti-rationalism is inevitably the enemy not only of religion and morality, but also of science. In the early centuries the church made one historic blunder, and one only, in its treatment of scientists, the notorious case of Galileo. The Marxist revolution in Russia, which exploited the prestige of science in the endeavour to dethrone God has ended in a general persecution of all scientists who do not conform to Marxist dogma. There is no reason to suppose that the persecution described in Chapter XVIII of this book have not increased in intensity.

Many chapters of this book are devoted to the great heresy of the nineteenth century, the doctrine of mechanistic evolution. Whether the body of man be descended from simpler forms of life is a relatively unimportant question, infinitely less important than the question as to whether the origin of life on this planet and the development of species can be explained within the framework of natural law without invoking supernatural creative power. It is a paradox of the present situation that whereas mechanistic evolution finds fewer and fewer supporters among the scientific elite, the man in the street still talks the language of the nineties, still believes in the reality of a conflict between religion and science, and still considers that those who reject Darwinism, a term which is popularly used as an equivalent of "evolution", are only fit to be classified as people who believe that the earth is flat. Spengler, one of the most stimulating thinkers of this century, was certainly no Christian, and was indeed hardly a theist in the conventional sense of that term, but he was quick to discern a change of mental climate, and to foresee the coming collapse of materialism. "Materialism, Monism and Darwinism," he wrote in *The Decline of the West*, "which stirred the best minds of the last century to such passion, have become the world view common to country cousins". There is an inevitable time-lag in such matters and it may be fifty years before the man in the street rejects the world view of country cousins, and discovers that materialism is no longer fashionable. Meanwhile, those in search of a "new look" for a moribund philosophy describe themselves as behaviourists in one decade, and as logical positivists in the next. How far I have been wise to devote any space to these ephemeral fashions in thought I cannot say, but I do not regret devoting the greater part of this book to the conflict between science and atheism, and I should be sorry if any potential reader of the later chapters would be deterred from reading them by the earlier chapters in which I have tried to suggest, if only in outline, the historical background to the greatest debate of modern times, the debate between fideists and rationalists. A reader who is uninterested in mediaeval thought should read the first chapter and then start again at Chapter VIII, and for the benefit of such readers it is important to define in this Introduction two terms which are used throughout this book, two words which are, I believe, the key to the greatest of modern controversies.

Catholic theologians describe as fideists those who deny the power of unaided reason to reach certitude, who affirm that the fundamental act of human knowledge consists in an act of faith, and who claim that the supreme criterion of certitude is authority, the ultimate foundation of which is divine revelation. In this book I shall use the words *fideism* and *fideist* in a wider sense than that in which these terms are employed by Catholic theologians. I shall describe as *fideists* all those whose philosophy is a matter of intuition rather than of reason, and who offer no reasoned argument in defence of their basic doctrines. I shall describe as rationalists those who do not base their arguments on personal intuition or subjective experience, but who appeal in support of their creed to reason and to objective criteria.

Catholicism, as is explained in Chapter III, is a rationalistic religion, and the Catholic claims to demonstrate by reason the existence of God, the deity of Christ, and the authority of the church. Anglicans such as Paley, Professor Salmon or Lightfoot are heirs to the rationalistic tradition of the Catholic Church. And it was because they were rationalists in the correct sense of that much abused word that they were able to make an outstanding contribution to Christian apologetics. Lutheranism, on the other hand, is a form of fideism. Luther, as I shall show in Chapter VII, is the father of the modern revolt against reason.

Throughout this book the word "Rationalist" is never used in its popular sense. The nineteenth-century secularists who described themselves as "rationalists" offered no rational defence of their uncritical faith in the supremacy of natural law. They were, in fact, unconscious fideists who rejected without serious examination all evidence which conflicted with their intuitive conviction that modern science had rendered belief in miracles untenable. The Victorian rationalists were, in reality, inverted Lutherans, "justification by faith" rather than by reason being the motive of their negative dogmas.

The thesis of this book is that the tragic bankruptcy of the modern world is the consequence of the revolt against reason. Political remedies are, at best, panaceas for spiritual maladies. Nothing but a return to the rationalism of Christianity can save our disintegrating civilisation from complete collapse.

"Within that household the human spirit has roof and hearth. Outside it is the night."

THE REVOLT AGAINST REASON

CHAPTER I

IN SEARCH OF DEFINITIONS

(1)

"THE success and enduring influence of any systematic construction of truth," writes Archbishop Trench, "depends as much on an exact terminology as upon close and deep thinking itself." "Terms," says Whewall, "record discoveries . . . hardly any original thoughts assume their proper importance in the minds of their inventors until aptly selected words and phrases have nailed them down and held them fast."

It is equally true that the success and enduring influence of a systematic construction of falsehood depends very largely on *inexact* terminology. Both the advance of materialism in the nineteenth century, and the retreat from Christianity were accelerated by the fact that the orthodox were outmanœuvred in the battle of words. The Christians imperilled the whole campaign when they conceded by implication that those who rejected Christianity had the right to describe themselves as "rationalists".

The *Concise Oxford Dictionary* offers a definition of rationalism with which no Christian can quarrel:

"Rationalism, n., practice of explaining the supernatural in religion in a way consonant with reason, or of treating reason as the ultimate authority in religion as elsewhere; theory that reason is the foundation of certainty in knowledge (opp. empiricism, sensationalism)."

Rationalism owes much of its success not only to its name, but also to the folly of Christians who should never have described their opponents as rationalists, thus labelling themselves by implication as anti-rational. The question at issue is not whether reason is to be preferred to unreason, but whether the theistic or atheistic conceptions of the universe is the more rational, in other words whether the theists are right. Equally mischievous in its influence is the misuse of the word "science", and the readiness of too many Christians to admit the reality of the alleged conflict between science and religion.

"Science" is derived from the Latin *scientia*, which means knowledge, and in the Middle Ages "science" covered all forms of knowledge, supernatural and natural, but even if the word be used in its modern popular and inexact sense, and restricted to the knowledge of nature, there is no justification for the loose talk about the conflict between religion and science. On the contrary, it is as true as in Bacon's time that "a little philosophy inclineth a man's mind to atheism, but depth in philosophy bringeth man's mind to religion."

The greatest scientists, with few exceptions, have insisted that nature is not her own explanation, and that natural forces are insufficient to account for the universe in which we live.

"I cannot admit," wrote Lord Kelvin, who was among the greatest scientists of the nineteenth century, "that with regard to the origin of life science neither affirms nor denies creative power. Science positively affirms creative power which it compels us to accept as an article of faith." The real conflict is not between science and religion but between the majority of scientists who believe in the conflict between science and atheism, and the minority who believe in the conflict between science and religion.

The acquiescence of Christians in an inexact and inadequate terminology—inadequate because "no words and phrases have nailed and held fast" the distinction between scientists as such and the sect of scientists who rejected the supernatural—had disastrous results. On the one hand, timid and ill-informed Christians tended to regard science with distrust. On the other hand, thousands rejected Christianity because they had been misled into accepting the reality of the alleged conflict between the science which they equated with truth, and the religion which, so they were assured, could not be reconciled with science.

The battle of words was lost because the Christians failed to invent an apt word to describe the fashionable heresy of the nineteenth century, the doctrine that the realm of natural science is co-terminous with reality, and that it is "unscientific" to believe in the supernatural. The mischievous consequences of a defective terminology are apparent in my book, *The Flight from Reason*. "Throughout this book," I wrote in the Preface, "I have used the term 'Victorian scientist' to describe those who assented to the creed which dominated the outlook of Victorian science." But, however careful I might be to explain that many Victorian scientists were orthodox Christians, and that only a minority were definitely committed to atheism, the use of the words "Victorian scientist" in this particular context implied that the majority of Victorian scientists rejected the supernatural.

Since I wrote *The Flight from Reason*, an unknown benefactor has enriched our language with the convenient word *scientism*. Scientism is the philosophy of those who believe that science confirms the supremacy of natural law, and refutes the belief in the supernatural. Unfortunately there is, as yet, no generally accepted word to describe those who accept the tenets of scientism. Throughout this book I have described the believers in scientism as *scientians*. I do not like this word but have failed to invent anything better, and I hope that those who dislike the word *scientian* as much as I do will not content themselves with underlining my own antipathy but will make some constructive suggestions for a substitute. One thing is certain. The lack of a word to describe the champions of scientism is not only a lacuna in the language but helps to confuse the issue, and thus to handicap the true rationalists in their controversy with the neofideists who have usurped that name.

(II)

Since men first began to speculate about the mystery of life they have followed one or other of two roads to truth, the subjective or the objective. The subjectivists have been recruited from the prophets, mystics and poets. The prophets seldom felt any need to prove that they were the recipients of a direct revelation from God. "Thus saith the Lord" is the only credential which they offered for the authenticity of their message. Mystics and poets are content to report what they have seen or felt. Wordsworth added no argumentative footnotes to his greatest poem:

> "Hence in a season of calm weather
>   Though inland far we be
> Our souls have sight of that immortal sea
>   Which brought us hither."

He offered no proof for the things of which "our souls have *sight*." His certitude was founded on "sight" not on reason.

Subjective experience may be completely convincing to the man who experiences it, but unless reinforced by objective evidence carries no conviction to those who have enjoyed no such moment of illumination. Only one man knew that Christ had appeared to him on the road to Damascus, and, for that one man, the experience was decisive, but what modern sceptic would be converted to Christianity by reading the ninth chapter of Acts? And if there were no other evidence but this chapter we too might be tempted to accept the sceptic's theory that St. Paul's vision was an hallucination due to an epileptic fit.

No argument is possible, as St. Thomas Aquinas fully realised, until you and your opponent have discovered a common premise. "Faith" is not common to the believer and the sceptic, but reason, which from its very nature is impersonal and objective, must be the starting point of rational apologetics. It may be true that no man has ever been *wholly* convinced by reason, but the operative word is "wholly", for the discovery that Christianity can be defended without invoking the appeal to faith has often been the first and decisive factor in the return to the Faith.

It is arguable how far men can be converted by sound arguments, but it is certain that they can be perverted by unsound arguments. Many of the Victorians for whom the loss of faith was a real tragedy would have continued happy in their beliefs had they been aware of the obvious answers to the arguments of agnostics like Leslie Stephen. But most of those Victorians left school not only unaware of the arguments by which Christianity can be defended but even unaware that such arguments exist. In recent years, I am told, the situation has improved partly as the result of Mr. C. S. Lewis's success in popularising Christian apologetics.

Even so, it would probably be more difficult for a Catholic than for an Anglican to leave school unaware of the fact that Christianity can be defended by reason without appealing to faith. However uninterested a Catholic may be in apologetics, and however unable to answer the simplest arguments against the faith, at least he has attended classes in apologetics and re-

tained some dim recollection of the unsuccessful efforts of a
teacher to impress upon him the rational case for his religion.

The knowledge that a rational case for Christianity exists
inspires, even in those who have never taken the trouble to
study that case, a certain confidence. It is not necessary to
handle or even to see the gold reserve upon which a paper currency is based to believe that a banknote is reliable, but it is
difficult to stop the inflation either of doctrine or of currency
once men lose faith in the reserves of reason or of gold, as the
case may be.

It is not, of course, reason which creates the spiritual
appetite of which St. Augustine speaks, that disquiet of the
heart until it finds rest in him who made it. *Fecisti nos at et
inquietum est cor nostrum donec requiescet in te,* and it is not reason
which convinces a hungry man that he needs food, but reason
guides us in the choice of food, and helps us to distinguish
between nourishing food and poison, be that food physical or
spiritual.

It is not only the prophet to whom the Lord has spoken who
invites our assent by the formula "Thus saith the Lord", and
even those who do not accept Father Philip Hughes's criterion
of objective theology will not necessarily disagree with this distinguished historian of the Catholic church when he writes:
"For the mystic especially it is important that theology
should flourish and good theologians abound, for in the guidance which objective theology supplies lies the mystic's sole
certainty of escaping self-illusion."

Gerson, perhaps the greatest religious writer and preacher of
the fourteenth century, "notes actutely as a matter that can be
observed every day, the contemplative's temptation to be his
own guide . . ." and also "how often false mysticism and a
certain looseness about sex morality go together," as for instance
in the case of the beghards whose doctrines were condemned at
the General Council of Vienna in 1311.

The beghards maintained that man, even in this life, can
attain to perfection. When he reaches this stage, he need
neither pray nor fast, for his spirit has achieved such complete
dominion over his senses that he can freely yield to the desires
of his body. Once a man has reached this stage he is emanci-
pated from human authority or from the authority of the

church. "Where there is the spirit of God there is liberty, and the practice of the virtues is a mark of the imperfect man: the perfect soul emancipates itself from the virtues . . . whoever kisses a woman unless led by sexual impulse sins mortally, while no sexual act is sinful if it is done from a sexual motive; such acts are especially free from blame if they are yielding to temptation."

The beghards were the precursors of the antinominians whose revolt against the sexual code was the direct consequence of Luther's revolt against reason, for reason acts as a check on the tendency of erring man to substitute for objective codes with their exacting standards, a code in conformity with his own desires and lusts.

In modern times the cult of irrationalism has nowhere been preached with greater fanaticism than in nazi Germany, and nowhere has the collapse of all objective standards of behaviour been more complete.

CHAPTER II

THE BIRTH OF RATIONALISM

CHRISTIAN rationalism had its roots not in the Old Testament but in Greece. The Hebrew prophets had far more in common with fideists than with rationalists. A rationalist might conceivably introduce his message with the words, "Thus saith the Lord," but only if he were prepared to support by rational arguments three propositions: (1) The Lord exists (2) The Lord has spoken, (3) My report of what the Lord said is accurate.

To the Hebrew prophet it would have seemed a pure waste of time to prove the first of these propositions, for his message was addressed to those who had no temptation to atheism. Polytheism and idolatry were the fashionable errors which the prophets felt constrained to denounce.

Most of the great prophets also assumed that it was quite unnecessary to produce evidence in favour of the second and third of these propositions. One of the rare exceptions was Elijah's challenge to the priests of Baal when he offered to submit his claims and theirs to the test of experiment, the experiment being the ordeal by miracle.

That God reveals himself in the majesty and beauty of the external world is a theme which recurs again and again in the psalms and in the prophets, but it is not until the Jews came into contact with hellenism that we find in their literature the first recognition of the fact that reason alone is capable of inferring from the external world not only the fact that God exists but also some knowledge of his character. It is significant that the dawn of rational apologetics should be found in Wisdom XIII, 5, 8, 9, which was written in Greek by a hellenized Jew.

Humanly speaking, there might never have been a Christian philosophy but for Greece. In Europe there is no philosophy which is not derived directly or indirectly from Greece, even Marxism, for Marx's debt to Hegel is no greater than Hegel's debt to Greek philosophy, but though there was no Hebrew equivalent of Aristotle or Plato, the Hebrew prophets were at home in a realm to which the Greek philosophers did not attain. To the prophet God was revealed. To the Greek, God could only be inferred as a conclusion at the end of a chain of syllogisms. The contrast between Isaiah and Plato is a contrast between vision and inference. The essence of religion for the Jew was that it was revealed. The Greek demanded not that religion should be revealed, but that religion should be explained. "The Jews", said St. Paul, "require a sign and the Greeks seek after wisdom."

Now there is a place in religion not only for the prophet, but also for the philosopher, not only for experience, but also for rational inference. St. Thomas Aquinas realised that no argument is possible until a common premise has been discovered with one's opponent. The prophet never tries to find a common premise for the prophet is not interested in argument.

The essential contrast between the hellenic and the Judaic outlook was the contrast between a people with a passion for hearing both sides of a case fully stated, and a people whose only interest in other people's views was to refute them.

Plato seldom gave complete victory to one side in the dialogues. He seemed more concerned to understand the different approaches to a controversial issue than to defend a particular thesis. Herodotus and Thucydides are at pains to give either in direct speech or in narrative the views of both contending parties.

Christianity owes an immense debt to hellenism, for the art of rational apologetics was a discovery of the Greeks. "Come now and let us reason together saith the Lord," but though Isaiah records this invitation there is no record of the invitation being accepted, as indeed Sir Ronald Storrs pointed out in the story of his own experiences in Palestine. The Greek was, and the Hebrew was not prepared "to reason together", and a whole world of thought and feeling separates, "Thus saith the Lord", from a Socratic dialogue.

It is indeed with a shock of surprise that one comes across St. Peter's "Be ready always to give an answer to every man that asketh you a *reason* of the hope that is in you."

λόγον περι, "a rational account" is a fragment of Greek feeling embedded in a Judaic epistle, for this good classical phrase, almost indentical as Dr. Selwyn points out, with a phrase in Plato, is almost without parallel in the New Testament.

(II)

So far at least as the west is concerned Aristotle may be described as the father of natural theology, that is of the theology which relies for its doctrines on reason alone, unaided by revelation. His system of physics compelled belief in a prime mover who was himself unmoved, and though Aristotle's God is very different from the Christian God, it would be difficult to exaggerate the influence of Aristotle's natural theology on St. Thomas Aquinas.

Many of the rational arguments for the existence of God which are still used by modern theologians can be found in the works of the Stoics. Stoicism was founded about 300 B.C. by Zeno who was born in Cyprus and who taught in Athens. Zeno's thesis which Cicero quotes is still valid against materialistic evolution. *Nihil quod animi quodque rationis est expers, id generare ex se potest animantem conotemque rationis.* "Nothing that is devoid of life and reason can give birth to a rational being" (Cicero quoting Zeno *De Natura Deorum* ii. 8). Elsewhere in the same book (ii. 37) Cicero makes Balbus reject the argument that the universe has originated by chance. "Balbus compares the man who believes that the universe came together by chance to a man who was prepared to believe that if a large quantity of each letter of the alphabet were thrown on the ground they might fall by chance in such an order as to form the Annals of Ennius." Marcus Aurelius, perhaps the greatest of the Stoics, anticipates the great argument from design: "Can order," he asks, "subsisting in yourself be consistent with disorder in the All?"

Christian rationalism had its roots in Greece. Greek rationalism, as Mr. Christopher Dawson reminds us, began by replacing the traditional religion of Greece, and then itself became a religion, a religion which found its ultimate expression in Logos worship, "in the deification of Intelligence as the supreme cosmic principle."

CHAPTER III

THE UNCERTAIN FRONTIER

(1)

THE popular view of the relations between religion and science might be summed up as follows:

"Roman Catholicism is a religion of authority. The Catholic has to believe what his church tells him to believe; Catholicism is, therefore, based, not on reason, but on blind faith. The ages of faith were uncritical, credulous and superstitious.

"The Reformation, a step in the right direction, was the first serious attempt to free reason from the shackles of faith, and to base religion, not on blind faith, but on reason. The attempt, of course, failed, and science, which alone is based on reason, has smashed the half-hearted compromise of Protestantism, just as Protestantism smashed Catholicism."

The popular view is wrong on all points. The reasonableness of Catholicism is, of course, a question of opinion. That the Catholic Church appeals to reason in support of its claims, and does not ask the convert to accept its authority on trust until its authority has been proved by reason, is a question of fact which can be settled by referring to any recognised work of Catholic apologetic, such as Monsignor R. A. Knox's *The Belief of Catholics*.

Medieval theologians, so far from distrusting reason, exaggerated the degree to which pure reason could solve the problems, not only of this world but of the next. The Lutheran Reformation, so far from being an appeal from faith to reason was, on the contrary, a violent reaction against the exaggerated rationalism of the later scholastics and to this day science, as the distinguished mathematical philosopher, Professor Alfred North Whitehead, F.R.S., insists, "has remained an anti-intellectualist movement based on a naive faith."

The Catholic argument may be summarised as follows:

Pure reason suffices to prove the existence of God, many of whose attributes can be discovered by philosophers without recourse to revelation; other facts about God, such as the nature of the Trinity, are not deducible by pure reason, but made

24

known through Revelation. Our next task, therefore, must be to discover whether God has revealed himself to man, and to test by pure reason the credentials of any alleged revelation. We cannot, for instance, appeal to the authority of the Bible unless we have proved by reason that the Bible contains the Revelation of God to man. And to do this, we must apply to the Bible the same critical tests which we should apply to any other book purporting to be historical.

The Catholic maintains that no unbiased reader can study the Bible without being impressed by the nobility of the view of God proclaimed in its pages, and by the contrast between the gods of Greece and the God of the psalmist or Isaiah.

The Old Testament, again, is the story of God's dealing with a particular and favoured nation. We are impressed by the sublimity of its teaching, and by the reiterated message of God's wish to save the world from the consequences of sin. We find scattered throughout its pages recurring hints and prophecies of a coming Messiah, the Saviour of the world. When we turn to the New Testament we find these prophecies miraculously fulfilled. The portrait of Our Lord carries conviction. The evidence of the miracles which he performed is very strong. It is impossible to explain the transformation of the apostles from a broken, dispirited company of disillusioned men into the triumphant evangelists of a gospel which conquered the world, if we deny the Resurrection. There is no satisfactory explanation of the empty tomb other than the Christian explanation. Nobody has ever produced a plausible hypothesis to explain why the Pharisees could not produce the body of Jesus when the apostles began to preach the explanation. No other hypothesis but the Christian fits the facts.

We find, moreover, that Christ declared his intention to found a Church which should endure till the end of time and which should guard his teaching from corruption. The subsequent history of the Church may fairly be described as miraculous, for in spite of its despised origin in a despised race, in spite of the most bitter persecution, it has gradually extended its sway throughout all the western world. The Church again fulfils the rôle which Christ prophesied that the Church would fulfil. It has guarded his teaching from corruption. Heresy after heresy has raised its head in vain against the rock of Peter.

The Church in its nineteen centuries of existence has fulfilled the promises of the New Testament just as the New Testament fulfils the Old Testament.

The true Church again will be distinguished from its rivals by the possession of certain 'notes'. She will be universal, and will claim to teach all nations; she will be one, that is, her members will agree in one faith and will be united under one head. No church but the Catholic Church possesses all these 'notes' nor fulfils all these qualifications.

The Catholic Church is, therefore, the Church which Christ founded. Her most important mission is to preserve from corruption the message which Christ came down among men to deliver.

The Catholic claims that he has proved her credentials without appealing to faith or to authority. "The approach to the Church is," as Father Hugh Pope remarks, "through faith in the Bible regarded as a purely human narrative." But once the authority of the Church is established by reason, it is, of course, rational to accept on the authority of the Church doctrines which reason cannot independently prove or disprove provided that the authority of the Church can first be established by rational proof.

If a martian reached this planet in a martian plane, our first task, once we had contrived to master his language, would be to test by a rational process his claim to have come from Mars. If he could establish his case by reason it would not be irrational to accept on his authority beliefs about life in Mars which the human reason had no independent means of verifying.

Let me repeat once more, that I am not concerned—at least in this book—to argue that the credentials of the Catholic Church can, in point of fact, be demonstrated by rational argument, but only to clarify the contrast between the Catholic rationalism and that distrust of the rational approach which characterises, not only Lutheranism and neo-Lutheranism but also the Victorian sect which usurped the name of "rationalist".

Whether or not St. Thomas Aquinas succeeded in proving the existence of God by pure reason is a question of opinion, but it is a question of fact that a vast gulf separates St. Thomas Aquinas from Luther who, as we shall see in a later chapter, was intemperate in his abuse of rationalism, and also from modern Lutherans such as that distinguished scholar and theologian, Dr. Emil Brunner, who writes:

"From the standpoint of the Christian faith there are two things to be said about the proofs for the existence of God in general. First, faith has no interest in them. The way in which the divine revelation produces the certainty of faith is quite different from that of proof, and it is completely independent of the success or failure of the process of proof. Secondly, the content of the knowledge 'secured' by these proofs is something quite different from the content of the knowledge of faith."

There is only one statement in all this with which a Catholic rationalist would disagree, the statement that "faith has no interest" in the fact that the existence of God can be proved by reason. Such proofs are necessary to meet the pretended rationalist on his own ground and to reassure the Christian troubled by foolish doubts.

Dr. Brunner's disdain for rational proof is mild compared with the angry scorn of Kierkegaard, the great Danish Lutheran, who writes:

"So, rather, let us mock God, out and out, as has been done before in the world—this is always preferable to the disparaging air of importance with which one would prove God's existence. For to prove the existence of one who is present is the most shameless affront, since it is an attempt to make him ridiculous; but unfortunately people have no inkling of this, and for sheer seriousness regard it as a pious undertaking. But how could it occur to anybody to prove that he exists, unless one had permitted oneself to ignore him, and now makes the thing all the worse by proving his existence before his very nose? The existence of a king, or his presence, is commonly acknowledged by an appropriate expression of subjection and submission—what if in his sublime presence one were to prove that he existed? Is that the way to prove it? No, that would be making a fool of him; for one proves his presence by an expression of submission which may assume various forms according to the customs of the country—and thus it is also that one proves God's existence by worship."

(II)

An interesting thesis for a D.D. degree would be a history of Christian apologetics. In the course of centuries the apologetic technique has been developed to meet changing conditions. The emphasis on reason has become more and more pronounced in proportion as those to whom the argument was addressed had become more and more sceptical. St. Peter and St. Paul could take the basic doctrines for granted, the existence of God, for instance, because those whom they sought to convert believed in God, but the modern Christian can take nothing for granted. Just as the great dogmatic definitions of the Church were hammered out in answer to particular heresies, so particular denials evoked new developments in apologetics. Beyond one contemptuous reference to what the fool hath said in his heart, there is no concern with formal atheism, as distinguished from idolatry, in the Old or the New Testament, for atheism is in the main a disease of old and urban civilisations, and the infidelity with which the prophets had to contend was not atheism but idolatry.

Mr. C. S. Lewis has written an excellent book on miracles because he lives in a world in which it is necessary to prove first that there is no *a priori* reason why miracles should not occur and secondly, that the evidence for particular miracles is impossible to refute, but the Pharisees who crucified our Lord would have regarded both these propositions as self-evident. Nay more, they were quite prepared to believe that Jesus wrought miracles and, indeed, tempted him to perform a miracle of healing on the sabbath in the hope that he would succeed "that they might accuse him" (St. Matthew xii, 10). And when he did succeed, instead of accepting this miracle as evidence in support of his divine claims, they "made a consultation against him. . . ."

It is even possible that the Pharisees believed that Jesus had risen from the dead. The brilliant camerilla who engineered the trial and forced reluctant Pilate to convict were not so stupid as to believe the official explanation which was the best they could invent to explain the empty tomb. They knew very well that the disciples had not stolen the body, and may well have reflected that if Jesus could work miracles during his lifetime by the power of Beelzebub, Beelzebub might have worked a supreme miracle after his death.

Be this as it may, the fact that the Pharisees, so far from denying the miracles of our Lord accepted them but attributed them to Beelzebub, may explain the absence from the New Testament of the arguments with which the reality of the Resurrection is defended by a modern Christian. St. Paul and the apostles are content to affirm, but make no attempt to prove the Resurrection. There is no evidence of their rounding on the Jews and asking "What is your explanation of the empty tomb?" Those whom they sought to convert took for granted not only that God existed but also that God from time to time performed signs and wonders.

The second chapter of "The Acts" is an admirable illustration of apostolic apologetic, and the value of this chapter as an illustration does not depend on whether in point of fact those assembled on the day of Pentecost heard every man "speak in his own tongue", and therefore not only the Christian who accepts "The Acts" as historic, but the sceptic who rejects the miracle of the tongues can agree at least in regarding this chapter as evidence of the kind of argument which the author of "The Acts" regarded as persuasive.

Now on what does St. Peter base his argument? On the fulfilment of prophecy and on nothing else. The miraculous gift of tongues was important because it was the fulfilment of what had been "spoken by the prophet Joel". Instead of attempting to *prove* that Christ rose from the dead, St. Peter uses the *fact* of the Resurrection as evidence that Jesus was the Messiah, of whom David was speaking when he said: "Because thou wilt not leave my soul in hell, nor suffer thy Holy One to see corruption." For David was a prophet, and knew that God had sworn to him with an oath, that of the fruit of his loins one should sit upon his throne. Foreseeing this he spoke of the resurrection of Christ. For neither was he left in hell, nor did his flesh see corruption.

Again, instead of summarising the evidence for the miracles of our Lord, he takes those miracles for granted and cites them as evidence that Jesus was "a man approved of God". St. Peter, because he was speaking to Jews who were eye witnesses or friends of those who had been eye witnesses of these miracles, felt no need to *prove* the miracles "which God did by him in the midst of you, *as you also know*."

The casual way in which St. Peter takes it for granted that all his audience are aware of the fact that Jesus worked miracles is a clear indication that even the enemies of the Christians were quite ready to admit that Jesus possessed supernormal powers.

(III)

Apart from the New Testament, the works of St. Justin Martyr (A.D. 150) are the earliest contributions to Christian apologetics, but as he starts from the assumption that revelation is the only source of divine knowledge, his writings would be of little value to a modern defender of the faith. It is not easy to find much of apologetic value in his writings, though indirectly his work, as I have shown in *The Third Day* (p. 92), is important as evidence of the fact that, in the century which had passed since the Resurrection, the Jews had not concocted a more plausible explanation of the empty tomb than the theory that the disciples had stolen the body.

Tertullian, who was born just about the time when St. Justin Martyr was writing, was converted by the silent argument of the martyrs. Like others, he had been impressed by their *obstinatio*, that stubbornness which Marcus Aurelius condemned as perverse. "That very obstinacy which you condemn," writes Tertullian, "should be your teacher". *Illa ipsa obstinatio quem exprobatis magistra est.* And fourteen years later he wrote: "No man beholding that great endurance but is struck by a sudden scruple and on fire to find out the cause thereof, and when he has learned the truth, he promptly follows it himself." *Et ipse statim sequitur.* The saint and the martyr still make far more converts than the mere apologist, a fact which does not dispense those of us who are neither saints nor martyrs from doing what we can to convince the world that there is a rational cause for Christianity.

St. Augustine was perhaps the founder of religious apologetics. "He is the first of the Fathers," writes Harnack, "who felt the need of forcing his faith to reason." On the one hand St. Augustine insists that faith must precede the intelligent apprehension of the truths of revelation but, as Father Eugène Portalie, remarks, it is St. Augustine "who marks out with great clearness of definition and more precisely than anyone else the function of reason in preceding and verifying the witnesses' claim to credence and in accompanying the mind's act of adhesion. What would not have been the stupefaction of

Augustine if anyone had told him that faith must close its eyes to the proofs of the divine testimony under the penalty of its becoming science! Or if one had spoken to him of faith in authority giving its assent without examining any motive which might prove the value of the testimony! It surely cannot be possible for the human mind to accept testimony without known motives for such acceptance."

Among the early Christian apologists Aristides and Tatian made some attempt to defend Theism by rational arguments and though their reasons for believing in God were expressed in rudimentary form they have some claim to be considered as semi-rationalists. They were, however, the exception. Most of the earlier Christian apologists were fideists. In the technical sense in which this term is used by Catholic theologians* a fideist, as I have explained in the introduction, may be defined as a man who denies the power of unaided human reason to reach certitude and who affirms that the fundamental act of human knowledge consists in an act of faith. The fideists, whom the Church condemned, maintained that the supreme criterion of certitude is authority, the ultimate foundation of which is divine revelation. The popular error that the Church demands a blind acceptance of claims which she makes no attempt to justify by rational argument attributes to the Church the heresy of fideism which the Church has repeatedly condemned. In 1348 certain fideistic propositions of Nicholas d'Autrecourt were condemned by the Church, and more recently, on September 8th, 1840, a moderate fideist, Professor Bautain of Louvain, was required to subscribe to the proposition "Human reason is able to prove with certitude the existence of God; Faith, a heavenly gift, is posterior to revelation, and therefore cannot be properly used against the atheist to prove the existence of God. . . . The use of reason precedes faith and with the help of revelation and grace leads to it."

The essence of rationalism, in the proper sense of the word, is crystalised in the statement, "The use of reason precedes faith", but many centuries had to pass before the frontier between faith and reason was clearly defined, and the priority of reason

* May I ask the reader to re-read page 10 of the introduction and to note the more general sense in which the word "fideist" is used in this book?

C

firmly established. Most of St. Anselm's contemporaries, for instance, would have been horrified by the statement that "The use of reason precedes faith." Indeed, St. Anselm, who died in 1109, takes high rank among theologians precisely because he was a pioneer of Christian rationalism. True, he did not distinguish as clearly as the theologians responsible for the definition of 1840 between the realm of reason and the realm of faith. "Ontological argument" is unconvincing, but even if we reject his attempt to demonstrate the existence of God by reason, he must at least be given full credit for making this attempt.

His principal, but not his only argument for the existence of God was the ontological argument. God is that than which nothing greater can be thought. Now that which exists in reality is greater than that which exists only in the mind, therefore since God "is that than which nothing greater can be thought," he must exist in reality.

The ontological argument was severely criticized at the time, and subsequently rejected by St. Thomas Aquinas. A variant of the argument was adopted by Descartes. Leibniz maintained that the ontological argument might be valid with the addition of a supplement to prove that God is possible. Kant rejected it, but Hegel's system had an ontological flavour, and Bradley's principle: "What may be and must be is," is clearly derived from St. Anselm. None the less, as I have already suggested, St. Anselm's importance in the history of theology is not due to the merits of his arguments for the existence of God but to the fact that he was not content to assume that God exists, but made a serious attempt to demonstrate his existence by reason. He did not, however, make any attempt to defend the Catholic creed in detail. He took Catholicism for granted and therefore had as much or as little right to be considered a rationalist as a modern biologist who takes evolution for granted, and, like the modern evolutionist, he used rational methods for the systematisation of the truths which formed the basic structure of his philosophy.

Faith, according to St. Anselm, was not an end but a means, the necessary condition for a deeper understanding to be achieved by the application of *ratio* to the truths guaranteed by *auctoritas*. "I do not seek to understand," he writes, "in order that I may believe, but I believe in order that I may understand. For I believe this because if I did not believe it I should not understand." *Neque enim quaero intelligere ut credam sed credo ut intelligam. Nam et hoc credo, quia nisi credidero non intelligam.*

Rationalism, so St. Anselm believed, was of value for unbelievers, because by the proper use of their reason they might arrive at the truth. 'While they search for reasons because they do not believe, we search for reasons because we do believe."

It is more surprising to find the *farouche* Abelard, by temperament something of an iconoclast, by grace a Catholic, harnessing his passion for dialetics within the framework of revealed doctrine. "I do not wish," he exclaims "to be a philosopher if I must contradict St. Paul, or an Aristotle if I must separate myself from Christ." *Nolo sic esse philosophus, ut recalcitrem Paulo; nolo sic esse Aristoteles ut seculudar a Christo.*

Peter Abelard and St. Anselm wrote before the rediscovery of Aristotle, and their philosophy was neo-platonic, thanks in the main, to St. Augustine who had adapted Plato to Christian dogma. The basic doctrine of the eleventh and twelfth-century scholastics was that true wisdom does not proceed from reason to faith but from faith to reason. The supernatural was so real to them that they ceased to be fully conscious of the natural.

And it was not, as Professor Gilson points out, until Aristotle had convinced the mediaeval mind "that things have a certain existence in themselves" that rationalism could develop. "In one word, there can be no rationalism until nature has reconquered her reality and the natural reason her content."

At the beginning of the thirteenth century the frontier between philosophy and reason was still undefined, and the fact that the credentials of authority, human or divine, must be demonstrated by reason was still imperfectly recognised.

St. Bonaventure of the Friars Minor (1221 to 1274) was a contemporary of St. Thomas Aquinas and died in the same year as St. Thomas. His own philosophy was nearer the rationalism of St. Thomas than the semi-fideism of the earlier apologists. He distinguishes clearly between reason and faith, between what one believes by faith and what one can prove by reason. Reason, he argues, can command assent by an act of violence, but the purely scientific assent to a doctrine is dry and without merit. St. Bonaventure would have agreed with St. Gregory's

Nec fides habet meritum cui humana ratio praebet experimentum—"nor can a man claim any merit for faith in something which can be proved by human reason.

St. Anselm had pointed out that the philosopher bases his argument on the principles of reason whereas the theologian starts from the principle of revelation, but the uncertain frontier continues to confuse the apologetics of St. Anselm and St. Bonaventure, for both of them believed that a rational demonstration of a proposition was possible even if the premises of the proposition were furnished by a revelation, the veracity of which they felt no need to establish by rational arguments. "This confusion", writes Dr. Gilson, "is due to the fact that the distinction between the domain of philosophy and the domain of theology is felt and divined rather than defined."

CHAPTER IV

THE ULTIMATE HERESY

THE rational basis of Catholic apologetics could not be firmly established before the uncertain frontier between philosophy and theology had been clearly defined, and before the duty to establish the credentials of divine authority by reason had been admitted without reservation.

In the course of the struggle to secure for reason her rightful place in apologetics, it was necessary to condemn two great heresies, both of which were infecting the mental climate of the century, in the course of which St. Thomas Aquinas was to lay the secure foundations of Catholic philosphy.

It was necessary for the Church to condemn not only fideism but also a heresy for which fideism provides a congenial soil, the ultimate heresy that a doctrine may be true for religion but false for philosophy or science.

The ultimate heresy is not the denial of the existence of God but the denial, implicit or explicit, of the law of contradiction—a thing cannot be and not be—for the man who repudiates the law of contradiction repudiates the very basis of thought and commits himself to a scepticism even more fundamental than atheism.

Now the doctrine of the double truth (the doctrine that a statement may be true for religion but false for philosophy or science) is an implicit denial of the law of contradiction, and though this doctrine has been defended by men who claimed the Christian name, it is far more dangerous to Christianity than open scepticism.

We first hear of the doctrine of the double truth in the thirteenth century when Aristotle, as interpreted by the Arabs, suddenly became the dominant intellectual influence in western thought.

The principal works of Aristotle and also of many Moslem philosophers first became known to western Christendom through the latin translations made in the first half of the twelfth century on the instructions of Raymond, Archbishop of

Toledo, which had been the Moslem University city and which had only been annexed to Castile in 1085. The great Arab philosopher, Averroes, was born at Cordova in Spain in 1126 and his "Commentaries" on Aristotle became famous and attracted great attention throughout Europe.

Though the followers of Averroes were freely accused of teaching the doctrine of the two-fold truth, Averroes himself never maintained that a thing might be true in religion and false in philosophy. Admittedly, he taught that religion has one sphere and philosophy another, but philosophy is the ultimate criterion of truth, and nothing which is false for philosophy could be true for religion. Philosophy, however, is not for *all* men. It is for the chosen few, whereas religion is for the multitude. Now religion is not wholly false. It contains, amid much that is false, symbolical truths which are of great value, and therefore religion must be retained for the benefit of those who are incapable of receiving the highest truths of philosophy. It is to be retained, in spite of what is false in it, for the sake of what is true in it. This is a position which a rationalist might adopt and is infinitely removed from the theory that the same statement might be true in one context and false in another.

The immense prestige of the newly discovered works of Aristotle exercised a disturbing influence on Christian Europe, for it was widely assumed, even by Catholics, that the genius of Aristotle had travelled as far as the unaided human reason can travel along the road to truth. And if this were so, if human reason unaided by revelation, must inevitably accept Aristotle's conclusions, then either religion *or* reason is wholly unreliable, for the God of Aristotle is not the God of Christian revelation, but a God who knows nothing outside himself and remains completely detached from the universe which is co-eternal with him. Aristotle, it would seem, believed in a unique intelligence which alone was immortal. What was immortal in man was not his individual soul but the universal intelligence which had informed his body.

If such were the conclusions which the supreme genius of the race had established by pure reason, what value could we attach to a Revelation so inconsistent with those conclusions? In point of fact, Aristotle's beliefs about God and the soul, so far from being demonstrably true, might not unfairly be described as the product not of rational argument but of the Aristotleian variety of "the inner light", but such was the prestige of Aristotle in an age when, as Dr. Etienne Gilson remarks, "L'Aristotélisme n'était pas alors une philosophie, il était la philosophie", that Catholic philosophers, such as those who taught in the University of Paris, were inclined to assume that Aristotle's solution to any particular problem was the best that unaided reason could discover. Of course, they never failed to add, with varying degrees of sincerity, that theology was the final criterion of truth and that no solution could be true, even if approved by Aristotle, which conflicted with revelation.

Siger de Brabant, for instance, to whom Professor Maurice de Wulf of Louvain attributes belief in the doctrine of the double truth, has left nothing on record to justify the allegation that he maintained that a thing could be true in religion, yet false in philosophy. His professed readiness to submit the conclusions arrived at by pure reason to the judgment of theology may have been insincere, a prudent insurance against persecution, but all that he wrote is equally consistent with the hypothesis that he never doubted the Church's claim to be the authentic interpreter of a divine revelation.

It is far less easy to believe in the sincerity of another famous Averroist, Jean de Jandum, who also proclaimed his readiness to submit his conclusions to the arbitrament of revealed doctrine, for de Jandum seems to have taken an impish pleasure in stressing the apparent contradiction between revelation and reason.

To sum up, it has yet to be proved that any thirteenth-century philosopher genuinely believed in the doctrine of the double truth, a doctrine which was probably invented by the orthodox as a *reductio ad absurdum* of Averroism.

The so-called Averroists were divided into two classes: those who resolved the apparent conflict between Revelation and Aristotle in favour of revelation and those who only professed to accept Revelation as a prudent concession to the orthodox. In other words, the Averroists were divided into sincere Catholics and sceptics, who tried to camouflage their scepticism by an insincere profession of faith. Neither the former nor the latter really believed that a doctrine could be true in religion and yet false for philosophy. The former made religion the ultimate criterion of truth, the latter philosophy.

None the less, the suspicion that the Averroists taught the doctrine of a double truth had important consequences, for the Church was thereby forced to define her own position. St. Thomas Aquinas, for instance, declared that the conclusions which reason imposed were true and that the contrary of these conclusions was false; and that to oppose reason to faith was to affirm that faith was false and impossible.

The official condemnation of the Church was pronounced by Etienne Tempier, bishop of Paris in 1277. He attacked the *execrabiles errores* of *nonulli Parisius studentes* "for they say that those things are true according to philosophy but not according to the Catholic faith, as if there might be two contrary truths" (Chartul I, 543, texte 473).

It may well be that the *Parisius studentes* were falsely accused of the damnable heresy. Certainly the first Christian of whom we can affirm with certainty that he boldly proclaimed the doctrine of the double truth was Martin Luther. The evidence for his attitude on this point will be found in Chapter VI.

The doctrine of the double truth has been revived in our day by the more extreme modernists who, as Dr. Inge has pointed out, "are quick to see the strategic possibilities of a theory which separates faith and knowledge, and declares that truths of faith can never come into collision with truths of fact because they belong to different orders. . . ." "It does not follow", writes Tyrrell, "that harmony of faith with the truths of reason and facts of experience is the best or essential condition of its credibility."

Dr. Inge is a modernist and he rejects many traditional doctrines of historic Christianity, such as the virgin birth, but Dr. Inge has far more in common with conservative Christians than with those modernists who proclaim the standard of the double truth. There is, for instance, nothing in the following passage from Dr. Inge's essay on Roman Catholic modernism with which St. Thomas Aquinas would not have agreed:

"The dualism alleged to exist between faith and knowledge will not serve. Man is one, and reality is one; there can no more two 'orders of reality' not affecting each other than there can be two faculties in the human mind working independently of each other. The universe which is interpreted to us by our understanding is not unreal, nor are its laws pliant to our wills as the pragmatists do vainly talk. It is a divinely ordered system, which includes man, the roof and crown of things, and Christ, in whom is revealed to us its inner character and meaning. It is not the province of faith either to flout scientific knowledge, or to contaminate the material on which science works by intercalating what M. Le Roy calls 'transhistorical symbols'— myths in fact—which do not become true by being recognised as false, as the new apologetic seems to suggest. Faith is not the born story-teller of modernist theology. Faith is, on the practical side, just the resolution to stand or fall by the noblest hypothesis; and, on the intellectual side, it is a progressive initiation, by experiment which ends in experience, into the unity of the good, the true, and the beautiful, founded on the inner assurance that these three attributes of the divine nature have one source and conduct to one goal."

CHAPTER V

THE AGE OF REASON

(1)

THE firm foundations of Catholic rationalism were laid by Albert the Great (1206–80), the teacher of St. Thomas Aquinas, and like St. Thomas a Dominican. Albert began by defining the frontier between faith and reason. He was indebted to Alexander of Hales (died 1245) whose *Summa Theologiae* was the first contribution to philosophical and theological writing after the discovery of the works of Aristotle.

Albert clearly distinguishes between the truths, such as the existence of God, which the unaided human reason can discover, and the truths, such as the doctrine of the Trinity which we, learn from divine revelation.

Prior to the Albert-Thomist revolution in thought, theologians had made great efforts to prove that dogmas of the church which we accept on the basis of a divine revelation, the authenticity of which can be proved by reason, could be proved by pure reason. Albert the Great's rejection of these reasons as unsound caused no small sensation. St. Thomas Aquinas, greatest of the scholastics, not only supported him in this, but caused great scandal by pointing out that the attempts to demonstrate by philosophy that the world had been created at a particular point in time were valueless. We accepted this fact on the authority of revelation, and the pretended proofs that the world must have been created in time were worthless.

"To the contemporaries of St. Thomas," writes Professor A. E. Taylor, "the assertion that there are no sound philosophical arguments against the creation of the world from eternity involved at least as great a revision of traditional thinking as the doctrine of the origin of species by natural selection demanded of our grandfathers."

Whereas the predecessors of St. Thomas had been inclined to regard with indulgence, if not with positive approval, the *sancta simplicitas* of pious people who defended the faith with weak arguments, St. Thomas insisted that arguments which were not cogent merely provoked the ridicule of the unbelievers. *Cedit in irrisionem infidelium.*

St. Thomas accepted the papal principle *Philosophia ancilla theologiae,* philosophy the servant of theology, but he gave to the principle a new and original interpretation. Theology, as Dr. Gilson remarks, had to begin by freeing her slave in order the better to make use of her services—*Pour mieux s'assurer les services de son esclave la théologie vient de commencer par l'affranchir.*

St. Thomas warned his disciples that they had no right to expect the innate and intuitive knowledge of God, and that they should face the fact that the human intellect can only form a defective and imperfect conception of God by patiently examining the world of sense. It is significant that the immense structure of the *Summa Theologica* should rest on and begin with a simple fact of everyday experience. "It is certain and obvious to the senses that some things are in motion."

The ruthlessness with which St. Thomas condemned the approach of piety unanchored in reason provoked fierce opposition, but the opposition was defeated. "The Albertino Thomist philosophy," writes Dr. Gilson, "constitutes the only attempt at modernism which has ever succeeded." And he adds, "St. Thomas did not believe that religious sentiments were respectable unless they were rationally founded. He believed himself to be robbing them of nothing more than their illusions. Thomism is an attempt to achieve honesty in philosophy by the complete acceptance of the real and of reason . . . we should see in his work the first system of purely rational truths to which western philosophy has given birth and one of the direct origins of modern philosophy."

(II)

"Never before," writes Henry Adams of the thirteenth century, "have men shown equal energy in such varied directions or such intelligence in the direction of their energy. . . . To them, words had fixed values like numbers, and syllogisms were hewn stones that needed only to be set in place in order to reach any height or support any weight."

We have less confidence in reason and logic to resolve our difficulties, to explain, for instance, how a mother could be

happy in heaven knowing that her son was in hell. That is a
problem which we feel less competent to solve than did St.
Thomas Aquinas. To reject the doctrine of eternal punishment
is to reject Christ, for Christ taught that God became man to
save sinners from hell, but though the traditional eschatology
is an integral element of the Christian revelation, there has been
an immense and welcome change in the interpretation of that
doctrine.

The modern Catholic has neither the taste nor the talent for
the eschatological research which was so popular in the Middle
Ages. His difficulty is to understand why men should ever have
wasted time discussing whether the bodies of the Blessed are or
are not possessed of subtility, clarity and so forth, or whether "the
hair and nails will rise again on the Last Day". For we have all
been influenced to a greater or lesser degree by pragmatism;
St. Thomas, on the other hand, as Father Martin D'Arcy observes, "begins where pragmatism ends".

"St. Thomas Aquinas," writes Father D'Arcy, "takes sides in
the age-long quarrel between those who cherish experienced
mysticism, love or life as in some way superior to reason, and
those who trust only the lamp of the latter in a night where all
else may prove to be illusion. We shall see later that St. Thomas
is not so inhuman as to exclude the factor of love in his philosophy of life; his dislike is reserved only for those who put 'the
reasons of the heart before those of the head'."

If we are Christians we accept the fact that our ultimate des-
tination is eternal beatitude or eternal punishment, but we
have no confidence in the power of the human mind to explain
how a mother could be happy in heaven knowing that her son
was in hell. Such an attitude would have struck a mediaeval
theologian as deplorable, for he had been trained in public
disputes, such as those known as *Quolibets*, where any Master of
Arts could formulate a question for discussion, and where it was
a point of honour to offer a solution to any problem which was
soluble by the aid of reason and revelation. The mediaeval
philosopher was convinced that reason, making proper use of
the rich material provided by revelation, could provide accurate
answers, if not to all, at least to most of the questions that might
be asked about the conditions of life in the next world. An experienced theologian should, for instance, be able to define the

difference between an aurea and an aureole and prove that,
whereas virgins would wear an aureole in heaven, angels would
not, for 'it is not owing to virtue that angels abstain from the
pleasures of the flesh seeing that they are incapable of such
pleasures." And further, of course, no theologian with a reputation to lose would have dared to confess ignorance if asked
whether the blessed in Heaven rejoiced in the sufferings of the
damned. Here is St. Thomas's answer to this question:

"*We proceed to the First Article:*

"*Objection* 1. It would seem that the blessed in heaven will
not see the sufferings of the damned. . . .

"*I answer that:* Nothing should be denied to the blessed which
belongs to the perfection of their beatitude. Now all things are
the better known for being compared with their contrary. Consequently, in order that the happiness of the saints may be more
delightful and that they may give to God more copious thanks
for it, they are permitted perfectly to behold the sufferings of
the damned. . . .

"*We proceed thus to the Second Article:*

"*Objection* 1. It would seem that the blessed must pity the
sufferings of the damned. For pity proceeds from charity, and
the most perfect charity will be in the blessed. . . .

"*Reply to Objection* 1. Charity is the principle of pity when it is
possible for us, inspired by charity, to desire the termination of
a person's unhappiness. But the saints cannot wish this for the
damned, since this would be contrary to divine justice. Consequently the argument does not prove.

"*We proceed thus to the Third Article:*

"*Objection* 1. It would seem that the blessed do not rejoice in
the punishment of the damned. For to rejoice in another's misfortune pertains to hatred. But there will be no hatred among
the blessed. Therefore they will not rejoice in the unhappiness
of the damned. . . .

"*I answer that:* A thing may give cause for rejoicing in two
ways. First directly, when one rejoices in a thing for itself.
Second indirectly, on account of something annexed to it: and
in this way the saints will rejoice in the punishment of the
damned, for they will see in this the order of divine justice and
their own escape which will fill them with joy. And thus the
direct cause of the joy of the blessed will be the divine justice

and their own deliverance; whereas the punishment of the damned will cause it indirectly."

It is difficult to find any flaw in the logic of this careful argument. One cannot but admire the intellectual honesty which refuses to soften the austerity of this particular thesis. A man who is less half-hearted in his devotion to pure reason would have shrunk from pushing his syllogisms to so grim a conclusion. He might even have been tempted to question premises in which such conclusions are implicit.

St. Thomas, as Father D'Arcy remarks, was "coldly indifferent to the world of emotions and imagination except in so far as they subserve his purpose, a metaphysical account of the contents of reality."

The contempt of the modern humanist for the mediaeval theologian is partly due to popular misrepresentations of passages which he has never read, and partly to popular passages which have never been written. The passage I have just quoted is an example of the former, and the passage about angels dancing on the point of a needle is an example of the latter.

To conceive of St. Thomas teaching that the blessed would gloat over the sufferings of the damned is a complete travesty of his argument. The difficulty with which he was dealing was a difficulty raised not by the tough-minded but by the tender-minded. How could one be happy in heaven if one actually *saw* the torments of the wretched damned? (Be it remembered that mediaeval man believed that if he was lucky enough to escape hell fire, many of his friends would be less fortunate.) St. Thomas's task was to prove that happiness in heaven was compatible with the *sight* of the tormented, and not merely with the knowledge that they were being tormented.

"It would seem," suggests some tender-hearted inquirer, "that the blessed in heaven will not see the sufferings of the damned . . . ."

St. Thomas, being as Father D'Arcy remarks, "coldly indifferent to the world of emotions," transforms the nature of the problem from the human and emotional to the impersonal and metaphysical. His "blessed" and his "damned" are intellectual abstractions who neither rejoice (much less gloat) nor suffer, as we rejoice and suffer. They are impersonally aware of the ultimate mystery of God's justice and, because the sufferings of the damned vindicate the justice of God, it is a matter of no importance whether the awareness of the blessed takes the form of knowledge at a distance or of actual sight.

St. Thomas was a genius, but even the genius is limited by the mental outlook of his age. St. Thomas was interested in the fanciful speculations which fascinated his contemporaries and which bore us. We are interested in fanciful speculations which will probably bore our descendants.

The modern world is as uninterested in the aureoles of the saints as in Pythagoras's disquisitions on the mystical qualities of numbers. But we too enjoy exercising our minds with problems of no real relevance for practical life. Relativity has taken the place of eschatology. Would a man who travelled with the speed of light to Sirius and back be older than his father when he returned to this planet? How large is the universe? Is it finite or infinite? Are there several kinds of "time"? Perhaps seven hundred years hence these speculations will appear as fanciful as the reflections of St. Thomas on the "goodly humours" that fill the entrails of the blessed after the Resurrection.

It is also important to remember that though St. Thomas devotes a great amount of space to these fanciful speculations, he was far more concerned with the great issues of the religious life, the Church in its various aspects and with the practical problems which confront the faithful Catholic in his journey through the world.

The disrepute into which scholasticism fell at the Renaissance was due to what the late Professor A. N. Whitehead has described as "the rationalistic orgy of the Middle Ages". The schoolsmen of the decadence did not, contrary to what is so often asserted, sink so low as to debate how many angels could dance on the point of a needle—the origin of this myth is discussed in Appendix A—but their rationalism was utterly divorced from life. They filled their pages with futile subtilties about categorematices and syncategorematices, and they wrote as if the only road to truth was by the well-tried milestones of *formaliter*, *materialiter*, *fundamentaliter*, and *eminenter*.

The futilities of exaggerated rationalism were innocuous, which is more than can be said for the precursors of modern irrationalism, the men who within fifty years of St. Thomas's death were beginning to undermine his supreme achievement, the clear distinction between natural and supernatural knowledge.

The Thomist conception of the relation between philosophy and theology "guarantees the integrity of both schools, and the right of each to use the methodology natural to it. The philosopher is saved from the temptation to infidelity, and the theologian from reliance on rhetoric and emotion." Now it was, as Father Philip Hughes insists, "the unfortunate effect of the great thinkers who followed St. Thomas that their theories of knowledge destroyed the all-important nexus between the spheres of reason and faith, when they denied the power of reason really to prove the existence of God."

Of these thinkers the most mischievous was undoubtedly William of Ockham, an English Franciscan born somewhere about 1285. In spite of his open rebellion against the popes and the condemnation of his heresies, it was his mind which was to dominate the university world between the Middle Ages and the Reformation. Now Ockham maintained that the only knowledge which is certain and wholly reliable is intuitive knowledge, the knowledge which is self-evident.

Implicit in Ockham's theory of knowledge is the scepticism which denies the possibility of knowledge other than that of our physical sensations. Knowledge is no more than a mere system of useful mental conversations with no objective justification. Ockham has taken the first step which leads through the antirationalism of Luther to the final scepticism of Bertrand Russell:—"There is nothing but prejudice and habit for the view that there is a world at all."

Most of the troubles of the modern world are due to that separation of faith and reason for which Ockham and Luther are largely responsible.

(III)

Among the minor consequences of the repudiation of Catholicism by the University of Oxford were the separation of philosophy and theology in the schools, and the fact that the school of philosophy was thenceforward known as *Littera humaniores*. Why "*more humane*" Letters? Because the syllabus had been purged of all trace of mediaeval philosophy. The new humanist of the pagan renaissance despised gothic thought and gothic philosophy. This uncivilised attitude to the great centuries has only recently changed.

When Dr. Thomas Arnold, later of Rugby, was appointed Regius Professor of Modern History, he shrank from writing about the Middle Ages. "I could not bear to plunge myself into the very depths of that noisome cavern, and have to toil through centuries of dirt and darkness." The gothic revival in architecture was perhaps an essential condition of a gothic revival of philosophy, but even more decisive was the reaction against the Secular optimism of the nineteenth century. The miscalculations of those who believed in the perfectibility of man are so obvious to-day that men are far readier than they were to re-examine the political thought of those who, like St. Thomas Aquinas, believed in original sin.

We have less excuse than our forefathers for believing that the reformation of man will be the inevitable result of the reformation of our political system, and are readier to listen to philosophers like St. Thomas Aquinas, who insisted that the medium in which the statesman works is necessarily imperfect, for the best of political systems have to be worked by fallen men, for which reason power will almost always be abused by those who wield it. St. Thomas, after pointing out the demerits of absolute monarchy, oligarchy and pure democracy respectively, insists that only a mixed regime, in which neither the king nor the oligarchy nor the people had absolute power, could offer some insurance against the grosser abuses of power. There is nothing that dates in this advice.

To-day it is not only Catholics who regard St. Thomas as one of the master minds of all time, but non Catholics such as Professor T. F. Tout who describes him as "one of the foremost names in the history of thought", and Professor A. E. Taylor who insists that St. Thomas was "one of the great philosophers of human history, whose thought is part of the permanent inheritance of civilised Europeans and whose influence is still living and salutary." Again, it is doubtful whether the late Professor A. N. Whitehead, F.R.S., perhaps the most brilliant mathematical philosopher of his time, was even a theist, as theism is normally understood. "God," he writes, "is the ultimate limitation and His existence is the ultimate irrationality," but at least he had taken the trouble, unusual in a scientist, to study mediaeval theology before pronouncing judgment on its merits and demerits.

D

"The Middle Ages", writes Professor Whitehead, "formed one long training of the intellect of western Europe in the sense of order. There may have been some deficiency in respect to practice. But the idea never for a moment lost its grip. It was pre-eminently an epoch of orderly thought, rationalist through and through. . . . But for science something more is wanted than a general sense of the order of things. It needs but a sentence to point out how the habit of definite exact thought was implanted in the European mind by the long dominance of scholastic logic and scholastic divinity. The habit remained after the philosophy had been repudiated, the priceless habit of looking for an exact point and of sticking to it when found."

The chasm between modern education with its complete lack of any integrating principle and the mediaeval education with its clearly defined objective is the theme of one of the most surprising books which have appeared in America during the present century, *The Higher Learning in America* by Robert Maynard Hutchins, President of Chicago University. There is nothing in Dr. Hutchins's background or in the secular atmosphere of the great University of which he is President, which would predispose him in favour of, and much which might be expected to prejudice him against, mediaeval philosophy.

Dr. Hutchins attributes what he himself describes as the chaos in the higher learning to the fact that there is "no ordering principle in it." "Real unity," he continues, "can be achieved only by a hierarchy of truths which show us which are fundamental and which are subsidiary, which significant and which not. . . .

"The mediaeval university had a principle of unity. It was theology. The mediaeval theologians had worked out an elaborate statement in due proportion and emphasis of the truths relating to man and God, and man and nature. It was an orderly progressing from truth to truth. . . .

"Theology is based on revealed truth and on articles of faith. We are a faithless generation and take no stock in revelation. Theology implies orthodoxy and an orthodox church. We have neither. To look to theology to unify a modern university is futile and vain. . . ."

"If we cannot appeal to theology we must turn to metaphysics. Without theology or metaphysics a university cannot exist. Both are missing to-day. And with them has gone any intelligible basis of the study of man in his relations to other men. The truths of ethics, for example, are now merely common-sense teachings about how to get along in the world."

Dr. Hutchins was not content merely to theorise. He imposed upon his startled colleagues lectures on thomistic philosophy delivered by a brilliant Jew, Dr. Adler, who though as yet unbaptised has been the cause of many conversions among his pupils.

Let me conclude this chapter by reminding the reader that my object in this book is not to demonstrate the truth of any particular creed, but to write a preliminary study for a history of rationalism in the proper sense of that term, and to describe the consequences of the revolt against reason. Let me insist once again that the word rationalist in its correct sense defines a *method*. There are Catholic rationalists and there are also sceptical rationalists. Hume was a rationalist, for at least he made an honest attempt to base his rejection of miracles on a reasoned ground. Matthew Arnold was a fideist. He accepted by faith the dogma "miracles do not occur" and made not the slightest attempt to examine the evidence for the best attested miracles.

A rationalist is a thinker who draws logical and rational conclusions from a given premise, and who is guided by reason rather than by emotion in his search for truth.

The Catholic moral code is, for instance, a rational deduction from Catholic premises; for if our eternal happiness is at stake we should indeed be irrational if we refused to be guided, both in faith and in morals, by that Church which, if its claims are true, alone has authority to interpret the mind of God to men.

The code of the high-minded materialist, on the other hand, is an irrational deduction from materialistic premises, for if thought is a by-product of matter and if free-will is an illusion, morality, in the proper sense of the term, ceases to have any meaning. We do not describe machines as moral or immoral, and on the materialistic hypothesis we differ from machines only in the fact that we are conscious.

The rationality of any particular conclusion is, of course, unaffected by the truth of the premise from which the conclusion has been deduced. If the Catholic premises could be proved to be false and the materialistic premises could be proved to be true, the medieval theologian whose conclusions logically followed from his premises, would still rank as a more rational philosopher than the Victorian rationalist, whose conclusions were inconsistent with his premises. The Victorian rationalist, as I hope to prove in a later chapter, might more properly have been described as a muddle-headed mystic.

Again, the familiar contrast between the medieval theologian who appealed to Scripture texts in support of his views, and the Rationalist who appeals to reason, ceases to be impressive when we realise that the scholastic appealed to Scripture because he believed that the credentials of Scripture had been proved by reason.

You will not, of course, find in the *Summa Theologica* of St. Thomas Aquinas, greatest of all the scholastics, a reasoned defence of the authority of the Bible any more than you will find in a treatise on the differential calculus a reasoned defence of the binomial theorem. The *Summa Theologica* is not intended as an apologetic for the Catholic faith, but as a treatise on sacred science on the basis of an accepted Bible, addressed to readers familiar with the arguments for accepting the Bible as the Word of God. St. Augustine, who was the first of the Fathers fully to realise the necessity for a rational foundation for the faith, devoted much thought to proving the authority of the Bible. St. Thomas Aquinas took all this for granted. He was writing for people who were familiar with St. Augustine's arguments and consequently he felt justified in beginning where St. Augustine left off. He appealed to Scripture in much the same spirit that a mathematician would appeal to Euclid. St. Augustine believed that he had done for the authority of Scripture what Euclid had done for geometry.

Those who reject the authority of the Bible are, of course, logical in rejecting the conclusions which the medieval scholastics deduced from Scripture texts, but it is only the loose thinker who will deny theologians like St. Thomas a place among the rationalists simply because he accepts the first principles of medieval theology. Relativity is a challenge to the validity of Newton's laws, yet we do not condemn the Victorian physicists as irrational because they accepted those laws.

CHAPTER VI

REASON DETHRONED

(I)

MARTIN LUTHER has been uncritically praised by the enemies of the Catholic Church and uncritically attacked by ardent Catholics, and both his partisans and his enemies have been so pre-occupied with his relation to the Church of Rome that they have under-estimated his importance as the leader of the sixteenth-century revolt not only against Rome but also against reason.

Luther's principal supporters in England have been found among the nonconformists who have tended, with notable exceptions, to follow Luther in his over-emphasis not only on Faith as opposed to works, but also on faith as divorced from rational argument. Anglicanism, on the other hand, resisted the infection of this form of irrationalism with the result that the greatest works of Anglican apologetic have remained true to the tradition of Catholic rationalism. And though much that Henry VIII believed was discarded at the Elizabethan settlement, the King still uses the title "Defender of the Faith" which was bestowed upon Henry VIII by the Pope in recognition of Henry's defence of Catholicism against Luther.

No well-informed member of the Church of England believes that Anglicanism stands or falls with the Lutheran movement, and it is, therefore, perhaps not surprising that the author of a recent attack on Luther should have been able to quote in his support Dr. W. R. Inge's statement, "There is very little to be said for this coarse and foul-mouthed leader—of a revolution"— and also the late Archbishop Temple: "It is easy to see how Luther prepared the way for Hitler."

Mr. Peter Wiener, the author of the book in question—*Martin Luther, Hitler's Spiritual Ancestor*—arrived in England as a refugee from Germany and is, perhaps, inclined to overstress one of the great antipathies which Hitler certainly shared with Luther— anti-Semitism. But not only with Luther, for anti-Semitism was almost universal in Luther's Europe and did not vanish from modern Europe with the death of Hitler.

It is, of course, possible to interpret the Peasants' War as a sixteenth-century prototype of the Popular Front, but Luther's attitude in that struggle merely helps to classify him with those who sided with the oppressors against the oppressed. Mr. Wiener is on stronger ground when he traces German nationalism to Luther, but he missed, or at least failed to give proper emphasis to, the one outstanding link between Hitler and Luther—the deliberate cult of anti-rationalism. Hitler's scream, "We think with our blood" is merely a new version of Luther's description of reason as "the devil's whore".

Mr. Wiener's book was largely based on Denifle's *Luther und Luthertum*. Father Henri Suso Denifle, o.p., was a great Dominican scholar who, as even Lutherans have admitted, was perhaps the greatest authority of his time on the Middle Ages. The first volume of his book, which appeared in 1904, created an immense sensation, not only in Germany, but in other countries in which the book was translated. In England his book was not translated and was largely ignored, and M. Jacques Maritain's study of Luther in his book *Three Reformers* was not widely read outside of Catholic circles.

Denifle, Maritain and Wiener would certainly have been more effective had they been readier to recognise Luther's undoubted qualities. He had the makings of a great religious leader. He wrote one superb hymn. His translation of the Bible had those qualities of style, majesty, and beauty which are unusual in modern translations. Luther came of peasant stock. He had the coarseness and the courage of the peasant, and his readiness to face a painful death for his beliefs should have counted more with the intellectuals who have attacked him. Ordinary folk will give him a good mark for the courage of his *Hier stehe ich und kann nicht anders*. Now if Luther were judged by the same standards which we apply in the case of a militant Catholic layman and warrior, such as Don John of Lepanto fame, our verdict would be more favourable, but he is described as a "reformer" and the implied comparison is with Catholic saints who were content to live and to die in an unreformed church. And that is a standard of comparison which Luther cannot sustain.

Mr. Wiener's book evoked a brilliant reply from the erudite Methodist, the Rev. Gordon Rupp, who is in every way a worthy successor to that great Methodist historian of the Reformation, the late Dr. Workman. "Historians' English", writes Mr. Rupp, "is an industrial disease." A disease from which Mr. Rupp does not suffer. He is an accomplished writer, and his astringent invective will give particular pleasure to those who hold that it is equally unChristian to criticise Luther, or to show mercy to Luther's enemies, past and present. Luther, to quote an old gibe, has been accused by Peter Wiener of murdering three men and a dog, and Mr. Rupp triumphantly produces the dog alive. The happy bark of resurrected dogs gives a cheerful note to Mr. Rupp's book, but what about the three men?

Mr. Wiener quoted examples not only of Luther's coarseness but also of an obscene blasphemy in *Table Talk*, the like of which it would be difficult to parallel in the pamphlets of the atheist underworld—I have relegated these horrors to the notes on this chapter, so that no reader shall have cause to complain that he came across them unawares.

Denifle quotes letters from Luther in which he condones adultery and fornication. Mr. Rupp's general line of defence is to insist that Luther cannot have meant what he appears to say because his writings and statements to which Mr. Wiener draws attention, are inconsistent with Luther's teaching. Luther has certainly written many beautiful passages about marriage and chastity, but he is also responsible for statements which were the cause of great embarrassment to his supporters.

The fallacy of Mr. Rupp's line of defence is to assume that Luther was a consistent character. All the evidence suggests that he was an extreme case of a split personality. There were two Luthers—the Catholic Luther and the Luther who is in revolt not only against Catholicism, but against all external authority, including the authority of reason. The never-ending conflict between Luther the Catholic and Luther the anarchist, is the key to the inconsistencies of his thought. What remained of the Catholic Luther after his secession from the Church can always be quoted against Luther the anarchist.

Denifle maintains that Luther's secession from the Church was primarily due to a moral failure. That Luther was oversexed is probable, that he failed (as many contemporary priests and nuns failed) to observe the difficult commandment is possible, but by no means proved. And no such deduction can be drawn from Luther's insistence that "Concupiscence cannot be conquered."

Concupiscentia, in Luther's writings, includes not only sexual sin but all the sins of the unregenerate personality and may, therefore, mean no more than what St. Paul meant by "the flesh". M. Maritain quotes "I am but a man prone to let himself be swept off his feet by society, drunkenness, the movements of the flesh . . ." and adds "In a sermon of the same period on the state of marriage Luther writes, 'What is needed to live in continence is not in me'."

For the former quotation M. Maritain gives this reference (not in the text but in the footnotes at the end of the volume): "Sermon of the 16th January, 1519 (Weim. Lx 215, 13)." For the latter quotation he gives no reference. Both quotations are from a sermon which was printed by somebody who claimed to be present but which was repudiated by Luther both as to form and content and which, therefore, cannot fairly be quoted against Luther.

It would admittedly be easy to quote, as Denifle and others have done, authentic and unrepudiated passages in Luther's writings which suggest that Luther regarded sexual appetite as something which was all but invincible, but those who have maintained that Luther himself was guilty of immorality have failed to prove their case.

"In April 1525," writes Mr. Wiener, "he (Luther) refers to himself as 'a famous lover' who has three wives but 'no intent whatsoever to marry'." Mr. Wiener must have taken this quotation second-hand without checking it from the original letter to Spalatin of April 16th, 1525:

"As for your remarks about my marriage," the letter runs, "do not be surprised at my marrying, seeing that I am such an exceptionally skilful lover. It is more extraordinary, seeing how much I write about marriage and mix with women *in that way*, that I have not long ago become a woman, to say nothing of marrying. But if you will follow my example, you have the very best of reasons. For I have already had three wives at once, and loved them so intensely that I have lost two of them, who now want to marry other men. The third one I am just managing to hold fast by the left arm. She will probably be torn from me too. But you are such a sluggish lover that you will not even venture to marry one."

Luther was of peasant stock and this letter is characteristic of the cruder forms of peasant humour. Father Denifle, quoting from the same letter attaches undue significance to the phrase *et sic misceor feminis* (and mix with women in that way). Admittedly Luther in another connection uses *misceor* for sexual connection, but surely the *sic* is clear evidence that Luther only means "I write about marriage so much *and thus* mix with women."

Luther was a heavy eater, but the charge that he was an habitual drunkard, or even a persistently heavy drinker, is refuted by one fact alone, his unprecedented literary output. He published in all some 350 printed works which included many pamphlets and a series of translations. Of all authors ancient and modern, his only rivals for sheer productivity are the Jesuit Gretscher (268 works) and St. Augustine (232 works). And it is not only by the amount but by the quality of output that he can claim a high rank among great writers. In his case productivity was not identical with prolixity. He was a supreme pamphleteer with an amazing talent for effective expression.

To sum up, the charge of habitual drunkenness can be dismissed as absurd, the charge of sexual immorality as unproved. The case against Luther is based not on the alleged breakdown of his private morals but on his public utterances which led, as we shall see, to a collapse of moral standards throughout Lutheran Germany.

(II)

The conflict between Luther the Catholic and Luther the anarchist may be traced in his attitude to reason. It is, for instance, his Catholic background which emerges in "*ratio es pars divinae naturae*" and again in "man is especially gifted with the glorious light of reason and understanding so that men have thought out and discovered so many noble arts with ability and skill; all this comes from this light or from the Word which is the light of men." But the respect for reason which he had been taught as a Catholic was not strong enough to resist his later anarchism. There was, admittedly, every justification for attacking a debased scholasticism, but no such pretext could justify his description of reason as the "most atrocious enemy of God ('rationem atrocissimum dei hostem')" or his reply to the Anabaptists who had compared reason to a torch . . . "Does reason shed light? Yes, like that which filth would shed if it were set in a lantern."

That Luther's revolt against reason was due to his failure to refute by reason the rational argument for the claims of the Catholic church, or, alternatively, to produce a rational justification for Lutheranism, is a theory which Protestants will naturally not accept, but which at least offers a plausible explanation of the violence and intemperance of Luther's attacks on reason in passages such as these:

"God only gave us reason 'that she might rule on earth, that is that reason should control above all else the manner in which during this temporal life we should eat, drink and clothe ourselves, and have a respectable life'."

"But in spiritual and divine things reason is not only blind and darkness (blind und Finsternis) but the devil's whore . . . and she can only blaspheme and dishonour everything that God has said or done."

In the last sermon which he preached at Wittenberg towards the end of his life he abandons all restraint in his attack on reason.

"Reason is the devil's greatest whore; by nature and manner of being she is a noxious whore; she is a prostitute, the devil's appointed whore; a whore eaten by scab and leprosy who ought to be trodden under foot and destroyed, she and her wisdom. . . . Throw dung in her face to make her ugly. She is, and she ought to be, drowned in baptism. . . . She would deserve, the wretch, to be banished to the filthiest place in the house, to the closets."

The theory that a belief may be true for faith but false for philosophy originated, so far as Christendom is concerned, among the thirteenth-century Averroists, but was, as we have seen, repudiated by the Church. It was revived by Luther. "Reason" he insisted, "is contrary to faith. It pertains to God alone to bestow faith against nature and to enable us to believe against reason."

(III)

"The Sorbonne, mother of errors," writes Luther, "pronounced a very bad definition to the effect that the same thing was true in philosophy and theology, and impiously condemned those who maintained the contrary."

It was not, in point of fact, the Sorbonne that asserted this but Leo X on December 19th, 1513, against Pomponatius in the Fifth Lateran Council: "Cumque verum vero minime contradicat, omnem assertionem veritati illuminatae fidei contrariam omnino falsam esse definimus."

Elsewhere Luther cites "the Word was made flesh" as a doctrine which is true in theology but "impossible and absurd in philosophy." In modern times both Loisy and Tyrrell maintained that a belief might be true for faith and false for history, but since even modernists find it difficult to deny the law of contradiction, the practical upshot of such teaching is to camouflage the dogmatic denial of a particular doctrine by the formula that the doctrine in question is only false for history but not for faith.

The revolt against reason is in its ultimate essence the revolt of unbridled individualism against an external and objective code. The great leaders of this revolt have all been wishful thinkers who contrived to believe that reality could be forced to conform to the pattern shaped by their ambition or by their lust. And because it is impossible to reconcile subjective desire with an objective code, such as, for instance, the code which Christ imposed upon his followers in this difficult business of sex, the revolt against reason leads to a revolt against the moral code.

(IV)

The effect of Luther's teaching, which is far more important than the effect of his private life in so far as it remained private, made many converts to the seductive doctrine that concupiscence, in the sexual as well as in the more general sense of the word, is invincible. "Nothing can cure *libido*" he exclaims, "not even marriage" (*libido nullo remedio potest curari nequidem conjugio*). Elsewhere, he insists that "God condemns us all. We are all whoremongers, if not openly in the eyes of the world at least in our hearts; if we had room, time, place and opportunity, we should all commit adultery." It is passages such as these which lend colour to the charge that Luther's own life was immoral.

If the claims of the Catholic Church cannot be justified, a priest who leaves the Church cannot be censured for breaking a vow of celibacy which he made on the assumption that the Church was divine, but of those who, as Protestants, would applaud Luther's change of faith, not many would approve this systematic campaign to induce priests and nuns to break their vows, for it is one thing to marry after one has left the Church for reasons not connected with the burden of celibacy, and quite another to break such vows as the first step towards secession.

"There is only a moment of shame," writes Luther to those priests and nuns whom he urges to break their vows, "Then will come the good years full of honour. May Christ give you his grace that by his Spirit those words may become life and power in your heart. . . . Receive not the grace of God in vain." Surely we have crossed the frontier, not between Catholicism and Protestantism, but between decency and blasphemy when Luther can introduce his incitement to break the vow of chastity by words such as "Receive not the grace of God in vain."

The Lutheran revolt was followed by an outburst of sensuality among the apostate priests who had accepted Luther's invitation to break their vows. Where mere invitation to secession failed, cloisters were often invaded by gangs of apostate priests. After a rape of nuns which took place on the night of Holy Saturday 1525, Luther described Koppe, a burgher of Torgau, who organised the assault as a "blessed robber" and compared him to Christ—Yes, to *Christ*. "Like Christ, you have rescued these poor souls from the prison of human tyranny; you have done this at an epoch providentially indicated, at the moment of Easter." The word translated "rape" is, no doubt, a figurative expression but I cannot see Koppe, as Mr. Rupp does, in the role of a kindly courier who merely arranged for the transport of the nuns to decent lodgings. "The picture," writes Mr. Rupp, "is nearer *End of Term at Girton* than to *Mardi Gras in Montmartre*."

Denifle quotes a letter written by one of the apostate priests who organised a kind of trade in profaned nuns: "Nine have come to us. They are beautiful, fine and of noble birth. Not one that is fifty years of age. I have kept the oldest for you, my dear brother, for an honourable wife. If you would prefer a younger one, you can take your choice of the loveliest." Not *my* idea of *End of Term at Girton*.

Once you concede that continence is all but impossible, it follows logically that adultery must be condoned if either partner refuses the marital due. "One may well find," Luther writes, "a stubborn wife who is obstinate and doesn't worry herself even if her husband falls ten times into impurity. That is the time for her husband to say to her, 'if you won't, another will.' If the wife won't, let the maid come! Give yourself an Esther and send Vashti away."

It was this kind of thing which disgusted not only a saint like St. Thomas More, but a man of the world like the Duke George of Saxony. In one of his dialogues with the "Messenger," the advocate of the new heresies, St. Thomas More cites as characteristic of Lutheranism the teaching that "if a man be not able to do his duty for his wife, he is bounden secretly without slander to provide another to do it for him." To this the Messenger replied: "Forsooth, this was courteously considered of him; he is a very gentleman, I warrant you. It is no marvel though his wife be well teeming if he make her such provision." The Duke's protest must also be quoted. 'When were there more adulteries than since you wrote 'If a woman cannot bear children to her husband, she should go to another and bear him children which the husband must support'."

One can hardly blame pro-Lutherans for concealing all evidence of this aspect of Luther's teaching, but it is impossible to assess the influence of Luther if this important evidence is suppressed. As indeed is admitted by Dr. Coulton, the life-long opponent of the Church which Luther left, and himself the author of a book *In Defence of the Reformation*. Dr. Coulton writes:

"Denifle was perhaps the greatest medievalist of our time. I have only dipped into his *Luther*; it is outside my period of special study. But I saw that (apart from the fact that he here lays aside his usual objectivity) his 'case for the prosecution' is very formidable. He has dug out from Luther's *Table Talk* and letters passages which are not only repellent but grossly repulsive, and it is discreditable to Lutheran historians that these things should have remained so long unknown or unconfessed. As a fault of *omission* it seems to me as serious as those which I have often charged against the Roman Church. But it lacks, so far as I know, the further and far greater fault of refusing to recognise misstatement of fact, errors of *commission*. However, the neglect by Luther's special biographers of facts which, as now revealed, appear so patent and significant, seems inexcusable; and, writing now without verification, on the authority of Denifle and of the quotation you give, I feel heartily ashamed. If I myself had ever posed as an infallible historian, here is very plain proof of the contrary."

(v)

Luther's *Opinion on Monastic Orders* is perhaps one of the most influential (and disastrous) of Luther's works. It was in effect the proclamation of a new code of ethics. Concupiscence is invincible, the gratification of the sexual instincts is not only as natural but as inevitable as that of any other physiological function. The resistance to natural appetites was declared all but impossible and therefore the salvation of the soul no less than the health of the body demanded an instant abrogation of the laws of celibacy. This book was a trumpet call to priests and monks to desert the sanctuary and the monastery. Its effect was immense.

Chastity is at the best a difficult ideal, and it is easy to predict the inevitable consequences of teaching such as Luther's. His notorious *Si pecca pecca fortitur* (if you sin sin boldly) may be defended as an impulsive paradox, but the following passage from his works is less easy to explain away:

"Whenever the devil vexes you with that thought, immediately seek the company of men, or drink more deeply, or make jokes, or sport, and behave more cheerfully. From time to time one must drink more deeply, joke or commit stupidities, and commit some sin out of hatred and contempt for the devil, in order that we may not give him any room and have qualms of conscience over the smallest matters, for otherwise we shall be conquered if we are too anxious not to sin. Therefore, if the devil says, 'Don't drink', I shall answer 'Precisely for this very reason I shall drink the more deeply, speak with less restraint, carouse the more often, to mock and vex the devil, who has set about trying to vex and mock me.' Oh, if I could only designate some quite remarkable sin, to mock the devil, so that he should learn that I recognise no sin, and am conscious of no sin, we whom the devil so threatens and vexes must strike out of our eyes and understanding the entire decalogue."

When we compare this with the traditional advice to meet temptation by prayer and spiritual meditation and asceticism, we realise the length of the road that Luther had travelled. Luther's doctrine is the triumph of subjectivism. Justification by faith should more properly have been described as justification by feeling. If you *feel* that you are sinless you *are* sinless.

In 1525 Luther wrote, "You owe God nothing more than to believe and to confess. In everything else he gives you your freedom, that you can do what you wish, without any peril to your conscience. He who believes that Christ has taken away his sins is as sinless as Christ." It's as easy as all that.

I remember seeing in a French paper an advertisement of Artorogéne, a medicine which, so it was claimed, permitted all excesses and cured them. "L'Artorogéne permet tous les excès et les répare." The quest for Artorogéne will never cease. What Luther offered to his disciples was a kind of spiritual Artorogéne.

Luther was genuinely shocked when some of his followers drew from his teaching that good works do not promote salvation the logical conclusion that bad works do not hinder salvation. Johannes Agricola and his followers asserted that Christians are exempt from the teaching of the moral law. Thus antinomianism (ἀντι against νομος the law) was the logical consequence of the Lutheran revolt against reason, for the revolt against law is only one phase of the rebellion of subjective intuition against objective reason, and thus of the individual against all external codes.

Why not advise bigamy for reasons of state, as Luther advised and condoned the bigamy of Philip? If concupiscence is invincible, why should monogamy be enforced? "It is not forbidden," writes Luther, "that a man should have more than one wife. I could not restrain it to-day, but I would not recommend it (*Ich könte es heute nicht wehren, aber raten wollteich's nicht*)."

Luther's apostles were largely recruited from those who were in search of "the freedom of the flesh". So, at least, Luther himself asserted. "I see," he wrote, "that many of our monks only left the cloister for the same reasons that they entered, that is for the sake of the belly and the freedom of the flesh, and through them Satan will raise a great stink against the good reputation of our teaching."

We have Luther's own authority for the fact that the first effect of his teaching was a general collapse of morals. Here are some passages from Luther's writings:

"Now that one devil is driven out of us, seven worse devils are entered in."

"People are to-day more avaricious, more pitiless, more lecherous, more impudent and wicked than under the papacy."

"Avarice, usury, leudness, carousing, swearing, lying and deceit are present at full strength, even more so than under the papacy. Such disorderly living provokes with regard to our Gospel and preaching the rejoinder, if this teaching were true, then the people would be more pious."

"The more one preaches the worse the people, and the weaker the faith."

Such was, in fact, the state of affairs, writes Denifle, "that Luther already in 1527 expressed the doubt whether he would have begun had he foreseen all the great scandals and disorder. 'Yes, who would have begun to preach', he said twelve years later, 'Had we known before that so much misfortune, scandal, slander, thanklessness and wickedness would follow. But as we are in it, we must hold on.' . . . Little wonder that the reformed regretted that he had been born a German, and complained 'if one were to paint Germany now, one would have to paint her like a sow'."

In support of his contention that the immediate effect of the Lutheran movement was a rapid decline in morals, Denifle quotes many witnesses drawn from the ranks of Luther's apostles. The apostate Franciscan, Heinrich von Kettenbach, exclaimed in 1525, "Many people behave now as if all sins and wickedness were permitted, as if there was no devil, no hell and no God, and are worse than they ever were." And another Franciscan apostate, von Günzberg, said that the new evangelists were "twice as evil as the papists, yes than Tyre and Sidon and Sodom." And one of Luther's followers, Pirkheimer, exclaimed, "We hoped that the Roman knavery would disappear, and the roguery of monks and priests, but to judge by what we have under our own eyes, the blackguards of the new Gospel make those of popery seem pious."

German history, said Heinrich Heine of this period, is almost entirely composed of sensual disturbances, and yet, as we know,

Lutheranism gradually developed a characteristic and attractive type of piety. Denifle explains the contrast between Lutheranism in the age of Luther and the later Lutheranism by the fact that Germany never ceased to be partially Catholic and that the old Catholic instincts revived and influenced the later Lutheranism. This may be a partial explanation, but I am inclined to suspect that even more important was the fact that, whereas the first apostles were in the main apostate priests and monks who fully merited the contempt with which Luther spoke of them, the later Lutherans were born Lutherans, whose moral sense had not been weakened by apostasy, and broken vows of chastity. Luther's own denunciation of so many of his first apostles makes it difficult to believe that these men left the Church as the result of a sincere and honest conviction.

That the Church was in need of reformation was admitted by contemporary Catholics, but that the so-called "Reformation" was in fact a "deformation" was admitted by Luther in one of those not infrequent moments of candour when the submerged Catholic came to the surface. Of his own followers he said, "They exchange the abuses of the Church with greater. Often we refuse to bear a small evil and summon a greater evil into being."

Germany recovered from the wave of sensual disturbances which, as Heine said, were the direct consequences of the Lutheran revolt, but the political influence of the movement may not unfairly be said to have prepared the way for the more unbalanced forms of German nationalism.

Mr. Wiener spoiled a sound case by exaggeration, for it is not fair to imply a close resemblance between Luther and Hitler. Luther and Hitler were born Catholics, but whereas the Catholic Luther never wholly vanished, there is no trace of a Christian background in the later Hitler. Moreover, Luther remains, whether we like him or not, "One of the giant voices of history" whereas Hitler is remembered not as a voice but as a scream, the scream of a sadist.

Luther undoubtedly broke down barriers which, had they remained intact, would have prevented the emergence of the more violent forms of German nationalism and the more unrestrained forms of dictatorship. Such is the conclusion which emerges from the study of a readable and erudite book *From*

*Luther to Hitler** by Professor William Montgomery McGovern, Professor of Political Science at the Protestant Northwestern University and visiting lecturer at Harvard University.

Professor McGovern points out the paradoxes in Luther's career. He began as a reformer of the Church; he ended as a reformer of the state. He began as the champion of individual liberty and freedom of conscience, yet his doctrines led to the belief in the divine right of kings (and dictators). He began as an internationalist; he ended by formulating the doctrine of the all-powerful state, the citizens of which should be subject to the iron will of their secular Lord.

"Among the followers of other Protestant leaders, such as Calvin and Zwingli, there was a certain democratic tendency. This was completely lacking in Luther's philosophy of the state. Luther had a very poor opinion of the political abilities of the average man. The average man, to him, was full of wickedness and needed to be restrained by the strong arm of temporal authority. All human souls might be equal in the sight of God, but the temporal state must rest upon inequality. To Luther, it was the duty of every subject to know his place and keep it, fulfilling the law of God within his own sphere. When the peasants of Germany rose in rebellion against their lords, Luther was filled with wrath and commanded that the rebels be shown no mercy, that the insurrection be put down with fire and sword.

"Luther believed that the monasteries should be suppressed, and this belief had political as well as religious significance. Luther was opposed to the monastic ideal not only from the religious point of view but also because he regarded with dislike the existence within the state of semi-independent corporations such as the monastic communities. The feudal idea of the state as a corporation of corporations was to be displaced by the state as a single corporation having direct control over all its subjects as individuals."

The influence of Lutheranism was even more disastrous on apologetics. In England the Lutheran revolt against reason had no effect on the succession of Anglican divines who remained faithful to Catholic rationalism. Bishop Butler and Paley in the eighteenth century, Salmon, Lightfoot, Gore and, in more

* Published in England by Harrap.

modern times, Mr. C. S. Lewis, have all based their defence of the basic doctrines of Christianity on rational grounds. I may perhaps be forgiven for a personal digression if I record at this point my own debt to Salmon's *A Historical Introduction to the Study of the Books of the New Testament* and to Bishop Lightfoot's crushing rejoinder to a pretentious anonymous book *Supernatural Religion*. I was an agnostic at the time and those books were the first which introduced me to the rational case for Christian miracles in general, and for the Resurrection in particular.

The Lutheran depreciation of reason influenced the Evangelicals in the Church of England and the Nonconformist communions. John Wesley, for instance, was not only an Anglican clergyman, but he was also in many ways a characteristic child of the eighteenth century in his respect for reason, but Wesley, and through Wesley, Methodism, was greatly influenced by the Moravians, a German Lutheran body. Peter Böhler, a young Moravian graduate from Jena, succeeded in convincing Wesley that every man, however moral or orthodox he may be, is in a state of damnation until he suddenly perceives by a process of supernatural insight, wholly divorced from human reasoning, that the sacrifice of Christ has been applied to him and that he has expatiated his sins. Böhler listened patiently to Wesley's arguments and remarked quietly, "My brother, this philosophy of yours must be purged away." His advice to Wesley was "Preach faith until you have it, and then because you have it you will preach faith."

There is one aspect of the flight from reason which has not attracted as much attention as it deserves. The man who is convinced not only that his case can be rationally defended, but also that he himself is fully qualified to defend it, seldom crosses the well-defined frontier which separates spirited controversy from mere abuse. So far as controversy is concerned, the flight from reason usually coincides with a flight from manners. In the modern world Hitler and the rulers of Russia illustrate the organic relationship between anti-rationalism and the coarsest of invective. But Lenin, Stalin and Hitler were courteous controversialists compared with Luther, examples of whose lavatory invective are quoted (but not translated) in the notes on this chapter.

It is curious to find a theologian of Karl Barth's eminence praising in Luther something which is so infinitely foreign to his own courteous and scholarly dialectic. "He who wishes", Dr. Barth writes, "to be certain with Luther and as certain as Luther . . . must not only allow himself to be reproached but must—and this is more difficult—have sufficient self-confidence himself to reproach, to curse and to damn with great force (*mit grosse Kraft zu schelten, zu fluchen zu verdammen*), to call lies lies and abomination abomination, without consideration, without sentimentality and without any readiness to receive offers of a truce." Dr. Barth would be the first to condemn not only a modern Catholic who wrote of Luther as Luther habitually wrote of Catholics, but also a modern Protestant who descended to Luther's controversial level in his attacks on the papacy.

I admit that in this chapter in which I am only concerned with Luther's attack on reason and with objective standards, I have not been able to do justice to those aspects of Luther's character and teaching which alone can explain the devotion which he inspires in men as revered as Dr. Barth himself, but it would be easier to arrive at an accord with scholarly Lutherans if they were readier to admit that justification by feeling is not an adequate substitute for rational apologetics.

CHAPTER VII

THE PEDIGREE OF MODERN SCIENCE

(1)

"THE scientific movement began in Greece, but the triumph of Christianity was followed by the decline of science. The mediaeval church discouraged scientific research and it was not until science liberated itself from the despotisms of the Church that the modern scientific movement began." This is the kind of paragraph which was common form in the writings of the nineteenth-century scientians. The late Professor A. N. Whitehead, F.R.S., and Mr. J. W. N. Sullivan, who have proved that a populariser of science need not be unscholarly, have had some effect in weakening the hold of this myth, but secularists have a vested interest in representing the Church as the enemy of science and can therefore hardly be expected to admit the plain fact that it was from the despotism of Aristotle and not the despotism of the Church that science was freed at the renaissance.

It is true that the scientific movement began in Greece, but also true that it would not be easy to decide whether Greek thought had on the balance a greater influence in stimulating or in retarding scientific research. The decisive advance of science began when science liberated itself from teleology, and the teleological outlook did not begin with the mediaeval theologians. Plato and Aristotle were teleologists, and the Greek bias in favour of the deductive as opposed to inductive reasoning was certainly one of the influences responsible for the stagnation of science in the Middle Ages.

A deductive or *a priori* reasoner deduces either from truths universally admitted, or from truths deduced from truths universally admitted, their necessary consequences. Thus St. Thomas Aquinas starting from the universally admitted truth that "it is certain and obvious to our senses that some things are in motion" proceeds to deduce the existence of God.

Inductive or *a posteriori* reasoning is the attempt to discover the nature of a general law from its observed consequences.

Astronomers observed that certain planets did, in point of fact, move in elliptic orbits. They inferred by inductive reasoning that the movements of these particular planets was a consequence of a general law that all planets move in elliptic orbits. Induction will thus often create a strong presumption in favour of a general law, the proof of which depends on deduction or on mathematical processes. From the fact that certain planets move in elliptic orbits, it is impossible to infer with certainty that all planets move in such orbits. Observation must be supplemented by mathematics in order to achieve exact proof.

The deductive approach to truth is usually preferred by the philosopher, the inductive by the scientist. I shall describe those who prefer the deductive approach as *apriorists* and those who rely on inductive reason and experiment as *empiricists*.

The contrast between the mediaeval and the modern outlook may be illustrated by Galileo's retort to Sarsi. Sarsi maintained that motion invariably produced heat, and in support of this theory he quoted a statement, which he had seen in print (and which he therefore assumed to be infallible), that the Babylonians cooked eggs by whirling them in a sling. Galileo made the obvious reply that it would be perfectly easy to test the truth of this statement by repeating the experiment. Sarsi, we may be sure, had never thought of that, for the very idea of appealing from authority to experiment, and from *a priori* reasoning to empiricism was foreign to the mediaeval mind.

Galileo, like the modern scientists, was mainly interested in the "why", the mediaevalist in the "how" of phenomena. In other words, he was a teleologist. Teleology is the doctrine of final ends rather than of efficient causes. The teleologist explains phenomena, not by trying to discover how things work, but by attempting to show why things are. To the mediaeval thinker the "why" of natural phenomena was solved once you had discovered their usefulness to man.

Nature is the work of God, and since God made man only a little lower than the angels, it was reasonable to deduce that Nature has been created purely for the benefit of man. From this assumption the scholastics deduced that the best method of understanding nature was to interpret nature with reference to man's eternal destiny.

Ruskin was in the direct descent from the great mediaeval teleologists. His "geology", if indeed it can be described as such, is gloriously mediaeval in outlook. Mountains, for Ruskin, were not the inevitable result of certain physical changes on the surface of the earth. No, they are appointed to fulfil "three great offices", which he proceeds to describe in detail, "in order to preserve the health and increase the happiness of mankind." Nor is their arrangement haphazard. The great peaks are set back on a vast Alpine plateau. They "are not allowed"—a teleological phrase—"to come to the edge of this plateau for fear lest the stones and snow-slides from their slopes should fall on inhabited ground and cause death and destruction." "It is hardly necessary to point out," adds Ruskin, "the perfect wisdom and kindness of this arrangement as a provision for the safety of the inhabitants of the high mountain regions." Aquinas himself might have concluded as Ruskin concludes, "Now that such a structure is the best and wisest possible is indeed a sufficient reason for its existence and to many people it may seem useless to question further respecting its origin."

(II)

Teleology such as Ruskin's can only retard the advance of science, but though teleology is associated with deductive reasoning it would be absurd to suggest that deductive and *a priori* reasoning is of no value in science. This is very far from being the case. All that we are entitled to affirm is that the value of induction increases in proportion as science comes down to earth. The propositions of Euclid, to cite a classic example, are concerned with pure abstractions, with timeless truths which are eternally valid for the only kind of space with which Euclid is concerned. It might well be the case that Euclidean space only exists in the mind of God and that Euclid's propositions are not true of our space, for our space it would seem is not Euclidean. It is possible that some of Euclid's theorems may have originated in observation or experiment, but Euclid never strengthens his argument by the appeal to experiment or by the faintest suspicion of inductive reasoning. Euclidean geometry, the supreme example of triumphant deductive logic, occupies a border region midway between philosophy and science, and we are indebted to the Greeks not only as pioneers of pure mathematics but also for the first stirrings of the scientific spirit. "zetesis" (ζήτησις), which literally means "searching", is perhaps the first word to suggest that eager disinterested curiosity which is the very essence of scientific research.

The Greeks were interested in knowledge for the sake of knowledge. The Babylonians and the Egyptians had mastered the rudiments of space and time measurement, but their interest in science was purely pragmatic. Their rudimentary science was designed to provide an agricultural population with a reliable calendar and an accurate system of land measurement. It was left to the Greeks to develop the technique of mathematical reasoning.

"The land-surveying formulae of the Egyptians," writes Mr. J. W. Sullivan, "gave rise in the hands of the Greeks to a deductive geometry. This was an immensely important step forward. Mathematical reasoning, the most powerful of man's intellectual instruments, was created. Overwhelmed by the almost magical power of this new instrument, the Greeks thought that in mathematics they had discovered the key to all things. To the Pythagoreans in particular, number was the principle of all things. Everything, whether physical properties or moral qualities, was a manifestation of number. This outlook has played a very large part in the development of science. Leonardo da Vinci's remark that a science is perfect in so far as it is mathematical has been very generally accepted by scientific men. If a complete mathematical description of the world could be given it is felt that science would be complete."

Pure mathematics belong to philosophy; it is only when we cross the frontier which separates pure from applied mathematics that we enter the realm of science. If the Greeks had been as interested in applied as in pure mathematics they might have anticipated Watt's invention of the steam-engine, but though they were attracted by mathematics, especially by geometry, it is only the exceptional Greek who is prepared to submit to the discipline of patient and systematic observation. They were interested in the fundamental problems: What is the basis of the physical world? Water? Fire? Or a perpetual flux? and their preoccupation with these problems, which belong to philosophy rather than to science, distracted their attention from the specific problems with which the scientist deals.

The development of science along observational and experimental lines was checked by the great influence of Socrates. Socrates (470–399 B.C.) assumed a position of scepticism with regard to the validity of all human knowledge. He was interested in ethics rather than in physics, and he neglected, as Aristotle remarks, the world of Nature. His supreme interest was in conduct. Plato followed his master in concentrating on the ethical motive. His book *Timaeus* gives us, according to Dr. Singer, "a picture of the depths to which natural science can be degraded in the effect to give a specific teleological meaning to all parts of the visible Universe. . . . In its decay Platonism dragged science down and destroyed by neglect nearly all earlier biological material. . . . The mighty figure of Aristotle (384–322) stayed the tide for a time."

Plato was an impenitent fideist. He distrusted all knowledge received through the senses and maintained that intuition was the sole basis for certitude. Aristotle might be described as a semi-fideist. On the one hand he was certainly an empiricist, a firm believer in the value of experiment and observation. He practised what he preached, for he was a great naturalist with remarkable gifts of observation. His work gives evidence of profound knowledge of the animal kingdom, more especially of fishes, knowledge based on close and prolonged observation.

"The principles," he writes, "which lie at the basis of any particular science are derived from experience." (ἐμπειρία) He makes some very contemptuous references to the apeiría (ἀπειρία) induced by indifference to facts and undue preoccupation with abstract reasoning. "It is easy," he writes, "to distinguish those who argue from facts and those who argue from notions," and he held that the scientific study of Nature is more likely to lead to truth than the dialectical method of abstract deduction from unproved premises. He anticipated the doctrine that induction will often create a strong presumption in favour of a general law (see page 68). Through sense experience we discover particulars and we proceed from these particulars to universals by induction (ἐπαγωγή).

Aristotle, however, was not only an empiricist. He was also a fideist. For though observation was the dominating influence in the development of his system, the system itself had constantly to be readjusted to suit the requirements of certain *a priori* beliefs which Aristotle made no attempt either to prove or to check by observation, or indeed by reason.

Thus the fundamental bases of the Aristotelean system of physics depended among other things on the following beliefs:

That all matter is made up of the four elements, earth, air, fire and water. That the earth is at the centre of the universe which is itself spherical, and that the circular movement is the *most perfect conceivable, and that for this reason* the stars and planets move in concentric circles round the earth.

There is, of course, no pretence of scientific justification for the words which I have italicised, but the fideism which finds expression in these words is the link which connects Aristotle the Greek, Roger Bacon the mediaeval Catholic and Kepler the Protestant. The fideistic assumptions which handicapped Kepler in his scientific research were derived not from the medieval church but from the Greeks. Kepler revived the mathematical mysticism of Pythagoras. He believed that the universe was not merely explicable in mathematical terms, but is itself governed by mystical mathematical relations. At that time only six planets had been discovered. Kepler was immensely elated when he found that the "five regular solids" could be inserted between the spheres of the six planets. He believed that this fact, which even if it was true we should regard as absolutely irrelevant, was sufficient explanation of the planets being six in number. This in itself provides an interesting example of the conflict between the apriorist and empiricist standpoint. Kepler was influenced by apriorist considerations when he endeavoured to prove that the orbit of the planets was circular. At that time it was considered more dignified for a heavenly body to follow a circular orbit than an orbit in the shape of an ellipse. The circle was considered to possess more "perfection". Kepler made eighteen successive attempts to adapt the planetary movement to circular orbit before he finally adopted ellipses. The empiricist finally triumphed over the apriorist. "His faithfulness to observation", as Mr. Sullivan puts it, "overcame the aesthetic preferences."

It would be a great error to suppose that Kepler was the last of the aesthetic fideists and that "aesthetic preferences" had less influence on modern scientists than on Aristotle, Roger Bacon or Kepler. The circular orbit was probably thought more "perfect" because it is simpler than the elliptic. It is the aesthetic rather than the scientific appeal of simplicity which tempts us to prefer a simple to a complex solution. The doctrine that all living forms originated from a single cell has nothing but aesthetic charm to recommend it. It satisfies the aesthetic critic and is therefore accepted in spite of and not because of any scientific evidence. The prejudice against the doctrine of special creation is aesthetic rather than scientific. The constant interference of the Creator with the creation is felt to be untidy and therefore unaesthetic. The principal source of prejudice against psychical research is the aesthetic prejudice. A tambourine floating in mid-air cannot be reconciled with our *a priori* conviction that the supernatural is dignified. We would find it far easier to believe in spirits if the spirits which manifest themselves through mediums behaved and talked with greater dignity, but there is no scientific reason why discarnate spirits should be more intelligent or more dignified than the spirits which are incarnate in human bodies, some of whom as we know to our cost are not notably better company than "Feda" or "Great Hawk".

There are of course other reasons than the aesthetic for rejecting the claims of spiritualists to be in communication with the other world, but there is no scientific justification for refusing to examine, as Huxley refused to examine, these phenomena because they offend aesthetic susceptibilities. It is important that we should realise that aesthetic prejudices are as influential to-day as in the time of Kepler, Roger Bacon or Aristotle.

(III)

Aristotle's works on biology were not recovered for the west until his logic had penetrated and permeated the universities, and for this reason Aristotle the philosopher had far more influence on Christian thought than Aristotle the biologist, but it was not until the twelfth century that Aristotle's influence was decisive. It was Plato rather than Aristotle who dominated the first centuries of the Christian era, with disastrous results for science. Stoicism which found "incentives to piety in the established order, the universal harmony, the magnitude, the colour, the form, the arrangement of the world," ceased to be a living force after the end of the second century, and it was neoplatonism and not Stoicism which was to influence the church when the church emerged from the catacombs.

Sir Edmund Whittaker, f.r.s., one of the few great scientists who is also a philosopher, has summed up the mischievous influence of neoplatonism in the Donellan Lectures which he delivered in June 1946 in Trinity College, Dublin, and which have since been published under the title *Space and Spirit* (Thomas Nelson & Sons Ltd.).

"The Stoics more than any other school," writes Sir Edmund Whittaker, "had recognised the reign of law in nature and had attached a high importance to scientific investigation. To the neoplatonists, on the other hand, the material world was the lowest and vilest element in the scheme of things, and matter was a cause and embodiment of evil; their greatest teacher Plotinus (so we are informed by his disciple Porphyry) blushed because he had a body. So far as they took any notice of natural knowledge, they followed Aristotle: but their supramundane metaphysical system, in which no historical event could have any significance, left empirical knowledge aside, and focussed attention entirely on the One, the superessential supreme principle, and its various emanations. Incidentally it starved mathematics by depriving it of any contact with experimental science and created an intellectual atmosphere in which scientific research of every kind was abandoned. . . ." Neoplatonism affected the Christian attitude to empirical science, for St. Augustine who acknowledged his debt to Plotinus insisted that the only type of knowledge to be desired was knowledge of God and the soul, and that no profit was to be had from investigating the realm of nature.

"About 1120," writes Sir Edmund Whittaker, f.r.s., "an English monk, Adelard of Bath, secured in Cordova an Arabic edition of the *Elements* of Euclid and translated it into Latin. This work, and a Translation of the Algebra of Al-Khowarizmi made in 1145 by Robert of Chester, were the real beginnings of modern exact science" (*Space and Spirit*, p. 16).

Albert the Great (1193–1280) was one of the first of the mediaeval thinkers to display a real interest in scientific research. He wrote a book about animals and another book about vegetables and plants. Albert recommends the reader to study the best works of ancient writers, but their conclusions ought to be re-examined and above all supplemented by individual observation. Albert practised what he preached. Phrases such as "I have established", "I have observed", "I have proved", occur again and again in his works. He not only made positive contributions to existing knowledge but also helped to eliminate hypothetical monsters from the subjects worthy to be discussed by naturalists. There is a touch of genial irony in his remarks about the Phoenix:

"The phoenix is a bird of East Arabia, as those writers affirm who have done more research in mystical theology than in nature."

(IV)

Albert the Great had the making of a scientist, but the great Franciscan Roger Bacon was the first thinker of modern Europe to base his system of natural knowledge on observation and on experiment. Like his great namesake, Francis Bacon, he advocated the experimental method, but unlike Francis Bacon, he was himself an experimenter. He wrote a book on optics which was used as a textbook for two hundred years, and it is probable that he actually invented the primitive telescope which he described. He was an enthusiastic astronomer; the Gregorian reform of the calendar was based on ideas which Bacon had advocated without success in his own day. He gives us the first-known description of the composition of gunpowder. He was keenly interested in all mechanical problems, and his writings contain pregnant hints of future discoveries:

"Machines for navigating are possible without rowers, so that great ships suited to river or ocean, guided by one man, may be borne with greater speed than if they were full of men. Likewise cars may be made so that without a draught animal they may be moved *cum impetu inaestimabili*, as we deem the scythed chariots to have been from which antiquity fought. And flying machines are possible, so that a man may sit in the middle turning some device by which artificial wings may beat the air in the manner of a flying bird."

Nor were his interests confined to science in the strict sense of the term. He was the first to collect systematic data for a geography, and one of the first to insist on the importance of a scientific study of languages. He projected Greek, Hebrew and

Arabic grammars, and laid down the principles of textual criticism which were not fully developed until the nineteenth century.

Roger Bacon was in some respects very modern, and in other respects a true child of the Middle Ages.

Nothing, for instance, could be more mediaeval than Roger Bacon's insistence that all branches of knowledge must serve theology, and must find in that service their justification. The chief value of mathematics, so he tells us, is the light which it throws on many problems in the Holy Scriptures. The mathematician can, for instance, help to determine the exact position of heaven and hell, and the exact measurements of the Tabernacle, the Temple and the Ark. Roger Bacon could, indeed, be described as the spiritual father of the Anglo-Israelites; for, like the Anglo-Israelites, he believed that messages of great significance lay implicit in scriptural measurements.

Again, even in his hymn of praise of "experiment" he betrays the influence of his age.

"Experimental science," he writes, "teaches *experiri*, that is to test by observation or experiment the lofty conclusions of all science . . . the *fidelis experimentator* has considered that the eagle, and the stag, and the serpent, and the phoenix prolong life, and renew their youth." On which Dr. Taylor observes, "It may be pertinent to our estimate of Bacon's experimental science to query where the *experimentator* ever observed an eagle or a phoenix renewing its youth."

These were, however, the limitations of his age, and in spite of those limitations Roger Bacon can clearly be described as the first man of science in the modern sense of the term.

"His legacy to thought," writes Dr. Singer, "may be regarded as accuracy of method, criticism of authority, and reliance on experiment—the pillars of modern science."

Roger Bacon, indeed, was the first great empiricist of the Middle Ages. He has a far greater claim than his great namesake, Lord Bacon, to be considered the real father of modern science.

Roger Bacon initiated no scientific movement. He was an intellectual "sport" with no apparent influence on his contemporaries so far at least as science is concerned. How then can we explain the failure of his contemporaries to react to the stimulus of this great pioneer of scientific thought?

This is a question which the semi-educated can answer with ease. Bacon failed because the Church was hostile to science. There has never been a period when the Church was hostile to science; there have been periods when churchmen were uninterested in science. Aristotle and the Bible, so the mediaeval theologians believed, have all the answers. What the unaided human reason can discover has been discovered by Aristotle. The Scriptures contain divine revelation about matters which the unaided reason cannot discover. Everything worth knowing can be known by synthesising the truths which are accessible in Aristotle and the truths which have been revealed in the Scriptures. It was the logical rather than the spiritual and temporal relations between phenomena which interested mediaeval man. Natural phenomena illustrated the same general principles which were taught in theology. The principle on which the orderly universe had been constructed could be learned not by experiment and observation but by synthesising Aristotle and revelation. The *raison d'etre* of all phenomena was to be sought in their bearing on the eternal destiny of man. Nothing had any meaning except in so far as it fitted into this great logical scheme.

In this atmosphere it is obvious that science would appear to be a trivial activity. It could be of no real importance for the reason that it was concerned with merely secondary questions. *How* things happened was of no importance compared with the question of why they happened. "Even Roger Bacon," writes Mr. Sullivan, "the one man of his time who insisted on the experimental investigation of Nature, agreed that the importance of this investigation was that it would assist in elucidating theology. It was only when faith in the all-pervading purposefulness of natural phenomena had faded that the scientific method of enquiry became important."

It is often asserted that science stagnated in the Middle Ages, an assertion which fits very neatly into the propaganda pattern of the secularist, but which is only the starting point for the research of a history more concerned to understand the past than to minister to the self-satisfaction of those who congratulate themselves on their superiority to their forefathers. Admittedly the Middle Ages added little to the elementary scientific knowledge which they inherited from the past, but they "had a great deal to do," as Mr. Sullivan admits, "with the formation of the modern scientific outlook." The mediaevalist, like the scientist, believed in a universe subject to the reign of law, a universe unlike that of the Babylonians in which the arbitrary and the capricious predominated. Moreover, men like Bunden, Rector of Paris University, Nicholas of Oresine who became Bishop of Lisieux and Albert of Saxony, Bishop of Halberstadt were not molested for propounding scientific ideas very different from those of Aristotle. One need not be a Catholic to recognise the very real contribution of the mediaeval church to the scientific movement.

Harnack, the Liberal Protestant, was no friend to Catholicism, but he was a scholar who had a scholar's knowledge of the Middle Ages. "Scholasticism," he writes, "is simply nothing less than scientific thought, and it is merely perpetuating an unwarranted prejudice when it is thought that this part of the general history of science should be designated by a special name . . . the science of the Middle Ages gives practical proof of eagerness in thinking and exercises all its energy in subjecting all that is real and valuable to thought to which we can perhaps find no parallel in any other age."

"The Middle Ages," to quote the late Professor A. N. Whitehead, F.R.S., who had not the slightest sympathy with Catholic doctrine, "formed one long training of the intellect of Europe in the sense of order." There may have been some deficiency in respect to practice, but the idea never for a moment lost its grip. It was pre-eminently an epoch of orderly thought, *rationalist* through and through. The very anarchy quickened the sense for a coherent system; just as the modern anarchy of Europe has stimulated the intellectual vision of a League of Nations. But for science something more is wanted than a general sense of the order of things. It needs but a sentence to point out how the habit of definite, exact thought was implanted in the European mind by the long domination of scholastic logic and scholastic divinity. The habit remained after the philosophy had been repudiated, the priceless habit of looking for an exact point and of sticking to it when found. . . . The greatest contribution of mediaevalism to the formation of the scientific movement was the inexpungable belief that every detailed occurrence can be correlated with its antecedents in a perfectly definite manner, exemplifying general principles."

". . . The faith in the possibility of science generated antecedently to the development of modern scientific theory is an unconscious derivation from medieval theology."

Galileo is the only scientist who has been persecuted by the Church for his scientific opinions. The systematic persecution of scientists as scientists dates from the foundation of the first government in history to adopt atheism as a state philosophy. The mediaeval churchmen were neither hostile to nor interested in science. The mental energy of the Middle Ages was directed into other channels. They were preoccupied with the fundamental problems, the nature of ultimate truth and the destiny of man; they were not interested in what makes the wheels go round. Religion was to them the supreme reality, and therefore, yes *therefore*, the Middle Ages enriched Europe with its noblest art.

Great art and a dogmatic religion are as characteristic of the springtime of a culture as scepticism and scientific achievement of the winter of a declining civilisation. "Culture", writes Spengler, "is synonymous with religious creativeness. . . . Of great painting or great music there can no longer be for Western people any question. . . . In the shareholders' meeting of any limited company or the technical staff of any engineering works, there is more intelligence, taste, character and capacity than in the whole music and painting of modern Europe."

In the Middle Ages the creative genius of many found expression in art and song. To-day they find expression in applied science. The *Summa Theologica*, *The Divine Comedy* and the cathedral of Chartres are organically related, products of a religious philosophy. "Because we have no dogmatic theology of our own," writes the distinguished hellenist Professor Gilbert Norwood, "we have no cathedral architecture of our own," but we have instead the miracles of applied science. The communist manifesto, surrealism and the atom bomb are organically related, products of a secular philosophy.

"There are not bad things," said St. Thomas Aquinas, "only bad uses of things." In a Europe which was as Christian as the Middle Ages every new scientific discovery would be used *ad majorem gloriam nominis sui et utilitatem quoque nostram.*

L ?

(v)

There is no evidence in support of the popular myth which ascribes the alleged stagnation of science in the Middle Ages to the hostility of the Church. Roger Bacon was befriended by an enlightened pope who unfortunately died too soon to implement his promises of support. Bacon was suspected of heresy and towards the end of his long life was imprisoned for a few years by his own Order on the charge that his teachings "contained suspicious novelties".

Bacon, it must be admitted, asked for trouble. He was aggressive and tactless. He made sweeping attacks on the great leaders of Catholic thought whom he accused of "puerile vanity and ineffable falsity." He did not confine himself to attacks on rival Orders. His pointed references to the great Dominicans, Albert and Aquinas, might have been forgiven, but his own Order came in for its fair share of abuse. "Nullum ordinem excludo," he exclaimed in a fine outburst of impartial invective.

It was his controversial manners and not his scientific views which incensed his contemporaries. Original thinkers often find it difficult to conceal their contempt for their less brilliant colleagues. To convict the Church of persecuting science it is not enough to cite cases of scientists who got into trouble with the Church. Dentistry is a branch of medical science, and Dr. Crippen, a dentist, was hanged for murder when a Liberal government was in power, but nobody has accused Mr. Asquith of persecuting science. Bruno, a philosopher with an incidental interest in science, was burnt for heresy, but his scientific theories were not mentioned in the indictment on which he was condemned, and his case, greatly though we may deplore the action of the Church, has no relevance to the question which we are discussing, the attitude of the Church to science.

Both Joad and Haldane in their published controversies with me accused the Church of persecuting science. Haldane referred to scientific pioneers who had been "burned alive by their colleagues as some of them were at the instigation of the clergy." Joad was even more explicit. "The exponents of Christianity burned the men who discovered the earth's motion, burned the men who made the first tentative beginnings of physics and chemistry, burned the men who laid the foundations of our medical knowledge." Neither Haldane nor Joad when challenged could name a single scientist who was burned because his scientific views caused scandal among Christians.

The fact is that the alleged persecution of scientists by the Church is a propaganda myth. In the nineteen centuries of Christian history *there is only one case* of the Church taking action against a scientist because of his scientific beliefs.

The possibility that the earth revolves round the sun had been mooted by Aristarchus the Greek, but Aristarchus made no converts. The pioneers of heliocentric astronomy were not lay scientists but scientific churchmen, such as Nicole Oresme, Bishop of Lisieux from 1377 to 1382, who anticipated Copernicus in his commentary on Aristotle's *De Coelo*, and above all Canon Copernicus, whose book *De Revolutionibus orbium coelestium*, published in 1543, laid the foundations of "the modern history of the theories of the universe," to quote a distinguished modern astronomer, Sir Edmund Whittaker, F.R.S. The Canon's book, so far from encountering ecclesiastical opposition, would never have been published but for the active support of great churchmen, Cardinal Schömberg and the Bishop of Culm, support which was endorsed by Pope Paul III when he accepted the dedication of the book.

Neither Paul III nor any of the nine popes who followed him protested against the Copernican doctrine. In 1596, twenty years before Galileo got into trouble, the Protestant biological faculty at the University of Tübingen censured Kepler for writing a book in support of the Copernican doctrine. They made things so unpleasant for Kepler that he fled. And to whom? To the Jesuits of Gratz, who welcomed him warmly. Both Luther and Melanchthon inveighed against the blasphemy of a moving earth long before Rome itself was infected by this general alarm. Had Galileo been content to maintain the Copernican theory as a convenient hypothesis which explains phenomena in a simpler manner than the Ptolemaic, he would have been left in peace. He got into trouble because he invaded the sphere of the theologian and maintained that the Scriptural account of the sun standing still to facilitate Joshua's victory was in conflict with established facts.

Specialists, whether these be theologians or scientists, resent the competition of amateurs and the name of Galileo should be included in the martyrology of amateurs rather than in the martyrology of scientists.

The decree of the Holy Office which censured these views was, of course, a great blunder. But it must be remembered that, on the evidence available at the time, the case for the Copernican system was by no means overwhelming. Huxley, who looked into the matter, came to the conclusion that on the available evidence "the Pope and the Cardinals had rather the best of it." Directly after the trial of Galileo, Cardinal Bellarmine, perhaps the most influential of the cardinals, sent a letter to Foscarini in which he said that, had Galileo been content to show that his system explained celestial phenomena without denying the truth of Scripture, all would have been well. He added that if it could really be proved that the sun was fixed, a possibility which he clearly contemplated, it would be necessary to consider carefully the passages in Scripture which seemed to prove the contrary, and that it would then be necessary to admit that these passages had been misunderstood, rather than "to pronounce that to be false which is demonstrated."

So great was the respect of the Church for science that Galileo was treated with consideration far greater than that which would probably have been accorded to a priest who had sponsored his theories. "In the generation which saw the Thirty Years War", writes Professor Whitehead, "and remembered Alva in the Netherlands, the worst that happened to men of science was that Galileo suffered an honourable detention and a mild reproof before dying peacefully in his bed."

CHAPTER VIII

THE AGE OF NAIVE FAITH

Science has remained predominantly an anti-rationalistic movement based on a naive faith . . . it has never cared to justify its faith or to explain its meanings.

A. N. Whitehead, Science and the Modern World

(1)

SHORTLY after Renan left the church he contributed a preface to a book, *L'Avenir de la Science*. "It is no exaggeration," he wrote, "to say that science contains the future of humanity, and that it also can say the last word on human destiny, and teach mankind how to reach its goal . . . science is only valuable in so far as it can take the place of religion."

Here we find the essence of *scientism*, which was to be the fashionable creed of the nineteenth century.

Thirty years later Renan wrote a new preface to the same book. He was still a scientian but his seminary training had not been wholly wasted. The rationalism of the seminary had gradually eroded the emotional utopianism of the scientian. The rosy dawn which he had predicted was beginning to look suspiciously like a sunset, and science had not yet taken the place of religion. The evolutionary doctrine had filtered down to the man in the street, whose reactions to the good news that he was nothing more than a super-gorilla were not wholly encouraging.

"It seems possible," wrote Renan in more chastened mood, "that the collapse of supernatural belief will be followed by the collapse of moral convictions, and that the moment when humanity sees the reality of things will mark a real moral decline. Under the influence of illusions the good gorilla succeeded in making an astonishing moral effort. Remove the illusions and a part of the factitious energy which they aroused will disappear. . . . We are living on the perfume of an empty vase."

But the second thoughts of Renan could do little to arrest the Utopian optimism of the scientians, an optimism inspired by emotional deductions from the unproved dogma of evolution, by faith in the perfectibility of man and the inevitability of progress. "Man's progress," wrote Herschel, "towards a higher state need never fear a check, but must continue till the very last existence of history." "Progress," writes Herbert Spencer, "is not an accident but a necessity. What we call evil and immorality must disappear. It is certain that man must become perfect. . . . The ultimate development of the ideal man is certain —as certain as any conclusion in which we place the most implicit faith." "Men are borne along through space and time," writes Mr. H. G. Wells, "regardless of themselves as if to the awakening greatness of man."

Mr. H. G. Wells was the most uncritical of all the Scientians, but the optimism of his youth did not endure to the end. Just before he died he gave way to despair. His last testament is the tragic book *Mind at the End of its Tether*.

It is interesting to compare the pronouncements of the nineteenth-century scientians with the encyclicals of the popes. The prediction value of a philosophy is a useful test of its truth, and by that test scientism fails. The popes approached the problems of human nature with the detachment of the true scientist. Whereas many nineteenth-century scientists wrote like emotional revivalists in their predictions of man's inevitable progress to perfection, the popes based their predictions not on man as they would wish him to be but on man as he is. They did not forget the basic fact of original sin.

"In like manner," wrote Leo XIII, "the pains and hardships of life will have no end or cessation on earth; if the consequences of sin are bitter and hard to bear and must accompany man so long as life shall last, to suffer and endure that is the lot of humanity. . . . If there be any who pretend differently and who hold out to a hard-pressed people the boon of freedom from pain or trouble, an undisturbed repose, and constant enjoyment, they delude the people and impose upon them, and their lying promises will undoubtedly bring forth evils worse than the present. Nothing is more useful than to look upon the world as it really is."

Who were more scientific in their social outlook, the Utopian scientians or the pessimistic popes? The fact is that the popes were rationalists whereas the scientians were fideists. Scientism is a nineteenth-century variety of fideism. We have seen that the fideism which the church condemned affirmed "that the fundamental act of human knowledge consists in an act of faith." The nineteenth-century fideists would have repudiated with indignation the charge that they were fideists, and they would have been even more surprised had they been challenged to produce a rational proof of their philosophy. Whereas the Christian rationalist is prepared to support by proof and by rational argument his belief in the basic dogmas of Christianity, the existence of God and the deity of Jesus Christ, the scientian has "never cared to justify his faith or to explain its meaning."

A scientian would, far instance, be very surprised if he were challenged to give reasons for his instinctive belief that scientific research was its own justification irrespective of the practical importance of the results of such research. When Leverrier discovered the planet Neptune, he received the plaudits of the scientific world. He was recognised as a man who had enriched science with an epoch-making discovery, but it would be difficult to prove that his discovery has been of the slightest practical benefit to any inhabitant of our planet.

Professor Julian Huxley, whose book, *Religion without Revelation*, is a characteristic by-product of the scientism which has never cared to justify its faith, would reply by insisting that the pursuit of truth is an end in itself.

"Truth," he writes, "is not merely truthfulness; it is also discovery and knowledge. I believe that the acquisition of knowledge is one of the fundamental aims of man; that truth will, in the long run, prevail, and is always to be preferred to expediency."

St. Thomas, a rationalist living in an age of reason, did not begin by assuming, but by proving the articles of his creed. He developed his system, not from a highly arguable proposition such as the theorem that truth is always to be preferred to expediency, but from such modest premises as the axiom that nothing moves unless it has been set in motion.

No pupil of St. Thomas would have been allowed to *assume* that truth should always be preferred to falsehood. He would have been expected to prove his proposition, and if he had been unable to do so, he would have been sent to the bottom of the class and required to write out in a fair flowing hand the twenty-third chapter of the second book of the *Summa Contra Gentes*, in which St. Thomas proves that the first cause of the universe is mind, and that the last end of the universe must be the good of mind, that is truth, and that in the contemplation of truth man finds the principal object of wisdom.

Again, it is interesting to compare the fideism of Julian Huxley with the rationalism of Hilaire Belloc, for Mr. Belloc is not content merely to make a profession of faith in the allegiance which we owe to truth, but offers a rational ground for that allegiance. "The truth to which I am sure we owe a sort of allegiance not because it is the truth—we cannot owe allegiance to an abstraction—but because whenever we insist upon a truth we are witnessing to Almighty God."

Indeed it is only theism which can provide a rational basis for Professor Huxley's conviction that "truth is always to be preferred to expediency." Where theism is repudiated as in Soviet Russia, truth has to toe the party line, and a sincere Communist would feel very ashamed of himself if he permitted a bourgeois prejudice in favour of truth to conflict with his duty to the party.

Naturalism which is defined by the *Concise Oxford Dictionary* as "a view of the world which excludes the supernatural or spiritual", provides the scientian with no justification for the first article in the creed of the true science: "I believe that truth is to be preferred to falsehood." Theism, on the other hand, far from being in conflict with science, is required as a working hypothesis without which science itself has no justification. This view had, indeed, been put forward as early as 1894 by Mr. Arthur Balfour, who wrote as follows:

"Theism, then, whether or not it can in the strict meaning of the word be described as proved by science, is a principle which science, for a double reason, requires for its own completion. The ordered system of phenomena asks for a cause; our knowledge of that system is inexplicable unless we assume for it a rational author. . . . On the naturalistic hypothesis, the whole premises of knowledge are clearly due to the blind operation of material causes, and in the last resort to these alone. On that hypothesis we no more possess free reason than we possess free will. As all our volitions are the inevitable product of forces which are quite alien to morality, so all our conclusions are the inevitable product of forces which are quite alien to reason."

A quarter of a century later, Professor Eddington had developed Mr. Balfour's contention that unaided science is impotent to justify its existence or to vindicate its criteria, or even to prove that truth should be preferred to falsehood.

"If, for example, we admit that every thought in the mind is represented in the brain by a characteristic configuration of atoms, then if natural law determines the way in which the configurations of atoms succeed one another it will simultaneously determine the way in which thoughts succeed one another in the mind. Now the thought of '7 times 9' in a boy's mind is not seldom succeeded by the thought of '65'. What has gone wrong? In the intervening moments of cogitation everything has proceeded by natural laws which are unbreakable. Nevertheless we insist that something has gone wrong. However closely we may associate thought with the physical machinery of the brain, the connection is dropped as irrelevant as soon as we consider the fundamental property of thought—that it may be correct or incorrect. The machinery cannot be anything but correct. We say that the brain which produces '7 times 9 are 63' is better than the brain which produces '7 times 9 are 65'; but it is not as a servant of natural law that it is better. Our approval of the first brain has no connection with natural law; it is determined by the type of thought which it produces, and that involves recognising a domain of the other type of law—laws which ought to be kept, but may be broken. Dismiss the idea that natural law can swallow up religion; it cannot even tackle the multiplication table single-handed."

(II)

The basic doctrine of scientism is the sanctity of natural law, the basic emotion of scientism a quasi-mystical deification of science. Materialism is the most logical form of scientism, but many Scientians would categorically refuse to be classified as materialists, however resolutely they may continue to assume that all phenomena will ultimately be explicable in terms of natural forces. The more extreme modernists might be described as the fellow travellers of the scientians, for they too believe in the sanctity of natural law and are inhibited by emotional and irrational prejudices from embarking on the scientific investigation of the evidence for alleged miracles.

Modernism in its more extreme form is merely a revival of that eighteenth-century deism which was the theological reflection of the prevalent political fashion. Deism, the theory that God created the world, and then left it severely alone, became fashionable in England at the time of the 'Glorious Revolution' of 1688, the revolution which substituted a limited for an absolute monarch. The god of deism is a constitutional monarch. The king of England has a theoretic right to veto laws approved by Parliament, and the god of deism has a theoretic right to veto the laws of nature, but neither the king of England nor the King of Kings would venture to exercise these theoretic rights. Miracles are as objectionable to the deist as the arbitrary acts of an absolute monarch to the historian of the Whig tradition. Deism, in fact, might be defined as constitutional theism.

It is clear that the question as to whether higher intelligences are responsible for phenomena inexplicable within the framework of natural law is a question which can only be decided by evidence. Neither philosophy nor science can disprove the possibility that such high intelligences exist or that such higher intelligences are responsible for supernatural and supernormal phenomena.

The distinguished French scientist, Professor Richet, was a sceptic. He tried to explain the phenomena of psychical research within the framework of his materialistic philosophy, but though a sceptic he was not an obscurantist. His mind was not obscured by an invincible prejudice against evidence which conflicted with his materialistic bias. "Why should there not be intelligent and puissant beings distinct from those perceptible to senses? By what right should we dare to affirm on the basis of our limited senses, our defective intellect, and our scientific past, as yet hardly three centuries old, that in the vast cosmos man is the sole intelligent being, and that all mental reality always depends upon new cells irrigated by oxygenated blood?"

The scientian who is challenged to justify by reason his conviction that miracles do not occur, often falls back upon Hume. "A miracle," wrote Hume, "is a violation of the laws of nature, and as a firm and unalterable experience has established those laws, the proof against a miracle, from the very nature of the fact, is as entire as any argument from experience can be." Hume begged the question at issue, for those who believe in miracles assert that "a firm and unalterable experience" has proved that the so-called laws of nature are not absolute but are subject to influence by supernatural agencies.

John Stuart Mill was a rationalist, but like Richet he was not an obscurantist. He shocked contemporary rationalists by insisting that the question could "only be stated fairly as depending on a balance of evidence: a certain amount of positive evidence in favour of miracles and a negative presumption from the general course of human experience against them." And he added, "The interference of the human will with the course of nature is not an exception to law: and by the same rule interference by divine will would not be an exception either."

Professor J. B. S. Haldane, F.R.S., and I collaborated in a series of controversial letters published under the title *Science and the Supernatural*. Haldane is not only an exceptionally distinguished biologist but he has also enjoyed the benefits of a training in metaphysics. He took first-class honours in the Oxford school of *Litterae Humaniores*. It is reasonable to assume that a scientist with such versatile qualifications would state the case against miracles as effectively as it could be stated. And this is what he writes:

"Now, firstly, this hypothesis can be used to explain any phenomena you like. The motions of the stars were at one time explained as due to spirits guiding them (see *St. Thomas, passim*). It was a complete explanation, but unscientific because it could not be tested. These motions have since been explained by gravitation plus a series of 'miserable subterfuges', such as light pressure in the case of comets, the Friedmann-Lemaître effect for distant nebulae, and so on.

"Secondly, the historical argument appeals to me. In primitive societies such as those of West and Central Africa, all phenomena not understood, e.g. all non-violent deaths, are put down to the activity of spirits. As knowledge increases more and more of them are explained in other ways. There are now rather few left over in which the intervention of spirits is in the least plausible. A hundred years ago the best we could do to cope with an epidemic of cholera was to say prayers, and thus obtain aid from the spiritual world. It has since been discovered that the cause of cholera is to be found in the material world, and is readily destroyed by boiling. I am sufficiently impressed by the history of science to suppose that this sort of thing will go on."

Now in point of fact mediaeval theologians did *not* believe that the motion of stars was due to spirits guiding them. When asked for a reference Haldane could only reply that St. Thomas had quoted St. Augustine who did not consider it "certain whether the sun, moon and all the stars belong to the same company," i.e. of the angels, " 'though some think them to be bodies endowed with light, without sense or intelligence'."

"On the whole," writes Haldane, "I think it fair to say that, owing to the great respect paid to Aristotle's opinions, most mediaeval philosophers would have regarded the theory of angelic movers as very plausible." Haldane's standards of what is or what is not "very plausible" will be subjected to a closer examination in connection with Darwinism. Meanwhile we note his standard of an adequate reference, his readiness to generalise about the beliefs of mediaeval theologians from non-existent evidence, and the confusion of the issue which is characteristic of scientism, for the point at issue is not whether the hypothesis of miracles "can be used to explain any phenomena you like" but whether the hypothesis of naturalism is adequate to explain phenomena alleged to be caused by supernatural agencies.

What Haldane describes as "the historical argument" is in reality an invalid deduction from facts which in themselves are evidence neither for nor against the supernaturalism. If phenomena may be divided into those which are due to supernatural agencies and those which can be explained by natural causes, what should we expect to find? We should expect to make occasional mistakes in classifying borderline phenomena, and we should expect primitive peoples to classify as supernatural many things which a more scientific age would assign to natural causes.

But for the life of me I cannot see why the very developments which are inevitable if the supernatural be a reality are solemnly trotted out as a "historical argument" against the supernatural.

The "historical" argument, stripped of unnecessary details, boils down to this: If A is true B must happen. But B happened, therefore A is untrue.

Again there is no justification for the theory that the belief in miracles declines as the faith in science increases. On the con-

rary we believe in miracles precisely because we believe in
cience. It was, for instance, because men accepted the scientific
doctrine that bodies are attracted to the ground by the law of
gravity that they suspected a miracle when they witnessed the
phenomenon of levitation, a not unusual phenomenon in the
lives of the saints. It is, again, completely unhistorical to suggest that until comparatively recently a vast mass of phenomena
of which modern science has discovered the cause has been
attributed to supernatural agencies. Many phenomena which
we now understand appeared inexplicable to our mediaeval
ancestors, but it is absurd to suggest that they attributed to
supernatural agencies all phenomena which they could not
understand. Even if Haldane could show that they exaggerated
the influence of the supernatural, this would no more prove that
the supernatural is an illusion than the fact that the Darwinians
grossly exaggerated the effects of natural selection would prove
that natural selection is an illusion.

Finally, I dissent from Haldane's view that the process of
transferring phenomena from one class to the other, from the
supernatural to the natural, for instance, has been a one-way
process. Far from it. The process of attempting to transfer
phenomena from the supernatural to the natural category
reached its climax in the nineteenth century, but the ebb of
materialism has resulted in a re-transfer to the supernatural
category of many phenomena which Victorian scientists
attempted to interpret within the framework of naturalism.
There is indeed an increasing tendency to admit the genuineness of many phenomena, such as telepathy and certain pyschic
phenomena which the Victorian scientians thought it beneath
their dignity even to examine.

Modern science with its technique of investigation has
strengthened the case for supernatural and supranatural phenomena. I distinguish between supernatural phenomena, such
as the miracles of our Lord, and the supranatural phenomena
associated with spiritualism. The technique of testing such
phenomena has been greatly improved during the last half century not only at Lourdes but also in the national laboratories of
psychical research. The Bureau des Constatations at Lourdes,
for instance, has been in existence for over seventy years.
Hundreds of miracles have been examined. If Haldane's theory

were correct a large proportion of these alleged miracles would already have been transferred from the supernatural to the natural class, for the advance in medical science has been very striking during these fifty years. This, however, is not the case.

There has been no steady transference of phenomena from one class to the other. Science is as impotent to-day as it ever was to explain miracles which have occurred in every century and in every country. Science is as powerless to-day as it ever was to explain the evolution of life from lifeless matter, the evolution of mind, the vast array of religious phenomena, or the miracles which we accept as such on evidence vastly stronger than anything which is produced to justify faith in evolution. A few borderline phenomena may have been transferred from the supernatural to the natural class, but the vast mass of phenomena, originally classified as supernatural in origin, still remain obstinately inexplicable by science.

Haldane's argument against miracles has, however, one obvious advantage: it can never be refuted. If a modern saint, after being guillotined in the streets of Paris, walked down the boulevards carrying his head in his hands, Haldane would still be able to reply that the science of the future would one day be able to provide a purely natural explanation for an apparently supernatural event.

If it were true, as Haldane seems to think, that it is inconsistent for those who believe in prayer to boil water during an epidemic of cholera, it is surprising that the popes should have been so active in the promotion of the study of medicine and that religious Orders should have been so prominent in the foundation of hospitals. It is not easy to deal patiently with such frivolous dialectics or to understand the mental processes which lead to the conclusion that the belief in miracles means the end of natural science. If Bishop Barnes, as Monsignor Knox somewhere remarks, had been present at the feeding of the five thousand, he would have said "That is the end of all rational bakery". A miracle, so Christians believe, is an exceptional favour for which no man has the right to budget. It would be just as irrational to abandon the study of natural medicine because we believe that diseases are sometimes cured supernaturally at Lourdes, as to give up using the telegraph because exceptional people in exceptional circumstances have communicated with each other by telepathy.

"The Victorian agnostics," writes Dr. Inge, "had a strong case against supernaturalism which claimed for the miracle exactly that kind of actuality which science cannot allow it." Note in passing the unscientific identification of "science" with a particular sect of scientists, the scientians. "If," Dr. Inge continues, "an epidemic of cholera may be caused either by an infected water supply or by the blasphemies of an infidel mayor, there is an end of natural science."

On the contrary the proper course would be to instruct the natural scientists to investigate all possible natural causes for the epidemic of cholera, for it would be bad theology even to consider the possibility that the cause of the cholera might be supernatural until we had explored every possible natural cause.

The rôle of the scientist is *more* not less important in the Christian economy than in the scientian, for it is his task not only to investigate the natural causes of phenomena but also to investigate alleged supernatural phenomena and to make every effort to explain them within the framework of natural law.

CHAPTER IX

THEOPHOBIA

(1)

THE mediaeval fideists made an act of faith in the existence of God. The modern fideists make an act of faith in his non-existence. The new fideism, like the old, is not the result of a careful examination of the available experience and arguments. On the contrary the new fideism is the product of theophobia, to borrow Father Wasman's useful term. Theophobia was in part a natural reaction against Calvinism.

"If you can realise," writes Mr. Shaw, himself a product of and a reaction from Irish Protestantism which has many affinities with Calvinism, "how insufferably the world was oppressed by the notion that everything that happened was an arbitrary personal act of an arbitrary personal God of dangerous, jealous and cruel personal character, so that even the relief of the pains of maternity by means of chloroform was objected to as interference with his arrangements which he would probably resent, you will understand how the world jumped at Darwin."

The "jump" was unnecessary, for it is possible to reject Calvinism without rejecting theism, but Mr. Shaw's outburst is characteristic, for again and again arguments which have no relevance to the question as to whether nature is its own explanation or whether nature can only be explained within the framework of a theistic philosophy are advanced in support of Atheism. Of these by far the most popular and the most difficult to refute is the argument which is based on the problem of evil.

Now the problem of evil is only a difficulty if we believe, as Christians do believe, that God is both all-good and also all-powerful. Suffering and misery present no problem to those who believe, as many theists have believed, that God is good but *not* omnipotent. There are religions in which the universe is regarded as the battleground between a beneficent God and a malevolent Devil, neither of whom are omnipotent.

Even if the scientian could disprove the Christian conception of God he would be no nearer establishing the principal dogma of his faith, the sanctity of natural law, or of explaining the origin of species without postulating some kind of creative power, though not necessarily an omnipotent creative power.

The evidence of nature may not point irresistibly to a belief in a deity who is both omnipotent and perfect, but the evidence does suggest that things have been, in the main, arranged to ensure the happiness of living creatures. "The popular idea," writes that eminent Darwinian, A. R. Wallace, "of the struggle for existence entailing misery and pain on the animal world is the very reverse of the truth. What it really brings about is the maximum of life and enjoyment of life with a minimum of suffering and pain. Given the necessity of death and reproduction—and without these there could have been no progressive development of the animal world—and it is difficult to imagine a system under which a greater balance of happiness could have been secured." And he adds elsewhere, "The probability is that there is as great a gap between man and the lower animals in sensitiveness to pain as there is in their intellectual and moral faculties."

Political theophobia is the result of an identification in the public mind of the established Church with the established order of society. The rebel against the existing order tends to become a rebel against the form of religion associated with that social order.

"The term *Bog*, God," writes Bukharin, "comes from the same root as the word *Bogaty*, rich. God is therefore strong, powerful and rich. What other names has God? He is called the Lord, that signifies lord in contrast to slave; God is also called the Ruler in Heaven, and all the other titles of God, such as Governor and the like, point in the same direction. . . . Faith in God is thus a reflection of loathsome earthly conditions; it is faith in a slavery which exists, presumably, not only on earth but throughout the universe."

Scientific theophobia is partly due, as Sir Arthur Eddington has pointed out, to a "tidiness of mind which rebels against the idea of permeating scientific research with religious implication."

"Creation," writes P. Broca, "implies the permanence of miracles, that is nature subjected to a will and not to laws. And if there be no more laws there is no more science." This is merely a variant of Haldane's antithesis, prayer versus boiling the water. Clearly it is the duty of the scientist to be very chary of admitting the possibility of a supernatural intrusion into the natural realm. It is his business to make every effort to discover the natural causes of the phenomena which he investigates, for as Sabatier remarks "God who is the final reason of everything is the scientific explanation of nothing."

But it is one thing to be reluctant to admit that a particular phenomenon is inexplicable within the framework of natural law, and quite another matter dogmatically to assert that natural law is supreme and inviolable.

(II)

Theophobia, as Mr. Shaw admits, was the principal reason for the triumph of Darwinism. By Darwinism I do *not* mean the doctrine of evolution which, as we shall see, was promulgated in a far more plausible form by Darwin's great predecessor Lamarck, but the doctrine which is implied in the title of Darwin's famous work *On the Origin of Species by Means of Natural Selection, or the Preservation of Favoured Races in the Struggle for Life*. Note "By Means of Natural Selection" and *not* "Mainly by means of Natural Selection."

Now that even those who still describe themselves as Darwinists realise the absurdity of ascribing the origin of species to an agency which can only select what has already originated, there is an increasing tendency to quote stray sentences from the *Origin of Species* which attribute importance to use and disuse, the fact being that it is easy to quote from Darwin's writings passages which support almost *any* theory of evolution, for he was neither a clear thinker nor a clear writer, but the importance which Darwin attached to Natural Selection can hardly be exaggerated. In the concluding sentences of his book *The Variations of Animals and Plants under Domestication* he elaborated a striking metaphor in which he compared Natural Selection to a human builder.

Natural Selection, Darwin argued, may be said to create new species out of fortuitous variations as truly as a man may be said to create a building out of the material provided by stones of various shapes.

It was this dogma that "Natural Selection may be said to

create a new species" which explains the attraction of Darwinism for those suffering from the fashionable complaint of theophobia. In his saner moments Charles Darwin might declare: "This grand sequence of events the mind refuses to accept as the result of blind chance. The understanding revolts from such a conclusion," but elsewhere he is just as insistent on the fact that it is unnecessary to postulate a mind behind creation to explain the evolutionary process.

According to Darwin the transformation of species is effected by the mechanical action of environment blindly selecting for survival fortuitous advantageous variations. Paley, in his classic *Natural Theology*, had argued that it would be no more difficult to believe that a watch represented a mere chance aggregation of matter than that the human eye, so exquisitely adapted to the purpose which it serves, is not the creation of an intelligent being. The popularity of Darwinism was due very largely to the fact that Darwin was said to have refuted Paley. "The old argument from design in nature," wrote Darwin, "as given by Paley, which formerly seemed to me so conclusive, fails, now that the law of Natural Selection has been discovered. We can no longer argue that, for instance, the beautiful hinge of a bivalve shell must have been made by an intelligent being, like the hinge of a door by man. There seems to be no more design in the variability of organic beings, and in the action of Natural Selection, than in the course which the wind blows."

It was this determination to eliminate design from nature which alone explains the triumph of Darwinism. Darwinism, as the great scientist von Uexhull said, *"is more a religion than a science*. Its logical consistency leaves as much to be desired as the accuracy of the facts on which it is based. That is why all arguments against it remain ineffective. It is nothing but the embodiment of the determination to rid nature at any cost of the principle of design (Planmässigkeit). In this way the idea of evolution has become the sacred conviction of thousands, *a conviction that has no longer anything to do with unbiased scientific research"* (italics mine).

Theophobia as the motive for the acceptance of Darwinism emerges very clearly in the following quotation from du Bois-Reymond: "Whoever does not place all activity wholesale under the sway of Epicurean chance, whoever gives only his little finger to teleology will inevitably arrive at Paley's discarded *Natural Theology*, and so much the more necessarily the more clearly he thinks and the more independent his judgment. . . . The possibility, ever so distant, of banishing from nature its seeming purpose, and putting a blind necessity everywhere in the place of final causes, appears, therefore, as one of the greatest advances of the world of thought, from which a new era will be dated in the treatment of these problems. To have somewhat eased the torture of the intellect which ponders over the world-problem will, as long as philosophical naturalists exist, be Charles Darwin's greatest title to glory."

Nothing but the irrational influence of theophobia can explain this hysterical worship for "blind necessity". If men like machines are governed by "blind necessity" there is no place for virtue or vice in our philosophy, for we do not speak of moral motor-cars. Why should we describe as "one of the greatest advances in the world of thought" a philosophy which robs life of significance and which deprives man of dignity and condemns him to final extinction?

Du Bois-Reymond is not the only scientist who seems to think that Darwin established his "greatest title to glory" by misleading the public. Professor Yves Delage, after drawing attention to the weak points in Darwinism, adds: "Whatever may befall this theory in the future, Darwin's everlasting title to glory will be that he explained the seemingly marvellous adaptation of living things by the mere action of natural factors without looking to a divine intervention, without resorting to any finalist or metaphysical hypothesis."

Du Bois-Reymond's "greatest title to glory" has evolved into "everlasting title to glory" perhaps because the evidence *against* Darwinism seemed even stronger to Delage than to Reymond, with the result that Darwin's heroic effort to prove that God could be dispensed with seemed all the more deserving of praise.

"We must assume," wrote Weismann, "Natural Selection to be the principle of the explanation of the metamorphoses because all other apparent principles of explanation fail us, and it is inconceivable that there should be another capable of explaining the adaptation of organisms *without assuming the help of a principle of design.*"

The italics, which are Weismann's, emphasise the horror with which he contemplated the appalling alternative.

We must accept, so he argues, a theory which we have every reason to distrust because the only alternative implies the existence of God.

We must assume. And yet it was the Victorians who contrasted the theologian who assumes, with the scientist who proves.

We must assume is the first commandment in the decalogue of the devout scientian.

"Spontaneous generation," wrote Weismann, "in spite of all vain efforts to demonstrate it remains for me a logical necessity." "Logical", because it is the only possible conclusion once we have assumed that God does not exist.

Fideism is a product of *feeling*, rationalism of thought. The most candid admission of the fact that the acceptance of evolution is a matter of *feeling* is to be found in the work of a distinguished scientist, Lecomte du Noüy, who writes in his book *Human Destiny:* "The same holds true of the appearance of homiothermism (constant temperature) in birds. This is an immense and unquestionable liberation from the servitude to the environment and has, it must be admitted, all the unsatisfactory characteristics of absolute creation, whereas we *feel* that such cannot be the case". ("feel" is italicised in the original).

That evolution has *not* been proved in the normal sense of that word is clear from the confessions of scientists who admit that they accepted or accept evolution for philosophical rather than for scientific reasons. Huxley realised that the fossil record did not suggest evolution. The expression "missing link" is most unscientific for it is not the *links* which are missing but the chains, the chains of fossils necessary to link one family with another. Huxley in his 1862 address to the Geological Society said:

"In answer to the question 'What does an impartial survey of the positively ascertained truths of palaeontology testify in relation to the common doctrines of progressive modification?' I reply: 'It negatives these doctrines, for it either shows no evidence for such modification or demonstrates that such modification has been very slight'."

In 1870 he repeated this passage but added that "the results of recent investigation" had provided "much ground for softening the somewhat Brutus-like severity with which in 1862 I dealt with a doctrine for the truth of which I should have been glad enough to be able to find a good foundation." Note the will to believe in evolution.

Huxley, when he first met Darwin, expressed his "belief in the sharpness of the lines of demarcation between the natural groups and the absence of transitional forms," but by 1857 he was searching for some hypothesis "to replace the untenable separate creation theory." By "untenable" Huxley, of course, meant "uncongenial". Yves Delage in 1903 admitted that he was evolutionist for "personal philosophic reasons" and that "if one takes his stand upon *the exclusive ground of facts* it must be acknowledged that the *formation of one species from another species has not been demonstrated at all*."

In more recent times Professor D. M. S. Watson who was the principal speaker in a series of broadcasts (October 2nd to December 18th, 1942) informed a body of scientists at Cape Town that "*Evolution itself is accepted by zoologists not because it has been observed to occur or can be proved by logically coherent evidence to be true*, but because the only alternative, special creation, is clearly incredible." (talics mine.)

It would be idle to ask a scientist why the theory of special creation is "untenable", for every scientist who can think is well aware of the fact that it is impossible either by science or by philosophy to demonstrate that the hypothesis of special creation is "untenable".

The emotional disgust provoked in certain minds by the hypothesis of special creation emerges very clearly in the exchange of letters between Douglas Dewar and H. S. Shelton which was published by Hollis & Carter under the title of *Is Evolution Proved?* The publishers, who specialise in educational works, invited me to edit and write an introduction to this book. It was my duty to do what I could to prevent Shelton and Dewar becoming too personal, for each regarded the other as an invincible fideist whose faith was unsupported by anything in the nature of scientific evidence, the truth being of course that there is a good deal to be said on both sides in the controversy. Dewar is a distinguished ornithologist, and the best-known critic of evolution in England. Shelton is the author of various books on science and on philosophy. The contrast between the urbane and rational tone of his contributions to papers such as *Mind* and the *Hibbert Journal*, many of which I have read with interest and profit, and the emotional petulance of his utterances on special creation was very striking.

Shelton is a theist and, as such, accepts creation, but when he was challenged to explain why the God in whose creative power he believes should confine his creative acts to the initial act of creating the universe on the understanding that thenceforward he would never again interfere, he was at first evasive, and when pressed became distinctly nettled; which is not surprising, for Shelton at his best is a clear and logical thinker, and no philosopher enjoys being forced to defend what he knows to be a purely emotional prejudice. "I regard," he writes, "the hypothesis of special creation as too foolish for serious consideration; indeed, I do not regard it as a hypothesis at all, but merely one of those peculiar confusions of thought which remove some anti-evolutionists from the class of people with whom it is possible to conduct a rational discussion."

When further pressed to explain why God, whose creative power he admitted, should confine himself to a single act of creation, he replied: "because one absurdity is better than a million absurdities," thereby inviting the obvious retort that he was, in effect, admitting that his own creed starts from the premise "credo quia absurdum est."

(III)

It is as difficult for modern man to accept special creation as it would have been for his mediaeval ancestor to disbelieve in the literal accuracy of Genesis. It is only the exceptional man who can resist the mental fashion of his age. We are all to a greater or lesser degree conditioned by a kind of snobbery which makes us reluctant to be classed with those who are mentally dressed in discarded fashions. *Noscitur a sociis*, and we shrink from association with Bible-belt fundamentalists. But there are other and less ignoble reasons for the prejudice against special creation, a prejudice which may have its roots not only in theophobic but also in theological reasons.

It is interesting to compare Mr. Shelton's emotional outburst when challenged to justify his objections to special creation with the calm rationalism of a modern disciple of that great mediaeval rationalist St. Thomas Aquinas. In *Blackfriars* (May 4th 1948) "F. S. T." writes:—

"To most scientists, including some Catholics, it seems very unlikely that God should be continually intervening in the course of biology and almost never in chemistry or physics. Such continuous interventions seems to them a less perfect mode of conducting a universe than the creation of a single primordial cell capable of actualising all the potentialities of life. Is such a feeling a mere fashion, as Dewar would have it, or is it a valid inference from the continuity and order of all the other phenomena with which we are acquainted? It seems that the Catholic need not positively reject or accept the theory of evolution, but rather take account of it as a likely account of the history of life and consider how it may be reconciled with the truths of faith. Let us remember the word of God to Job: 'Where wast thou when I laid the foundations of the world?' and refrain from positive assertions or denials concerning the manner in which we and other living creatures have, under God, come to be."

If it were not for reasons very similar to those mentioned by "F. S. T." in the passage which I have just quoted, many people including the present writer would be converted to special creation, but though I admit the force of F. S. T.'s argument it is a little rash to adapt our beliefs about creation to our own *a priori* conceptions as to what constitutes a "perfect mode of conducting the universe." If the scientific evidence be conclusive against the doctrine of a slow gradual evolution of species, we should have to subordinate our theological prejudices to demonstrated facts, however reluctant we might be to accept the doctrine of special creation. The fossil record is certainly difficult, but perhaps not absolutely impossible to reconcile with evolution, but there are, as we shall see, other slight indications of evolution which seem to me to absolve those who refuse to declare themselves evolutionists from the charge of cowardice or mental snobbery. None the less, the position of a person who adopts the agnostic attitude is not easy. The present writer, for instance, in his capacity as editor of the Shelton-Dewar controversy was attacked by Sir Arthur Keith in one review for his alleged anti-evolution bias and by Commander Acworth in another review for his bias against special creation.

(IV)

The modern revolt against reason owes more to Darwinism
than to any other single fact, and it will therefore be necessary
to discuss Darwinism in some detail. Our faith in reason is
bound up with our faith in the power of the human mind to
draw rational conclusions from reliable evidence, but "the
horrid doubt" to which Darwin confessed, "the horrid doubt as
to whether the convictions of a man's mind, which developed
from the mind of the lower animals, are of any value or at all
trustworthy" gradually infected his followers. Freudianism,
which starts from the premise that the mental processes are
mainly determined by irrational influences, is the logical consequence of Darwin's "horrid doubt".

The rejection of Darwinism does not necessarily involve the
rejection of evolution but the same fideism which inspired men
"to jump at Darwinism" is also responsible for the teaching of
evolution in our schools and universities, not as a tentative
hypothesis riddled with difficulties but as a dogma which only a
fundamentalist or a fanatic could possibly question. Biologists
who are well aware of the growing scepticism about evolution
have justified the official attitude on the ground that evolution
is "the only scientific hypothesis". Now the word "scientific" is
derived from the Latin word *scientia* which means knowledge,
and a scientific explanation, as I have already remarked, is an
explanation which is in accord with all the known facts. If,
however, "scientific explanation" means an explanation in
terms of natural agencies, the statement that evolution is the
only scientific explanation is a glimpse of the obvious, for clearly
the doctrine that the origin of species can be explained by
natural causes is the only explanation consistent with the doctrine that the origin of species was not due to supernatural causes.

But surely what matters is not whether an explanation is
"scientific", whatever that may mean, but whether it is correct,
and much confusion would be avoided if the old-fashioned
words "true" and "false" were substituted for "scientific" and
"unscientific".

Scientians have been very successful in suggesting that the
doctrine of evolution is only doubted by cranks. Even if we confine ourselves to the scientific élite of Great Britain, the Fellows
of the Royal Society, the name of the late Sir Ambrose Fleming,

F.R.S., who was a convinced creationist, could be cited in favour of special creation, and many another F.R.S. can be numbered among those who believe that evolution still lacks adequate proof.

The minority of those who have the courage to challenge the dogma of evolution is, of course, far smaller than the number of those who dare not express their doubts. It is, as a Fellow of the Royal Society once remarked to me, professional suicide for a biologist to attack organic evolution as such. "The tyranny of the *Zeitgeist* in the matter of evolution," wrote Dwight, Parkman Professor of Anatomy at Harvard, "is overwhelming to a degree of which outsiders have no idea. Not only does it influence (as I admit it does in my own case) our manner of thinking, but there is oppression as in the days of the Terror. How very few of the leaders of science dare to tell the truth concerning their own state of mind."

And now for a few quotations from the sceptics who *have* the courage to proclaim their scepticism.

Sir Ambrose Fleming, F.R.S., was a convinced creationist. He rejected evolution.

Sir J. William Dawson, F.R.S. (obit. 1899), Professor of Geology and Principal of McGill University, writes: "The evolutionist doctrine is itself one of the strangest phenomena of humanity, but that in our day a system destitute of any shadow of proof, and supported merely by vague analogies and figures of speech, and by the arbitrary and artificial coherence of its own parts, should be accepted as a philosophy, and should enable adherents to string upon its thread of hypotheses our vast and weighty stores of knowledge is surpassing strange."

Dr. Fairfield Osborn, former Curator of the American Museum of Natural History, an evolutionist troubled by doubts, writes: "Between the appearance of the *Origin of Species* in 1859 and the present time there have been great waves of faith in one explanation and in another; each of these waves of confidence has ended in disappointment, until finally we have reached a stage of very general scepticism."

Dr. Austin H. Clark, of the United States National Museum, Washington, writes: "Thus so far as concerns the major groups of animals, the creationists seem to have the better of the argument. There is not the slightest evidence that any of the major groups arose from any other."

Professor D. H. Scott, F.R.S.: "For the moment at all events, the Darwinian period is past. We can no longer enjoy the comfortable assurance which once satisfied so many of us, that the main problem has been solved, all is again in the melting pot."

Professor T. H. Morgan, Nobel prize winner in 1933: "Within the period of human history we do not know of a single instance of the transformation of one species into another, if we apply the most rigid and extreme tests used to distinguish wild species from each other. It may therefore be claimed that the theory of descent is lacking in the most essential feature that it needs to place the theory on a scientific basis."

European scientists have, on the whole, been less uncritical in their acceptance of evolution than British scientists. Oswald Spengler was not a scientist, but he was well informed about scientific opinion, and the following passage from his famous book, *The Decline of the West*, is evidence of the growing scepticism about evolution. Spengler's religious views are difficult to discover, but his theology seems to be pantheistic. In the following passage he uses "Darwinism" as a popular equivalent for "evolution".

"Palaeontology," he writes, "furnishes the most conclusive refutation of Darwinism. According to the laws of probability, fossil deposits are only test samples. Each sample should therefore represent a different phase of evolution, and in this case there would be no transitional forms, no boundaries, and also no species. Instead of this we find completely stable and unchanging forms persisting through long ages, forms which have not evolved in accordance with the principle of adaptation, but appear suddenly and at once in their final form, and thereafter instead of evolving towards more perfect adaptation become rare and die out, while quite other types emerge again." And Spengler sums up his own mystical interpretation of the origin of species in the memorable sentence: "It is fate which has summoned into the world, life above all, the ever-growing opposition of plant and animal, each single type, each genus and each species." *Es ist ein Schicksal welches das Leben überhaupt, den immer wachsenden Gegensatz von Pflanze und Tier, jeden einzelnen Typus, jede Gattung und Art in die Welt berief. . . .*

What is this but the translation into language inoffensive to modern ears of the old truth, "And God said, Let the earth bring forth the living creature after his kind, cattle and creeping thing, and beast of the earth after his kind. And so it was."

The most remarkable evidence of increasing scepticism about evolution is contained in the volume which lies before me as I write, the fifth volume of the *Encyclopédie Française*, which is devoted to *Les Êtres Vivants. Plantes et Animaux*. To this volume, published like its predecessors by the famous house of Larousse, eminent French scientists contribute. The editor, Paul Lemoine, was a former Director of the National Museum of Natural History at Paris. The concluding essay in this volume is by Lemoine and is entitled "Que Valent Les Théories de l'Evolution?" "What are the theories of evolution worth?" Lemoine answers, in effect, that they are worth nothing. "The theories of evolution," he writes, "in which our student youth was cradled, constitute a dogma which all the world continues to teach: but each in his speciality, zoologist or botanist, comes to the conclusion that none of the available explanations are adequate." Lemoine then analyses in detail the difficulty of reconciling evolution with palaeontology and biogeography. And he concludes his chapter with the following words: "Il resulte de cet exposé que la thêorie de l'évolution est impossible. Au fond, malgré les apparences, personne n'y croit plus. . . . L'evolution est une sorte de dogme auquelle les prêtres ne croient plus mais qu'ils maintiennent pour le peuple. . . ." "Cela il faut avoir le courage de le dire, pour que les hommes de la génération future orientent leurs recherches d'une autre façon." (It results from this summary that the theory of evolution is *impossible*. In reality in spite of appearances nobody believes in it any more. . . . Evolution is a sort of dogma in which the priests no longer believe but which they maintain for their people. . . . It is necessary to say this in order that future generations may orientate their researches in another fashion.)

It is of course a gross exaggeration even to imply that the majority of those who teach evolution do not believe in it, but the mere fact that such a statement could appear in Larousse's French Encyclopaedia is all the evidence that is necessary to refute the controversial trick of pretending that those who have doubts about evolution are fools or cranks.

(v)

Catholics are not free to believe in the evolution of the soul, but are free to support the hypothesis that man's body has evolved from simpler forms.

The belief in slow gradual evolution, though incompatible with belief in the special creation of the different types, is not incompatible with divine creation. The theory that mind is a by-product of matter is clearly inconsistent with divine creation, but the hypothesis that mind emerges when the cerebral organism has reached a certain stage is equally consistent with theism and with materialism. The popular modern phrase, "emergent evolution", is not, of course, an explanation but merely a label for an obvious lacuna in the knowledge of the scientist as such.

Though I myself do not believe that evolution has been proved, and though I refuse to recognise any compulsion to declare myself either for evolution or for special creation, I fully recognise the fact that the doctrine of slow and gradual evolution of all forms of life from a single cell is not incompatible with the Catholic doctrine of divine creation.

CHAPTER X

THE ESSENCE OF DARWINISM

D ARWIN's acquiescence in the conspiracy to represent him as the pioneer of evolutionary doctrine and his ungenerous attitude to his predecessors' doctrine are embarrassing to his admirers, for in point of fact the doctrine was first promulgated by Buffon (1708–88) who was born one hundred and one years before Darwin. The great French Naturalist Lamarck (1744–1829) and Darwin's own grandfather Erasmus Darwin (1731–1802) elaborated in complete independence of each other a doctrine of evolution which marked an advance on that of Buffon, and was slightly less difficult to defend than Darwinism.

In October 1838 Darwin read Malthus's *Essay on Population*, and was much impressed by his presentment of the struggle for existence. It was in this struggle for existence that Darwin believed that he had discovered the eliminating agent which his theory required. The means of sustenance are limited, and the competition for these limited means is very severe. The successful competitors survive, the less successful tend to die out. Malthus had given the clue and Darwin deduced that favourable variations are preserved and unfavourable variations are destroyed. "The result would be," wrote Darwin, "*the formation of a new species*." Here we have in outline the famous theory of natural selection.

The difference between Darwinism and Lamarckianism may be illustrated by the example of the giraffe. According to Darwin the long neck of this animal would be explained as follows: in times of drought or famine herbivorous animals with necks slightly longer than other individuals in that species would be able to reach the leaves of high branches which were out of reach of their less fortunate rivals. Consequently, animals with slightly longer necks have more chance of surviving than those with slightly shorter necks. The former would tend to survive and procreate offspring, and the latter to die. The process would be repeated in each generation, with the result that the average length of neck in each generation would tend to increase slightly, thus producing the giraffe in the course of geological ages.

Lamarck, on the other hand, would explain the giraffe's neck partly as the result of "use", partly as the reward of effort. The giraffe that keeps on stretching its neck develops a long neck, much as a blacksmith develops muscles in his arm. The giraffe that refuses to be beaten, that persists in trying to get the foliage just beyond its reach, will be rewarded by the acquisition of a long neck.

The great objection to Lamarckianism is the fact, if it be a fact, that acquired characteristics are not inherited. Use and disuse only affect the individual during his lifetime. The child of the blacksmith does not start life with an arm more developed than a child of yours or mine. The children of Jews whose ancestors have been circumcised for thousands of years are born wiihout any inherited trace of this operation. Darwin's half-hearted attempt to buttress the theory of natural selection with the Lamarckian theory of the effects of use and disuse contributes nothing of value to the apologetics of evolution.

According to Lamarck the more intelligent and the more persistent giraffes select themselves, so to speak, and survive as a reward of their efforts. According to Darwin, natural selection blindly selects in each generation the giraffes who happen to be endowed, not as the result of their efforts but by chance, with rather longer necks than their rivals. According to Lamarck, the long neck is the prize awarded to the best trier at the end of the race; according to Darwin, the long neck is the equivalent to, say, a start of fifty yards in a mile race, and it is pure chance which decides which competitors are to receive this start. "Stripped of detail," writes Samuel Butler, "the point at issue is this: Whether luck or cunning is the fitter to be insisted on as the main means of organic development."

Darwin's famous book is usually referred to as *The Origin of Species*. Its argument may be summarised as follows:

Individual members of a species vary. The variations may be slight, but they are none the less real, and moreover these variations affect the survival chances of particular individuals. Some individuals will be fleeter than others, and therefore better able to escape from their enemies. Other individuals will be slightly better protected against the cold, and will therefore

have more chance of surviving an unusually cold winter. The
progeny of favoured individuals will inherit the qualities which
enable their parents to compete with success in the struggle for
existence.

The gradual and progressive accumulation of small variations will produce first a distinct variety, and secondly a distinct
species—in other words, gradually transform one type of animal
or plant into a totally different type of animal or plant. In each
generation the individuals who are less fitted to survive will die
off more rapidly and thus presumably leave fewer progeny,
whereas their slightly more fortunate rivals will live longer and
consequently presumably leave a larger progeny.

Only a limited number in each generation will survive to procreate their offspring, and those which survive will perpetuate
the advantages which enabled them to compete successfully.
The gradual accumulation of infinitesimal differences will thus,
in the course of geological time, produce all the varieties of
living form. "The pivot upon which the argument for evolution
rested," writes Dr. Milum, "and by which it conquered men's
minds, was a train of thought, a logical syllogism, rather than
an observed sequence of events in the course of nature."

Samuel Butler declared that he could no more believe that
the adaptation of structures to needs throughout nature, adapta-
tions of the most delicate ingenuity, were the result of gratuitous
accumulation of favourable variations than he could believe
that a mouse-trap or a steam-engine "is the result of the accumulation of blind minute fortuitous variations in a creature
called man, which creature has never wanted either mouse-
traps or steam-engines, but has had a sort of promiscuous tendency to make them, and was benefited by making them, so
that those of the race who had a tendency to make them survived and left issue, which issue would thus naturally tend to
make more mouse-traps and more steam-engines."

CHAPTER XI

DARWINISM AND EVOLUTION

To us Darwin no more speaks with philosophic authority.
Professor Bateson, Presidential Address to the British
Association, 1914

We have now the remarkable spectacle that just when many scientific men are all agreed that there is no part of the Darwinian system that is of any great influence, and that, as a whole, the theory is not only unproved, but impossible, the ignorant, half-educated masses have acquired the idea that it is to be accepted as a fundamental fact. . . .
Thomas Dwight, Professor of Anatomy at Harvard
University

It is pretty clear that we must wholly abandon the Darwinian hypothesis.
Cuenot, LA GENÈSE DES ESPÈCES ANIMALES, 1921,
Second Edition

For men of clear intellect Darwinism has long been dead.
Driesch

Darwinism is a fiction, a poetical accumulation of probabilities without proof, and of attractive explanations without demonstrations.
DICTIONNAIRE ENCYCLOPÉDIQUE DES SCIENCES

IN SOVIET RUSSIA Darwin ranks second only to Marx in the calendar of Marxist saints. He is important not for his contributions to science, such as they were, but for his alleged refutation of the argument from design. It is therefore all the more significant that a Russian scientist, working under the aegis of the Soviet government, should have published in his book, *Nomogenesis*, some of the most effective criticisms that have yet appeared not only of Darwin in general but also of evolution in particular or at least of monophyletic evolution. Berg believes that the difficulties of monophyletic evolution, that is of the doctrine that all living things are descended from *a single primordial cell* are insuperable and that evolution can only be saved by substituting the doctrine of polyphyletic for monophyletic evolution, that is the doctrine of descent from many for the doctrine of descent from a single primordial cell.

I am only concerned in this book with Darwinism and evolution in relation to the points at issue between the scientian and the theist. The Christian is free to accept or to reject Darwinism as he pleases and his approach to the problem of evolution is necessarily more scientific than those for whom, as for Sir Arthur Keith, "Evolution is a basic dogma of rationalism."

It is only because of its exploitation by atheists that Darwinism is of vital importance in the history of European thought. It is amusing to contrast the "basic dogmatism" of the Darwinist when he is writing the kind of popular tract which is distributed by the editors of the so-called *Thinkers' Library* and the caginess of a Darwinist when cross-examined on his claim to have discovered an adequate substitute for the hypothesis of the Creator. The general public is conditioned to believe that Darwin had discovered the scientific key to the origin and evolution of species, and that the old argument from design had been rendered superfluous now that Darwin had proved that natural selection created new species out of fortuitous variations "as truly as a man may be said to create a building out of the material provided by stones of various shapes." Nobody seems to have noticed that the activities of an architect are not in themselves an explanation of the origin of stones. Natural selection is a negative and not a creative force. It can only select what has already originated and therefore offers no explanation of the origin of the variation. It is no explanation of the origin of weeds in a garden to reply that those particular weeds have not yet been uprooted by the gardener.

The dogmatic confidence of a Darwinist writing for a popular public disappears under cross-examination, and the impression is created that it is really most unreasonable to expect Darwin to throw any light on *origins*. Natural selection is great and Darwin is God's prophet but only infidel dogs will draw attention to the obscurities of the new Koran.

"Your first real argument," writes Professor Haldane, "is that Darwinism does not explain the origin of the fittest. It need

not. Heritable variation is an observed fact. Natural selection
is another. Darwin argued that the two together would explain
evolution, as Newton argued that gravitation and inertia (per-
sistence of motion) would together explain planetary movement. It is obvious that if no organisms ever perished, and all
could reproduce freely, all the existing species would be present
amongst a countless number of misfits. But on a finite planet
there is only room for a limited number of organisms. Natural
selection purports to explain why, of the countless possible
numbers of organisms, only a few have survived."

And is this really all that "natural selection purports to explain," this self-evident fact? Was Darwin's claim to greatness
based on nothing more than the enunciation of a truism? What
becomes of Darwin's claim to have refuted the argument from
design if Darwinism means nothing more than the truism that
the fittest to survive succeed in surviving? The analogy with
Newton would only be sound if Newtonians claimed that his
discoveries had rendered unnecessary the hypothesis of a
creator. "Heritable variation is an observed fact. Natural
selection is another." No doubt, but what light do these
'observed facts" throw on the *origin* of species? Darwinism was
the greatest confidence trick ever played on an unsuspecting
public, *for Darwin explains nothing*, nothing that has the least
bearing on the ultimate problem of *origins*.

Let us distinguish between an explanation for which proof is
offered and a theory which does not claim to be more than a
working hypothesis, a plausible explanation which can be pro-
visionally adopted until it is refuted or replaced. Those who
claim to have refuted the argument from design should at least
be able to *suggest* an alternative to the creative power of God.
Even if they can offer no exact proof for their hypothesis, they
should at least be able to produce a *plausible guess*, but all we
are offered is a series of confused evasions.

The true explanation of the origin of species is to be sought
in the origin of variation, and, as Butler remarks, a man who
refuses to explain variation should not imply that he has explained species. "Natural selection," as Mr. A. Harris remarks,
"may explain the survival of the fittest, but cannot explain the
arrival of the fittest."

Or, again, as Butler puts it, "The survival of the fittest is no more a cause of modification, and hence can give no more explanation concerning the origin of species, than the fact of a number of competitors in a race failing to run the whole course or to run it as quickly as the winner, can explain how the winner came to have good legs and lungs. What we want to be told is, not that a runner will win the prize if he can run 'ever such a little' faster than his fellows—we know this—but by what process he comes to be able to run ever such a little faster."

Darwinism, I repeat, as an alternative to creation, is nothing but a confidence trick, for Darwinism explains *nothing* which has any bearing on the mystery of life and its origins. He evaded *all* the difficulties of his theory. Of these difficulties the most important are summarised in the pages which follow:

1. *The Origin of Life*

Every attempt by skilled chemists to produce living matter out of inorganic matter has failed, and yet we are asked to believe that pure chance succeeded where chemists with all their knowledge and their apparatus and laboratory equipment have failed. "I venture to think," says Sir William Tilden, in a letter which appeared in *The Times* (September 10th, 1912), "that no chemist will be prepared to suggest a process by which, from the interaction of such materials (viz. inorganic substances), anything approaching a substance of the nature of a proteid could be formed. The idea that a chaos of unassorted elements and undirected forces could succeed where the skill of the chemist fails is preposterous. No known or conceivable process, or group of processes, at work in inorganic nature is equal to the task. Chance is an explanation only for minds insensible to the beauty and order of organic life."

It is important to note that the remarkable discoveries made at the Rockefeller Institute of the crystallisable viruses of rabbit papilloma by Wyckoff, and of the mosaic disease of tobacco which were once hailed as intermediaries between inorganic matter and living matter are not the link for which atheists have waited so long. Such at least is the opinion of that distinguished scientist (and convinced evolutionist) Dr. du Noüy who writes: "in no sense of the word are these substances alive. It is true that they reproduce, but only in contact with living matter, just like the toxins, known as ptomaines, which appear when living matter undergoes a process of decomposition."

2. *Why should the Process have Begun?*

Why should the evolutionary process have begun? "*The phrase 'survival of the fittest',*" writes Mr. W. J. Blyton, "*offers no explanation. For life itself has very little survival value compared with the inorganic matter from which it sprang. A rock survives for hundreds of millions of years, whereas even a tree lasts only a thousand years. If survival was what nature aimed at why should life appear at all? Again why should the trend of evolution be upwards so that higher and higher types are evolved?* The doctrine of evolution does not explain this. *The upward trend cannot be due to the influence of environment, for the lower types are just as well adapted to their environment as are the higher types.*"

3. *The Change from Asexual to Sexual Selection*

The "survival of the fittest" does not explain the change from asexual to sexual reproduction. On the contrary asexual cells are so fit to survive that "they do not know death as individuals," I am quoting from Dr. Nouy, "they are immortal."

No Darwinist has attempted to suggest how sexual reproduction could have originated.

4. *The Evolution of Complex Organs*

Darwinism fails to explain the evolution of very complex organs such as the eye, which consists of several parts, parts which cannot function unless they are very accurately fitted into each other. "One might possibly imagine," writes Wolff, "the adaptation between one muscle cell and one nerve end through selection among innumerable variations, but that such should take place in a thousand cases in one organism is inconceivable."

As Berg says: "The probability that all useful variations will simultaneously occur in all parts is the probability of a miracle. Recalling Darwin's words, it might be said, 'To admit all this is, as it seems to me, to enter into the realms of miracle, and to leave those of science. We might just as well expect that if the wheels, screws and other component parts of the mechanism of a watch were to be put into a vessel we could, by the simple process of shaking, get them to combine in such a manner as to become a watch that would function as such'."

Note Darwin's disarming technique. He states an insuperable objection to his doctrine and then says in effect, "well, well" and passes blandly on to the next point without making the slightest attempt to deal with the difficulty.

Is it conceivable that so complex an optical instrument as the eye could be improved by *pure chance?* Mr. Noyes, in his book, *The Unknown God*, quotes a Savilian professor of astronomy on this subject. "Suppose, for instance, one of the surfaces of the crystalline lens of the eye to be accidentally altered, then I say that unless the form of the other surface is *simultaneously* altered in one only way *out of millions of possible ways*, the eye would not be optically improved. An alteration in the two surfaces of the crystalline lens, whether accidental or otherwise, would involve a definite alteration in the form of the cornea, or in the distance of its surface from the centre of the crystalline lens, in order that the eye may be optically better. All these alterations must be simultaneous and definite in amount, and these definite amounts must coexist in obedience to an extremely complicated law.

"To my apprehension then that so complicated an instrument as the eye should undergo a succession of millions of improvements by means of a succession of millions of accidental alterations is no less improbable than if all the letters in *The Origin of Species* were placed in a box and on being shaken and poured out millions and millions of times should at last come together in the order in which they occur in that fascinating and, in general, highly philosophic work."

5. *Radical Transformations*

Darwinists are silent when challenged to suggest any natural mechanisms for the radical transformations required by the theory of gradual naturalistic evolution. Consider for instance the radical change from creatures which emerge from the egg to creatures which emerge from the womb. "We can hardly imagine," writes Macfie, "a shelled egg *gradually* giving up its shell, and its food supply, and *gradually* making a placental connexion, blood-vessels and all, with the parental uterus. It is one of these variations which—if it occurred in the course of reproduction—must have been sudden and complete in all its complex correlation." Whales are supposed to be descended from land mammals but no evolutionist has produced even a plaus-

ible guess, much less an explanation, as to the type of intermediary who could survive in the transition period before this
alleged transitional form took to the water. "The mother
whale," writes Dewar, "gives birth to her young one and
suckles it under water: both mother and young have to be
specially adapted to this. The mother has a receptacle into
which she can secrete milk; this receptacle is provided with
muscles, of which the contraction forces the milk into the mouth
of the young one. She has also a cap round the nipple into which
the snout of the youngster fits very tightly to prevent it absorb-
ing sea water with the milk she gives it. The young one has its
windpipe prolonged above the gullet to prevent any of the milk
ejected from the mother's receptacle getting into its lungs.

"Please bear in mind (1) that no gradual transition is possible
between the young one being born and suckled on land or in
the air and in being born and suckled under water; (2) the
latter would be impossible before the above apparatus was fully
developed; (3) therefore, *all the modifications of both mother and
baby would have to be complete before the first baby whale could be successfully suckled under water.*"

6. *Hit or Miss Phenomena*

What I have elsewhere described, for want of a better term
as "hit or miss phenomena" are impossible to explain by natural
selection or by the survival of the fittest. By "hit or miss
phenomena" I mean actions which have got to be right when
first they are attempted, actions which cannot possibly be the
result of gradual evolution. Feathers are a case in point. The
bird is supposed to have evolved from a lizard-like reptile. "I
regard feathers," writes Shelton, "not *in the first place* as an
adaptation to flight—as the bats manage very well without
them—but as an adaptation giving extra warmth. The pro-
longation of scales and their splitting up into fibres obviously
provides protection against cold even in rudimentary stages.
Lunn will get the idea if he will examine the feathers on newly
hatched birds, some of which, e.g. those of a pigeon, are very
simple indeed."

Shelton characteristically skates away from the difficulty.
You do not explain the transformation of scales into feathers by
the bland remark that feathers are an "adaptation to warmth,"

Still less do you explain how a feathery down could acquire the power to lift the transition reptile from the ground. Flight is definitely a "hit or miss phenomenon." Needless to say, Shelton, when challenged, made no attempt to produce even a guess as to the type of mechanism which transforms scales into feathers, or the process whereby feathers could be co-ordinated to produce flight.

"The immensely complicated structure of feathers," writes Dewar, "(some of which are said to contain more than a million barbules) is not necessary if their function is only to assist in the retention of body heat. You make no attempt to explain how the fore-leg of a reptile became *gradually* converted into the wing of a bird—an implement that in a fraction of a second can be changed from a surface impervious to air into one through which air passes almost without resistance."

Shelton replied, "I have no more to say," when challenged to explain (a) the mechanism by means of which scales turned into feathers, (b) the survival value of the first embryo feathers, (c) the process whereby feathers could be co-ordinated to produce flight. Please note that a slow gradual evolution in a feather direction is no use.

Flight is a "hit or miss phenomenon". The intricate and complex correlation of feathers, muscles and bones to produce the power necessary to lift the bird from the ground even for the smallest of flights could not possibly have evolved gradually.

Dewar gave a series of examples of complicated nest-building which must have originated *per saltum*, as for instance the hanging nest of the first sunbird which would have been useless as a nursery until almost as complete and as strong as we see it to-day. Even more remarkable is the case of the water-spider which builds under water a home for its young in the shape of a diving bell. "Its walls are of silk, manufactured by the spider. It is moored to submerged leaves or to stones on the floor of a pool by silken threads which the spider spins. Before it can be inhabited it has to be filled with air brought to it by the spider. The body hairs of this creature are so constructed as to entangle bubbles of air; this applies particularly to the hairs of the abdomen which are long and hooked at the tip. Thus the spider when it goes underwater is enveloped in air, and this causes it to look as if clothed in silver, hence its name Argyroneta, the silvery-spinner. The lower part of the nest is connected with a surface weed by a strong silken cord, spun by the spider, along which it runs between its home and the surface. After the bell is completed the spider makes many journeys from it to the surface where it collects air which it takes below and liberates under the nest, so that this replaces the water there. This process continues until the water in the nest is all replaced by air, and then the habitation is ready for occupation, and the family is reared in it and kept as dry as if the nest had been above water. By the same process used-up air is taken to the surface and replaced by oxygenated air. I assert that this habit cannot have been acquired by an ordinary land-spider by a gradual process of evolution. The ordinary spider cannot survive long under water. On being submerged it immediately curls up and is drowned if not rescued within a few minutes. Thus the spider could not have begun to operate under water until it had become fully adapted to this, and this adaptation would have been useless as such until nearly complete. And I find it difficult to see of what use it can have been above water while it was developing. Having acquired the adaptation, you presumably have to imagine that another set of haphazard variations caused the spider thus equipped to take to entering water. Even so your spider has a very long way to go before it constructed its nest under water. I cannot think of a habit half-way between that of rearing the young in the air above water and of rearing them in a receptacle under water. So far as I can see, the change of habit, if it occurred, must have been *per saltum*."

7. *Absence of Nascent Organs*
If evolution be true there must have been a period in the past when, to take one example, reptiles would have been wandering round with a nascent and imperfect wing. In the past the world must have been full of nascent forms, why then do we see no nascent forms to-day? Why does evolution appear to have stopped?

8. *Origin of the Sense of Beauty*
Darwinism offers no explanation of the origin of the sense of beauty. We are invited to believe that the emotion which a sunset on the Jungfrau or Beethoven's Ninth Symphony evokes in

us was implicit in the mud, rocks, mists and sea of the primeval planet. Darwin's attempt to meet this difficulty was characteristically evasive. He assumed what it was his business to explain, the existence of a sense of beauty, and then proceeded to discuss the influence of this sense on evolution. The female is attracted by a beautiful mate, with the result that ugly varieties leave a numerous progeny. No doubt, but *why does the peahen think the peacock beautiful?* Is it conceivable that a blind and fortuitous process, undirected by intelligence, could have evolved from lifeless matter of the primeval planet the power to create and the power to appreciate beauty? And clearly sexual selection does not explain our appreciation of inorganic beauty, the beauty of mountains or the sea.

Darwin believed that Darwinism stood or fell with his theory of sexual selection. He declared that if it could be proved that these beautiful patterns had been created to delight man or the creator, this conclusion would be absolutely fatal to his theory.

I agree. The complete breakdown of all materialistic attempts to explain beauty is one of the chief arguments against not only atheism but also Darwinism.

"When the materialist," writes J. B. Mosley, "has exhausted himself in efforts to explain utility in nature, it would appear to be the peculiar office of beauty to rise up as confounding and baffling *extra*." As indeed Darwin realised. "The sight of a feather in a peacock's tail," he wrote, "whenever I gaze at it makes me sick." Consider the lilies of the field, and if you are a Darwinist they will make you as sick as the peacock's feather. Gentians, primula, soldanella. . . . It may not be possible to "prove that these beautiful patterns had been created to delight man or the Creator," but it would be impossible to suggest any other explanation of their beauty. "I cannot even begin," writes Father Martindale, "to appreciate the beauty of one petal of one flower . . . there is here no question of thoughts that lie too deep for tears but of a perception too deep for thoughts," and certainly too deep for a materialistic explanation.

9.   *The Fossil Record*

Neither the evolutionist in general nor the Darwinist in particular can produce an adequate answer to those difficulties of the fossil record which so greatly impressed Huxley and which for so long delayed his own conversion to the doctrine of evolution. The reader who is familiar with the literature of evolution will, I hope, forgive me if my discussion of the fossil record is introduced by some elementary definitions.

Organisms are divided into two kingdoms, the animal and the vegetable kingdom. The animal kingdom is divided into phyla. Each phylum is divided into classes, each class into orders, each order into families, each family into genera, each genus into species, and each species into varieties. A fox terrier and a spaniel are different *varieties* of the same *species*, Canis Familiaris. The dog, wolf and jackal are different *species* of the same genus. The wolf and the fox are of different genera of the Canidae or dog *family*. This is one of the families of the *order* Carnivora. The Carnivora belong to the *class* Mammalia (animals that suckle their young), and the mammals belong to the *phylum* Vertebrata (backboned animals). Every animal belongs to a species, genus, family, order, class and phylum. Biologists give every species a double name, denoting its genus and species, thus the domestic dog is Canis Familiaris—the species Familiaris of the genus Canis.

I propose to describe as major evolution, evolution which transcends the limits of the *family*, as minor evolution evolution within the limits of the family, and as *differentiation* evolution within the limits of the genus.

Fossils. Fossils are the impressions made by animals or plants on the rocks. If an animal or plant is covered by sediment after death, before the hard parts have decomposed, these may be preserved as fossils, the original material of the hard parts being replaced by mineral matter such as oxide of iron; animals lacking hard parts are less easily fossilised though in some cases they leave traces in the form of impressions made in the soil before they decay. Fossils are not found in igneous rock, that is any form of rock which was once in an igneous condition. Granite for instance, is an igneous rock. Fossils are found in sedimentary rocks such as limestone or sandstone composed of sediments which were slowly deposited at the bottom of the sea, lakes or rivers.

Birds and bats owing to their powers of flight are less liable than ground animals to be drowned or buried by floods or falling cliffs or to be bogged, hence their fossils, although numerous, are not so abundant as those of mammals tied to the ground.

The first fossil-bearing rocks are those of the Cambrian. Many of the pre-Cambrian rocks which immediately precede the Cambrian are sedimentary rocks similar to those in which fossils have been deposited, *but not a single undisputed fossil has been found in them*.

"Suddenly in the Cambrian Period," writes Dewar, "we find the sea full of highly organised types. We find nothing which suggests slow evolution. We find no experiments in the production of new types, no experiments, for instance, in shell making. The first shells are fully developed. We find these earliest animals as sharply differentiated into species, genera, families, orders and phyla as they are to-day.

"So varied are these earliest known fossils that they include members of all the great phyla that possess hard parts, except the back-boned phylum, of which the earliest known fossil does not occur earlier than the later part of the Cambrian Period.

"Underlying the richly fossiliferous Cambrian rocks are vast masses of rocks in which not a single indubitable fossil has been found, rocks thousands of feet in vertical thickness and in many places identical in all their physical features with the overlying Cambrian rocks into which they fade imperceptibly, rocks beautifully preserved, undisturbed, unmetamorphosed, eminently suited to hold and retain fossils."

(i) Now if evolution were true we should expect to find in the earlier rocks a slow gradual progression from simple to complex forms. But what we actually do find is evidence of a sudden appearance on the surface of the planet of an immense variety of complex forms of life, which is difficult to explain on any other hypothesis than that of a sudden burst of creative activity.

(ii) Every new family of animals appears suddenly in the fossil record with all the attributes by which it is distinguished from other animals. There is no evidence in the fossil record of experiment, no evidence, for instance, of experiments in shell making or feather making. The first shell of which we have any record was almost perfectly suited to the task which it had to perform. The first feather was adapted to the compexity of flight. If evolution be true then nature resembles sensitive authors who carefully collect and destroy their juvenalia.

(iii) It is not the *links* which are missing but the *chains*. It is impossible to trace any family in nature into another family by a true lineage series of fossils, by which I mean a series of fossils connecting an alleged ancestral type A with an alleged descendant type B by a series passing by *small* gradations from A to B— a series the members of which can be placed in a definite chronological order.

"It is truly remarkable," writes Berg, "that palaeontology in no way displays transitional forms between phyla and classes, and, possibly, not even between orders. Thus, we are ignorant of transitional forms not only between vertebrates and invertebrates, fishes and tetrapods, but even between the cartilaginous (chondrichthyes such as sharks, etc.) and higher fishes (osteichthyes); *in spite of a wonderful affinity between reptiles and birds, no transitional forms between them are known hitherto*. Formerly, this circumstance was accounted for by the imperfection of the geological record; but it is none the less surprising that the deeper our knowledge penetrates into the domain of fossils, the farther back recede genetic inter-relations, which, as it were, ever elude our grasp."

The italics, which are mine, prove that Berg was too competent a biologist to pretend that Archaeopteryx was a transitional form between reptiles and birds.

THE ABSENCE OF CONFUSION IN NATURE

If Darwinism be true, if blind chance alone be responsible for the universe, if evolution has been a slow and gradual process in which simpler forms gradually yield to more complex forms, what should we expect to find? We should not expect to find the appearance of organisation and planning which, in point of fact, we do find. Darwin in the sixth chapter of his book tries to meet this difficulty. "Why do we not see everywhere," he writes, "innumerable transitional forms? Why is not all nature in confusion, instead of the species being as we see them, well defined?"

That is the point—"*well defined*". The species are well defined, organised in interbreeding communities. The sterility of hybrids is one of the great difficulties of any theory of evolution. If evolution be true we should expect to find the species ill-defined, grading into each through innumerable transitional forms. We should expect, as Darwin said, "to find all nature in confusion."

Darwin's answer to this difficulty was that the evolution of species is determined among other things "by the presence of other species, on which it lives, or by which it is destroyed, or with which it comes into competition, and as these species are already defined objects, not blending into each other by insensible graduations, the range of any one species, depending as it does on the range of others, will tend to be sharply defined."

Now, in the first place, as Kellogg remarks, this is a *petitio principii:* "The sharp definition of species, that we started out to account for, is explained by the sharp definition of other species." And, in the second place, Darwin ignores the fact that there must have been a time in the past when all nature was "in confusion", when the slow changes which he postulates were taking place. His explanation virtually assumes that evolution has ceased to operate.

There is one point which so far as I know has never been made, but which seems to be worth making. Darwinists seem to believe in what may be described as the *synchronisation of evolution.* They assume that the different phases of evolution were synchronised throughout the world.

There was, if Darwinists are right, a time when the scales of certain reptiles were becoming feathery. At a later stage the descendants of those reptiles had developed rudimentary feathers incapable as yet of flight. Finally, Archaeopteryx, the parent bird, acquired a wing which could lift him from the ground. But unless all these phases are synchronised in different parts of the world, there must have been a time when certain reptiles had feathery scales, others had definite feathers, but feathers which could not lift them from the ground, and others had efficient wings. Again, unless evolution has ceased we should find all these phases represented in the world in which we live. No Darwinist has ever suggested that the conditions which determined the alleged transformation of a reptile into a bird were peculiar to the Mesozoic age or tried to explain the fact that reptiles would seem to have lost the faculty of evolving into birds. But if evolution be a continuous process we should expect to find in the world in which we live feathery scales and scaly feathers and also all the other nascent organs which must at one time have existed.

No animal in the modern form possesses *any* of the nascent organs which uncounted millions of animals must have possessed in the past. No animal in the modern world possesses in an incipient and undeveloped condition *any* organ or structure which is found in a well-developed state in *any* animal.

If evolution has occurred it would have seemed to have ceased, for the species which we see in the world of to-day would seem to have congealed into permanent moulds.

Such then, are the principal difficulties to which the Darwinists have no answer. *Most of these difficulties are equally valid against any doctrine of evolution which denies the controlling activity of a divine intelligence.*

The Darwinists who claim that their theory renders unnecessary the hypothesis of a creation have completely failed to explain how a purely natural process could create the multiform varieties of living life from the mud, sand, mists and sea of the primeval planet.

CHAPTER XII

THE CASE FOR EVOLUTION EXAMINED

THE principal arguments for evolution are as follows:—

1. *Morphological Resemblances*

The resemblances between what may be called the fundamental structure of animals belonging to different families and even different classes and orders suggest a common descent. "Assuming species, families or even orders," writes H. S. Shelton, "to have been created separately, there is no intelligible reason why one group of flying animals (the birds) should be something like reptiles, a second (the bats) something like mice, and a third (the insects) something like crabs. These similarities are not surface resemblances, but the underlying plan on which the creatures are built. Even if we search the past to find if perchance some flying creatures had a structure specially designed for flying, we find one more group and they were reptiles. We may express this concisely by saying that animal life bears no sign of a structure specially designed for the conditions of its existence; the main structure of the groups with different environment is the same, but there is evidence of special *adaptation*. Descent with modification explains. I know of no other explanation."

But surely an intermediate type is as easy to reconcile with the creationist as with the evolutionist hypothesis. There is not *a priori* reason why the Creator should begin *de novo* with each type, or why he should not introduce into a new type some features which have occurred in earlier types. The human creator does not begin *de novo* every time he tries to design a new car or a new plane. The fighter bomber is an intermediate between the fighter and the bomber, but the fighter bomber is not a blood relation of the fighter.

Archaeopteryx is cited by many evolutionists as an intermediate between birds and reptiles. Dr. Lecomte du Noüy, though an evolutionist, does not accept the claim. "In spite of the fact," he writes, "that it is undeniably related to the two classes of reptiles and birds . . .we are not even authorised to consider the exceptional case of the Archaeopteryx as a true link. By link, we mean a necessary stage of transition between classes such as reptiles and birds, or between smaller groups. An animal displaying characteristics belonging to two different groups cannot be treated as a true link as long as the intermediary stages have been found, and as long as the mechanism of transition remain unknown."

2. *The Pedigree of the Horse*

The pedigree of the horse is impressive evidence in favour of evolution within fairly wide limits, the limits of the family. Eopippus the parent horse was a dwarf horse and differed in many important respects from the modern horse. For instance it had four functional toes instead of one. It is impossible to connect Eopippus with Equus by a lineage series of fossils, but it is almost equally difficult to deny that they are at least descended from a common equine ancestor.

The horse pedigree is all the proof a rational man needs of evolution within the limits of the family, but there is no proof in the fossil record of evolution transcending the limits of the family. The casts in the Natural History Museum are sufficient to convince even the layman that in spite of important differences between Eopippus and Equus their resemblances are even more striking.

3. *The Imperfection of the Fossil Record*

The fossil record, as we have seen (pages 120–123) is difficult, if not impossible, to reconcile with the doctrine of a slow, gradual evolution. Consequently the evolutionist is compelled to assume that the fossil record is very unrepresentative of the extinct species. I say "compelled to assume" for, strangely enough, there is no evidence that evolutionists have ever taken the necessary steps to discover how far the fossil record can be trusted. Whereas the scientific historian is at pains to test the reliability of the documents which he uses, the evolutionists would seem to have been restrained by subconscious doubt from any attempt to *prove* that the record was as imperfect as they assumed. And yet had they been inspired by genuine scientific curiosity they would have begun by comparing the fossil record with the record of living species.

I

"*Mirabile dictu neither Darwin nor any of his followers,*" writes Dewar, "*seems to have made any attempt to ascertain to what extent animals are fossilised.* Their attitude seems to be: The evolution theory is true; therefore these intermediate forms must have existed; as none of their fossils have been found the fossil record is exceedingly imperfect. But is not this to put the cart before the horse?"

It was left to Dewar to discover how far existing species and genera are represented in the fossil record. He proved that of the land mammals now inhabiting Europe every one of the forty-eight genera are represented in the fossil record. Doubtless many of these fossils are in strata which is rapidly being eroded, but even so it is sufficiently remarkable that whereas *all* existing genera of European land mammals are represented in the fossil record, *all* the millions of genera necessary to link family and family, class and class, order and order and phylum and phylum have disappeared. Is it unreasonable to suggest that the imperfection of geological record is a dogma invented to explain the absence from that record of the evidence which is necessary to support the evolutionary faith?

A Catholic priest, Father Burton, who later became the Bishop of Clifton, took part in a disputation at Rome and defended the dogma of the Immaculate Conception, a dogma which Mr. Wells and others confuse with the doctrine of the Virgin Birth. His opponent, who was acting the rôle of *advocatus diaboli*, remarked that there was no clear reference of this doctrine in the works of the early fathers. Father Burton replied: "In operibus quae supersunt, concedo. In operibus quae perierunt, nego." ("I agree that there are no references in the works which survive. I deny that there are no references in the works which have perished.")

Father Burton's reply is an example of the humour of the schools. It was not intended as a serious contribution to theology, for the standards of theological controversies are more exacting than those which enable evolutionists to draw conclusions from the "operibus quae perierunt".

GEOGRAPHICAL DISTRIBUTION
If life began on the mainland and if evolution be true we should, as Shelton points out, expect "that the higher verte-

brates will be distributed all over the continental mass, but that in the islands there will be a great dearth of them, the exceptions being such beings as birds and bats which fly, and rats and mice, and possibly dogs, which travel with man to such islands as are, or have been, inhabited.

"This is exactly what occurs. The one mammal found in New Zealand was a rat. The only placentals in Australia were bats, mice and the dingo dog. Most of the islands have no indigenous mammals except bats." And we should expect to find exactly the same distribution if the different types had been created on the mainland. In so far as the argument has any validity it tells against evolution for this reason. There is nothing in the doctrine of special creation which raises any difficulty against creative activity being confined to a particular area.

The traditional Christian view has always been that a particular human pair were created in a particular spot, but if the origin and evolution of life was a purely natural process it is not easy to see why evolution should have been confined to the Euro-Asiatic mainland. In what respect were New Zealand and Australia less adapted for evolution than the mainland? There is no fact of geographical distribution which is not as easy to reconcile with creation as with evolution, but there are many features which are more difficult to reconcile with evolution than with creationism.

THE ARGUMENT FROM ARTIFICIAL SELECTION

The human breeder can effect considerable changes in animals in a short period; therefore natural selection can effect even greater changes in millions of years. To this the evolutionist replies, first that whereas nature is alleged to eliminate all but favourite variations, the human breeder can select any variation which he fancies; secondly, that whereas in nature a new variation would be swamped by breeding with individuals which did not possess this variation, the human breeder can segregate the individual in which it appears and cross it with another individual which has varied in the same way.

Finally, no human breeder has produced a new animal species which is infertile with the species from which it is bred, and fertile with other individuals of the new species. The claim that new species have been created in plants (polyphoidy) is rejected by many competent evolutionists such as Professor MacBride whose views on this point are quoted on page 349 of *Science and the Supernatural*.

EMBRYOLOGY

The embryo according to some evolutionists recapitulates its ancestry. "There is no logical justification," writes G. R. de Beer, F.R.S., who is an evolutionist, "in regarding any embryological stage as evidence of the former existence of such a stage representing an adult ancestor. Equally well might a present adult stage represent an embryological stage of an ancestor. Embryology is therefore no guide to philogeny."

VESTIGIAL REMAINS

There are many vestigial organs, such as the vestiges of hind limbs in some snakes, the teeth under the skin in Platypus, etc. To this the special creationist replies: "If each type of animal be an independent creation, we should expect it to be endowed at the time of its creation with all the organs necessary for its existence in the conditions prevailing at that time. It might well happen that subsequently conditions changed and in consequence an organ originally useful ceased to be so and then disappeared or became vestigial."

The reader who suspects that the evidence for evolution must be far stronger than emerges from my summary of the case has the remedy in his own hands. He can read *Is Evolution Proved?* one of the only two books in which an evolutionist has been forced to defend his beliefs under cross examination, a form of defence which is less easy than uttering dogmatic remarks on the subject for the benefit of those who already accept the faith.

It is not inconceivable that the great difficulties of the evolutionary hypothesis will produce before long important modifications in the popular presentment of this doctrine. "The assumption of a monophyletic evolution of the whole kingdom of organic life," writes Wassman, "is a delightful dream without any scientific support." Even as far back as the turn of the century a botanist of the eminence of Wettstein and well-known palaeontologists such as Steinman, Koken and Diener had

anticipated Berg in their support of the doctrine of polyphyletic
evolution, but more important that the distinction between
those who believe that all living things are descended from one
primordial cell and those who believe in a multiple origin of
life is, as I have already said, the radical distinction between the
mechanists and the teleologists. The mechanists, among whom
may be numbered the explicit and implicit materialists, believe
that the phenomena of life can all be explained without invoking the supernatural. The teleologists believe that the process is
controlled and directed towards a pre-determined end (telos,
end) not by pure chance but by Intelligence, that is by God.

Many who, if challenged, would admit that they believed in
teleological evolution are indistinguishable in their writings
from the mechanists and consequently lend the prestige of their
names to a doctrine of evolution which they know to be untenable. Some are themselves undecided, teleologists in their more
thoughtful moments, and implicit if not explicit mechanists at
other times. The very man who argued that there was no more
design in the chance which determined the action of natural
selection than "in the course which the wind blows" also
declares: "This grand sequence of events the mind refuses to
accept as the result of blind chance. The understanding revolts
from such a conclusion."

It is easy to multiply quotations from those who accept evolution but who reject the fantastic absurdities of mechanistic
evolution, as for instance:

"There is something that is the order of the cosmos and the
beauty of the world, that lives in all things living and dwells in
the mind and soul of man. . . . You may call it the harmony
of the world: you may call it the 'élan vital', you may call it
the breath of life. Or you may call it, as it is called in the story
book of creation and in the hearts of men—you may call it the
Spirit of God." (*Professor d'Arcy Thompson.*)

"It looks as if nature were nature for a purpose, and as we
cannot predicate purpose in a vast system we must reverently
ascribe it to a creator." (*J. A. Thomson.*)

"The more we discover as to physiological activity and inheritance, the more difficult does it become to imagine any
physical or chemical description which could in any way cover
the facts as to persistent co-ordination. From the standpoint of

the physical sciences the maintenance and reproduction of a living organ is nothing less than a standing miracle, and for the reason that co-ordinated maintenance of structure and activity is inconsistent with the physical conception of self-existent matter and energy." (*J. S. Haldane.*)

"The existence of God must be the central feature in future developments of philosophy." (*J. S. Haldane.*)

The reader must not confuse that distinguished philosopher and scientist, the late Professor J. S. Haldane, F.R.S., with his son, Professor J. B. S. Haldane, F.R.S.

In more recent times the case for teleological evolution has been ably argued by Dr. Noüy, whose defence of what he calls telefinalism is discussed in Appendix B.

CHAPTER XIII

SCIENTISM THE ENEMY OF REASON

(1)

FIDEISM is not necessarily anti-rational. Many a man who is incapable of defending by reason the first great premise that God exists can draw rational and valid deductions from that premise. If, however, we argue from a premise which is false our reasoning processes are liable to corruption. It is the falsity of the premises from which the scientian argues which explains not only the irrational but the anti-rational element in the writings of eminent scientians. And it is, I believe, the fideistic atmosphere of evolutionary literature which alone can explain the disregard for principles which every scientist regards as binding in other branches of scientific work.

At this point I hope that I may be forgiven a personal digression. I have frequently received letters from correspondents who, on the strength of a scientific degree, rebuke me for my temerity in venturing into a field which, so I am assured, should be left to scientists. My correspondents overlook the fact that if my ignorance of the subject were as great as they suggest, it should be easy to refute my arguments or to convict me of error. Now as it happens I have made a detailed study of Alpine geology and lectured on the subject, and what is perhaps more to the point, my researches into the habits of snow and ice have led to discoveries which have been accepted as such by professional scientists such as my friend Gerald Seligman, who has written the classic text book on snow structure and whose work was sufficiently important to be endowed by scientific societies. He found much in my book which he could endorse and nothing which was palpably wrong.

I mention this fact not because of its intrinsic importance, but because of the importance of my theme. I should be sorry if a reader who was impressed by the argument against mechanistic evolution and thereby led to revise his views on the most important of all subjects, the existence of God, was subsequently influenced by the kind of remark which is often made by those who find it easier to denigrate my qualifications than to reply to my arguments. And in the second place my experiences during the twenty years in which I studied snow have some slight relevance to the theme of this chapter. When I was asked to revise my book I found nothing in it to correct, in spite of the fact that Seligman's work had appeared in the interval, and this for the very good reason that I had been ultra-cautious. I had never claimed that a problem was soluble when every solution was riddled with difficulty, and I was never ashamed to confess ignorance. The evolutionist on the other hand dares not confess ignorance as to whether evolution has occurred, and finds it almost impossible to admit that he knows nothing about the origin of man.

Any form of research which affects men's lives or pockets discourages irresponsibility. A rash diagnosis of a snowslope, or even a faulty theory about snow expressed in print may result in a fatal avalanche accident, but nobody is a penny the worse if an evolutionary pedigree proves to be false, all of which encourages a certain light-hearted irresponsibility, unknown in other branches of scientific research.

It is indeed this light-hearted irresponsibility which is one of the most striking characteristics of the evolutionary fideists. Consider for instance the voluminous literature on the links which continue to be missing, Pro-Avis for instance, the missing link between the reptile and the bird. Mr. W. P. Pyecraft in his book, *A History of Birds*, gives us a careful and scholarly description of the "axillary membrane" which Pro Avis possessed and on the influence of the forelimb on the inner digits. The picture of Pro-Avis in his book is not labelled "hypothetical reconstruction of a hypothetical transitional type" but quite simply "one of the Pro-Avis". After reading the pages which Mr. Pyecraft devotes to Pro-Avis it is easy to forget that he is describing an imaginary creature, not one bone or feather of which is to be found in the fossil record.

Faith it would seem is the substance of fossils hoped for, the evidence of links unseen. In this connection G. K. Chesterton's remarks on the subject of Pithecanthropus are very much to the point: "People talked of *Pithecanthropus* as of Pitt or Fox or Napoleon. Popular histories published portraits of him like the portraits of Charles the First and George the Fourth. A detailed drawing was reproduced, carefully shaded, to show that the very hairs of his head were all numbered. No uninformed person looking at its carefully lined face and wistful eyes would imagine for a moment that this was the portrait of a thigh-bone; or of a few teeth and a fragment of a cranium."

All this, as Boule remarks, is so much "pithecanthropomorphism."

In 1922 a single imperfect molar tooth was found in a Pliocene stratum at Nebraska. Professor Osborn, the distinguished palaeontologist, identified it as the tooth of an ape which had evolved a considerable way in the direction of man. The ape was christened *Hesperopithicus*. Dr. Gregory, another eminent scientist, examined *Hesperopithicus'* tooth and came to the considered, careful, and scientific conclusion that *Hesperopithicus* was much nearer to man than an ape.

Hesperopithicus was accordingly elected to that distinguished club, the Missing Link Club, and received a warm welcome from the Chairman, *Pithecanthropus*.

Meanwhile *Hesperopithicus'* "discoverer" was becoming quite lyrical on the subject of *Hesperopithicus'* tooth, and all that this tooth meant for progress and humanity. "The earth," exclaimed Professor Osborn with that shrill note which is characteristic of scientists in the pulpit, "the earth speaks loudly and clearly of the ascent of the bird from one kind of reptile, and of humans from another kind of reptile. . . . The earth spoke to Bryan (a disbeliever in evolution) from his own State of Nebraska. The *Hesperopithicus* tooth is like the still small voice, this sound is by no means easy to hear . . . this little tooth speaks volumes of truth. . . ." So it did, but not to Osborn. The "still small voice" suddenly decided to speak up, and the tooth turned out to be the tooth of a bear, and poor old *Hesperopithicus* was expelled with contumely from the Missing Link Club. A like fate appears to be in store for the latest member of that club, *Sinanthropus*.

(II)

Principles of evidence which the evolutionist accepts as binding in all other departments of science are cheerfully disregarded in the apologetics of evolution. If for instance we appeal to an authority we must first make up our minds whether that authority is reliable. If, then, we are to draw deductions from the fossil record we must first determine the degree to which that record is reliable.

The evolutionist assumes that it is reliable when it tells in his favour and imperfect when it does not. The fossil of a bird in Devonian strata or of man in the Jurassic would destroy his entire scheme. No such fossils have been found and he is confident that none will be found. He is equally confident that the millions of genera which are necessary to link phylum with phylum must have existed though they left no record on the rocks. In other words he maintains that he is entitled but that the special creationist is not entitled to draw valid deductions from the *absence* of fossils.

In a court of law evidence which was as easy to reconcile with the prisoner's innocence as with the prisoner's guilt would be regarded as worthless, but Shelton was not impressed when I suggested in the Introduction to the Dewar-Shelton controversy, that this self-evident principle should be applied in the argument about evolution. He quoted my remark "Facts which are equally consistent with both of two rival theories can be cited in support of neither of these theories" and added "Yes, if the theories are both scientific and both on the same level. But if one of them is a theory of miracles it does not apply at all."

Then why agree to debate evolution with a special creationist who believes that the origin of species can only be explained by an act of supernatural creation, that is by a miracle? Nothing of course, could be less scientific than to exclude by *a priori* dogmatism from the field of research any possible explanation, natural or supernatural, of the phenomena under investigation. See in this connection *Is Evolution Proved?*, pages 29 and 42.

The greater part of what is produced as evidence for evolution is equally valid as evidence for special creation. Thus, evolutionists frequently confuse succession with descent. The first chapter of the Book of Genesis is as definite as Darwin in its insistence on the fact that the simpler forms of life were the first to be created and it is therefore absurd to trot out proofs of succession as if they were equivalent to proofs of descent, as Sir Arthur Keith does in his book on Darwinism. Sir Arthur points out that there has been, in the course of ages, evolution in everything, in watches, for instance. But the question at issue is not whether men are different from fishes, or whether men appeared on the surface of the planet subsequent to fishes, but whether men are *descended* from fishes and unless Sir Arthur Keith could prove that my wrist watch is a blood relation of a sixteenth-century watch his analogy has not the least relevance to the issue which is in dispute.

(III)

Ever since Darwinism first became fashionable, materialists have been oppressed by the thought that natural selection can only *select* and cannot produce, but the determination to discover in natural selection a creative agency to take the place of God is too strong for them and often leads them into fantasies of irrationalism. As, for instance, the following statement by Professor Julian Huxley: "Selection is destructive in the sense that it eliminates the unfavourable; but equally it is creative in that it preserves the favourable." By parity of reasoning it could be proved that the *Luftwaffe* was creative, and that Westminster Abbey had been "preserved" by the "selection" of the bombers which failed to destroy it. Again it is a common trick to pretend that anti-Darwinists do not accept the *fact* of natural selection. "The assertion is sometimes made," writes Professor J. B. S. Haldane in *Possible Worlds*, "that no one has ever seen Natural Selection at work." This assertion could only be made by an ignoramus and, as Professor Haldane would be the first to admit, those who do not believe in Darwinism are not all ignorant. An epidemic is a case of natural selection at work; the fittest survive, and the least fit perish.

The attribution of creative power to natural selection would be dishonest if it were not in fact merely the kind of woolliness which clouds the reasoning powers of able men under the pernicious influence of scientism. A characteristic example of scientian logic may be found in *The Science of Life*, a work of popularisation by the late H. G. Wells, Julian Huxley and G. P. Wells. The authors quote the passage to which I have already referred from Haldane's *Possible Worlds*.

"The assertion is still sometimes made that no one has seen natural selection at work. It is therefore perhaps worth giving in some detail a case recently described by Harrison. About 1800 a large wood in the Cleveland district of Yorkshire containing pine and birch, was divided into two by a stretch of heath. In 1885 the pines on one division were replaced by birches, while in the other the birches were almost entirely ousted by pines. In consequence the moth *Oporabia autumnata,* which inhabits both woods, has been placed in two different environments. In both woods a light and dark variety occur, but in the pine wood over ninety-six per cent. are now dark, in the birch wood only fifteen per cent. . . . The reason for the difference was discovered on collecting the wings of moths found lying about in the pine wood, whose owners had been eaten by owls, bats, and night-jars. . . . The whiter moths, which show up against the dark pines, are being exterminated, and in a few more years natural selection will have done its work and the pine wood will be inhabited entirely by dark coloured insects."

Now the authors had already stated that selection is selection and not production. "There exists," they wrote, "a voluminous foolish literature of controversy in which Darwin is alleged to have taught that natural selection, in heaven knows what inconceivable way, *produced* variations. Thereupon he is trounced, disposed of, burnt in controversial effigy and generally made an end to. Some victim of such mephitic controversy may chance to breathe the purer air of this work."

The authors, therefore, must have realised that the passage that they quoted from Haldane merely reaffirmed the obvious truism that the fittest to survive survived, but however loudly they might assert that natural selection did not produce variations and however loudly they might boast that the "purer air" of their work was uninfected by the suggestion that natural selection *produced* variations, they were still sub-consciously influenced by the anxiety to find an answer to Paley and to prove that natural selection was *creative.* So the phrase "*in the production of new characters*" was quietly interpolated in the original quotation and Professor Haldane's opening sentence read as follows: "The assertion is still sometimes made that no one has ever seen natural selection at work *in the production of new characters* (italics mine).

In my review of *The Science of Life* I quoted the passage as misquoted by the authors, and added:

"Come, come, Mr. Haldane, this will not do. Poor Mr. Everyman will want his money back if the conjuror cannot produce something better than this out of the old Darwinian hat. natural selection, you told us, has been seen at work in the production of *new characters*. Where are these new characters? White moths are being exterminated—granted—but no new characters are being created. The black moths in the woods are the descendants of the black moths which were there before the birch were replaced by pine. What 'new character' has been produced in the process? What bearing have these facts on the power of natural selection to transform a reptile into a bird? All that you have proved is that moths which are badly camouflaged disappear, much as guns which were badly camouflaged were blotted out in the war. But the war would have had to last a very long time to transform a gun into an aeroplane, and natural selection would require another ally more potent than the mere passage of time to transform a reptile into a bird."

The next development was a letter from Professor Haldane in which he pointed out that he had been misquoted, and complained that I (or the authors) had attributed to him "an obviously silly remark."

After I had apologised to the readers of the *New English Review* for my rash assumption that quotations by a Darwinist from a Darwinist did not need to be checked, Mr. Wells replied by a short and angry letter, in which he stated that the passage interpolated as a quotation from Haldane had been "manifestly inserted for greater clearness."

The comedy may be briefly summarised as follows: The authors (a) denounce all those who assert that natural selection produces new characters; (b) hunt round for evidence that natural selection after all does produce new characters; (c) interpolate a statement to this effect in a quotation from Professor Haldane; (d) accidentally omit quotation marks; (e) state that they have inserted "for greater clearness" a phrase which struck Professor Haldane and myself as "obviously silly."

In their defence it might be urged that the interpolation merely developed an idea which was latent in the original passage. Professor Haldane's moths were described in an essay entitled *Darwinism To-day* and only a reader who was more alert than most of those who read the *Essays in Popular Science* would have realised that the story had no relevance whatever to the subject which Professor Haldane was discussing. The truism that black moths show up more against light trees than against dark trees was quietly smuggled into an article on Darwinism as if it was evidence for the creative power of natural selection, but it would take a great deal of natural selection to transform the story about the moths into an argument for "Darwinism to-day."

(IV)

It is difficult to estimate how far Darwin's writings may fairly be used as evidence for the de-rationalising influence of scientism, for it is not easy to decide whether Darwin was a scientian or even a consistent Darwinian. He had no gift of logical thought and no power to reason out his own position, and consequently it is easy to quote from his work passages in support of completely different positions. I have already shown that he could not even arrive at a final decision on the supreme problem as to whether "this grand sequence of events" is or is not wholly due to chance.

His academic career was undistinguished. He made no attempt to read for Honours and finished tenth among those who entered for a Pass degree. He abandoned mathematics because he was unable, in his own words, "to see any meaning in the early steps in algebra." In later years the criticism of natural selection which made most impression on him was contained in an article which appeared in the *North British Review* and which referred to "a vague use of an imperfectly understood doctrine of chance among Darwinian supporters, a misunderstanding which led Darwinians to believe that species could be changed by the survival of a few individuals in a century through a similar and favourable variation." Had Darwin been a mathematician he would have realised the immense odds against the possibility of a species being radically transformed by natural selection. The mathematical refutation of mechanistic evolution is summarised in Appendix B.

Here is a passage from one of Darwin's works: If an earthquake occurred in England, "what would become of the lofty houses, thickly parked cities, great manufactures (*sic*), the beautiful public and private edifices?" One need not be a genius to answer this question. If the earthquake was severe "the beautiful public and private edifices" would depreciate in value. "The greatest of living men," as Darwin was described by an enthusiastic contemporary, then proceeds to explain that if the earthquake continued for some considerable time "England would be at once bankrupt," and that "all papers, records and accounts would from that moment be lost." There is a great deal more in this strain, and it is difficult to believe that a man who at the age of thirty-three could cover paper with these dreadful commonplaces was a genius.

It is difficult to understand the great popularity enjoyed by the *Origin of Species* outside scientific circles excepting on the hypothesis that fashion will create a circulation of a book of the moment irrespective of the style in which it is written. "I have been reading the *Origin* again slowly," wrote Huxley, "with the view of picking out the essentials for the obituary notice. Nothing entertains me more than to hear people calling it easy reading. Exposition was not Darwin's forte—and his English is sometimes wonderful. But there is a marvellous dumb sagacity about him—like that of a sort of miraculous dog—and he gets to the truth by ways as dark as those of the Heathen Chinee."

And just as it would be easy to prove Darwin a theist, an agnostic or an atheist by suitable quotations from his work, so it would be easy to demonstrate that he was a Lamarckian or anti-Lamarckian—according to the passage selected. One moment, for instance, he expresses surprise that the case of ants working by inherited instinct had not been brought forward as a demonstrative argument "against the well-known doctrine of inherited habit as advanced by Lamarck." At an earlier stage of his career he refers to nature as "making habit omnipotent and its effects hereditary"—pure Lamarckianism.

It would seem then that Darwin was never a clear thinker and that scientism cannot be blamed for the inconsistencies of his writings, but scientism certainly aggravated an inborn tendency to woolliness. His writings betray the conflict in his mind between sense and nonsense. He was subconciously aware of the fact that a man who professes to explain the origin of species ought to offer some explanation of the origin of variations, and he was compelled to camouflage his failure by a mist of meaningless verbiage.

To the question "How do variations arise?" he replies: "In living bodies variation will cause the slight alterations." In other words, variation will cause variation. How illuminating! He continues: "Generation will multiply them almost infinitely and Natural Selection will pick out with unerring skill each improvement." How can the blind process of pure chance be described as picking out variations with unerring skill? Skill is the opposite of chance. Here we have a good example of Darwin's silly habit of personifying Natural Selection and of attributing to it the characteristics of the Creator. Samuel Butler selected from different editions of *The Origin of Species* the fortuitous variations of a sentence which indicates Darwin's hesitating advance towards the personification of Natural Selection. In the 1859 edition we read:

"Further we must suppose that there is a power always intently watching each slight accidental alteration."

In the 1861 edition Natural Selection makes its coy appearance between brackets, and the passage reads:

"Further we must suppose that there is a power (Natural Selection), etc."

In the 1869 edition we read:

"Further we must suppose that there is a power represented by Natural Selection, etc."

As Butler says: "Mr. Darwin probably said 'a power represented by natural selection' instead of 'natural selection', only because he saw that to talk too frequently about the fact that the most lucky live longest as 'intently watching something' was greater nonsense than would be prudent even for him to write, so he fogged it by making the intent watching done by 'a power represented by a fact' instead of by the fact itself. As the sentence stands it is just as great nonsense as it would have been if 'the survival of the fittest' had been allowed to do the watching instead of 'the power represented by' the survival of the fittest; but the nonsense is harder to dig up, and the reader is more likely to pass it over."

A glaring example of *petitio principii* in Darwin's writings has already been quoted on page 124. Even more striking is the evidence of loose thought in his remarks about theism.

He confesses that he is "impressed by the impossibility of conceiving this immense and wonderful universe, including man, with his capacity for looking far backwards and far into futurity, as the result of blind chance or necessity. Thus reflecting, I feel compelled to look to a first cause having an intelligent mind in some degree analogous to that of man; and I deserve to be called a theist. This conclusion was strong in my mind about the time, as far as I can remember, when I wrote *The Origin of Species*, and it is since that time that it has very gradually, with many fluctuations, become weaker. But then arises the doubt— Can the mind of man, which has, as I fully believe, been developed from a mind as low as that possessed by the lowest animals, be trusted 'when it draws such grand conclusions' . . .? But then with me the horrid doubt always arises whether the convictions of man's mind, which has been developed from the mind of the lowest animals, are of any value or at all trustworthy. Would anyone trust the convictions of a monkey's mind, and are there convictions in such a mind?"

A clear thinker would never have been guilty of such inconsistent reasoning. If Darwin was not prepared to trust his mind when it drew the "grand conclusion" that God existed, why was he prepared to trust it when it drew the depressing conclusion that a mind of such bestial origin could not be trusted to draw any conclusion at all?

Darwin's mind at different periods of his life led him to two firm convictions: (a) that God exists, and (b) that man is descended from the lower animals.

If, as the result of (b) he lost confidence in his own mental processes, he might well have rejected both beliefs, but to retain the latter belief, which was the source of his scepticism, and to reject the former was illogical. It was, indeed, absurd to state on the same page that he "fully believed" in the bestial origin of his own mind, and that this same bestial origin did not entitle him "fully to believe" in anything.

K

CHAPTER XIV

THE PROPAGANDA OF SCIENTISM

(1)

ATHEISM would have conquered far less mental territory in the nineteenth and twentieth centuries but for the success of the scientians in exploiting the prestige of science on behalf of atheism explicit or implicit. Men who were beginning to find the demands of the old religion too exacting for comfort were conditioned to welcome a substitute religion which offered them power in this world in place of a hypothetical beatitude in the world to come.

The appetite for religion, one of the strongest of cravings, can find temporary satisfaction in a false religion, but religion of some sort man must have, and with religion the inevitable priestcraft to interpret its mysteries. The priests of the new religion were the scientists or rather the scientians who exploited the prestige of science on behalf of atheism.

The Christians were handicapped in their struggle against the new religion by the fact that whereas Christianity offers to the faithful self-mastery and spiritual control but holds out no promises of material rewards, the scientians were less exacting in their demands and more generous in their promises, so far at least as material reward was concerned. I should like to quote in this connection an illuminating passage from Mr. C. S. Lewis's profound booklet *The Abolition of Man:*

"You will find people who write about the sixteenth century as if magic were a mediaeval survival and science the new thing that came in to sweep it away. Those who have studied the period know better. There was very little magic in the Middle Ages: the sixteenth and seventeenth centuries are the high noon of magic. The serious magical endeavour and the serious scientific endeavour are twins: one was sickly and died, the other was strong and throve. But they were twins. They were born of the same impulse. I allow that some (certainly not all) of the earlier scientists were actuated by a pure love of knowledge. But if we consider the temper of that age as a whole we can discern the impulse of which I speak. There is something which unites magic and applied science while separating both from the 'wisdom' of earlier ages.

"For the wise man of old, the cardinal problem had been how to conform the soul to reality and the solution had been knowledge, self-discipline and virtue. For magic and applied science alike the problem is how to subdue reality to the wishes of men: the solution is a technique; and both, in the practice of the technique, are ready to do things hitherto regarded as disgusting and impious (such as digging up and mutilating the dead).

"If we compare the chief trumpet of the new age (Bacon) with Marlowe's Faustus, the similarity is striking. You will read in some critics that Faustus has a thirst for knowledge. In reality he hardly mentions it. It is not truth that he wants from his devils, but gold and guns and girls. 'All things that move between the quiet poles shall be at his command' and 'a sound magician is a mighty God'. In the same spirit Bacon condemns those who value knowledge as an end in itself: this, for him, is to use as a mistress for pleasure what ought to be a spouse for fruit. The true object is to extend man's power to the performance of all things possible. He rejects magic because it does not work, but his goal is that of the magician.

"In Paracelsus the characteristics of the magician and the scientist are combined. No doubt those who really founded modern science were usually those whose love of truth exceeded their love of power: in every mixed movement the efficacy comes from the good elements not from the bad. But the presence of the bad elements is not irrelevant to the direction the efficacy takes. It might be going too far to say that the modern scientific movement was tainted from its birth: but I think it would be true to say that it was born in an unhealthy neighbourhood and at an inauspicious hour. Its triumphs may have been too rapid and purchased at too high a price: reconsideration and something like repentance may be required."

(II)

The conflict between scientism and science is nowhere more apparent than in the scientian doctrine of man. The scientian starts from the same false premise as the Marxist. The Christian, whose doctrine of man is based as all valid science is based, on a realistic appraisal of the facts as they are and not on facts as we might desire them to be, realised that political systems depend very largely on the human material of those who administer them. Good eggs can be spoiled by a bad cook and a bad political system can fail to exploit what is good in human nature, but it is the eggs that matter most. The Marxist (and the scientian) argue, as Mr. Frank Sheed remarks, that a specific method of making an omelette will turn bad eggs into good, and finally the disillusioned Marxist evolves into the despairing nihilist who maintains that eggs (and human beings) are so inherently rotten that it is no use trying to make an omelette at all. Similarly the scientian assumes that the mere pursuit of science will transform bad eggs into a good omelette, that the human beings who embrace science as a career will automatically be purged of the vanity and self-interest which cloud their judgment of objective truth.

"The scientist," writes Huxley, "unlike the theologian, is compelled to demand that rational ground for belief without which, to the man of science, assent is merely an immoral pretence." It would be unfair to describe Huxley's assent to that rubbish as "an immoral pretence," for scientians have always been prone to dogmatise about theology without any "rational ground for the beliefs" which they ascribe to theologians, and I need not repeat the evidence which I have elsewhere summarised in support of my contention that Huxley (on his own admission, see page 99) gave his assent to evolution without a "rational ground for belief."

The Christian doctrine of man is based on a scientific study of human nature. The Christian believes in the supernatural Grace which helps the priest to practice virtue in general and the difficult virtue of chastity in particular. But we do not pretend that ordination transforms the ordinand into a saint. Every priest makes public confession in the mass that he has sinned most grievously in thought, word and deed, and to no priest is the *Confiteor* an empty formula.

Scientists have been very successful in imposing on the public a false dichotomy. The man in the street has been conditioned to believe that whereas the scientist is only concerned to discover the truth, the whole truth and nothing but the truth, the casuistical theologian is only interested in rigging the evidence in support of incredible dogmas.

Now the scientific approach to the problem of human bias leads to the conclusion that man has a natural tendency to welcome facts which confirm and a natural temptation to reject facts which conflict with the beliefs which he already holds, and there is not the slightest justification for distinguishing between the attitude of born Christian in this respect and the attitude of the scientist born in an age which takes evolution for granted. Or rather the distinction tells in favour of the Christian, for I have never met a theologian who was as ignorant of the case against Christianity as the average biologist is ignorant of the case against evolution.

A Fellow of the Royal Society once confided to me that his conversion to Catholicism had been greatly influenced by the fact that St. Thomas Aquinas had stated the case against atheism with conspicuous fairness, whereas the case against evolution was either evaded or ignored in the text books in use at his school and university.

Men who are prepared to sacrifice their material prospects in defence of unpopular or unfashionable truth will always be in a minority. "The tyranny of the *Zeitgeist* in the matter of evolution," wrote Dwight, in a passage which I have already quoted in full (page 104), "is overwhelming to a degree of which outsiders have no idea."

Then again consider the following quotation from Alex Carrel, *Man the Unknown*. Carrel, a Nobel prize-winner, is not a Catholic but he is a scientian with a conscience, prepared to investigate phenomena which most scientists of his day preferred to leave unexamined. The italics in the quotation that follows are my own:

"Miraculous cures seldom occur. Despite their small number they prove the existence of organic and mental processes that we do not know. They show that certain mystic states, such as that of prayer have definite effects. *They are stubborn irreducible facts*, which must be taken into account. The author knows that miracles are as far from scientific orthodoxy as mysticity. The investigation of such phenomena is still more delicate than that of telepathy and clairvoyance. *But science has to explore the entire realm of reality*. He has attempted to learn the characteristics of this mode of healing as well as the ordinary modes. He began this study in 1902, at a time when the documents were scarce, when it was difficult for a young doctor and dangerous for his future career to become interested in such a subject."

(III)

Dr. Carrel's quiet statement to the effect that he began his study of miracles "at a time when it was dangerous for his future career to become interested in such a subject" is, in itself, a complete condemnation of the anti-scientific attitude of nineteenth-century scientians, for genuine science "has to explore the entire realm of reality." Every schoolboy has heard of Galileo, but text books are silent on the victimisation of modern scientists who were rash enough to explore "realms of reality", boycotted by the priestcraft of orthodox science.

The degree to which our assent to a man's opinions should be influenced, either favourably or adversely, by what we know of his philosophical beliefs and personal qualifications is clearly a matter of the first importance, and it is therefore strange that the scientians made no attempt to arrive at an objective and a scientific criterion for assessing the influence of bias.

Instead their estimate of the personal factor was determined by four fideistic axioms:—

1. *All Christians are Biased*

It was assumed that you could dispose of the arguments of an anti-Darwinian by the simple expedient of proving that he had a Christian bias. It would, of course, be equally rational to assume that the arguments of a Darwinian could be refuted by proving that he had an atheistic bias. Professor Hartog, in a book from which I have already quoted, refers to certain Roman Catholic priests "with a considerable natural interest in natural history, and a strong professional interest in anti-Darwinism." But is there no such thing as a strong professional interest in pro-Darwinism? Would not the chances of a candidate for a scientific fellowship in 1880 have been adversely affected had he been known to hold anti-Darwinian views or, worse still, to be a disbeliever in evolution?

Professor Hartog, for instance, tells us that Darwin's most formidable critic, that distinguished scientist, Professor Mivart, "was regarded as negligible since he evidently held a brief for a party standing outside the scientific world." It would be as rational to regard Huxley as negligible because he evidently held a brief for a party standing outside the theological world, or indeed, to regard the arguments of any barrister as negligible because he was clearly biased in favour of his client. All barristers are "biased", but a sound argument is no less sound because advanced by a barrister with a bias in favour of his client.

2. *Atheists are Unbiased*

3. *It is Legitimate for a Scientist but Illegitimate for a Christian to Appeal to Authority*

Phrases such as "science teaches" or "all scientists accept evolution" are very common in the apologetics of scientism, but if a Christian replies by citing the names of scientists who do not believe in evolution and who do believe in God, he must expect to be accused of appealing to authority.

4. *Professional Theologians and Amateur Scientists should both be Treated with Contempt*

Whereas the atheist and the Darwinian are regarded, exhypothesi, as unbiased, the professional theologian is suspected on the ground that he has a brief to defend. We must therefore take our theology from popularisers of science, such as Professor Julian Huxley, but our science only from professional scientists.

(IV)

Let us see if we can substitute a scientific for a scientian criterion in our attempt to arrive at an objective standard for assessing the influence of bias and personal qualifications.

I suggest that the law of bias might be formulated in some such terms as these:

"*Bias must be allowed for in estimating the value of evidence, but not in estimating the validity of arguments.*"

A few illustrations will, I hope, convince the reader that this law is sound.

In estimating the value of the evidence for a ghost story we must allow for the bias of a witness known to be a convinced spiritualist, for a spiritualist starts his investigations with a bias in favour of ghosts, and is, therefore, more likely than an atheist to mistake some natural for supernatural phenomena.

Similarly, we must allow for bias in estimating the evidence of the conjurer Houdini, who claimed to have exposed the medium "Margery", for Houdini, like many other conjurers, had a strong professional interest in exposing mediums.

On the other hand, it is childish to meet an *argument* by an accusation of bias. The question of bias arises only in connection with the evidence for the facts on which the argument is based, and it can therefore only concern the witnesses who have been cited in support of those facts. You may logically refute an argument by alleging bias against a witness, but you do not strengthen your case by alleging bias against the arguer himself unless he has gone into the witness-box.

Again, if the effect of the personal equation were more generally understood, we should be spared those acrimonious criticisms of arguments advanced by amateurs against the conclusions of specialists.

The Victorian scientist not only considered that he had refuted Mivart by showing that Mivart was biased in favour of Christianity, but he was equally convinced that he had refuted Samuel Butler, a no less formidable critic of Darwinism, by proving that Butler was an amateur with no scientific training. The law of bias may be adapted to this case. *The credentials of a writer must be examined in estimating the value of his evidence, but not in estimating the validity of his arguments.*

The evidence of an amateur experimentalist on some problem of research would not weigh heavily against the view of an expert researcher, but if expert and amateur are arguing on the basis of facts admitted by the expert, it is ridiculous for the expert to challenge the credentials of the amateur.

The specialist who has convicted an amateur of elementary blunders is entitled to attribute his errors to lack of technical training, but he is not entitled to say, "I am right because I am recognised as a specialist, and you are wrong because you possess no academic qualifications whatever." This is much as if an eminent Counsel were to urge the jury to ignore the arguments of a young barrister on the ground that he had just been called to the Bar.

Similarly, if you convict a writer of bad logic or weak reasoning, you are entitled to hold a post-mortem and diagnose
"bias," but the post-mortem must follow and must not precede
the "mors." I have collected in this book many examples of bad
logic which I attribute to an anti-religious bias clouding the
reasoning powers of men for whose intellect I have a profound
respect, but unless I could produce objective evidence in support of this charge, I should not feel entitled to mention the
personal factor. In other words, I have introduced the question
of bias to explain the weakness of an argument, the unsound-
ness of which has previously been demonstrated. Once a man
has been fairly convicted of unreason, it is often profitable to
seek for the explanation of his sin against sound logic, but you
must prove the crime before you begin to reconstruct it.

(v)

In a theocracy the freedom-loving layman would tend to join
the ranks of the anticlericals. *Atheocracy* which has already been
established in Russia and which is in a fair way to be inaugur-
ated elsewhere, has its own priesthood and will in due course
provoke the modern equivalent of anti-clericism, the revolt of
the amateur against the tyranny of the specialists. The trade
union mentality is not confined to the ranks of organised
labour. It was not Galileo's championship of the Copernican
theory which provoked the theologians but his blackleg activities in the sphere of Scriptural exegesis. It was his claim that the
miracle of the sun standing still would need to be re-interpreted
which caused all the trouble. The professional theologians reacted much as the professional scientists reacted some centuries
later when that gifted amateur Samuel Butler began to criticise
Darwinism.

"Gentlemen versus Players" usually results in a victory for
the professionals, and it is only the exceptional scientific
amateur who can beat the professionals, but it is as well to
remember that professional training can develop but cannot
create inventive genius.

"Of all forms of enterprise," writes Mr. A. H. Pollen, "that
which is the most wholly personal is the gift of suddenly per-
ceiving what is hidden from other men. It is this rare gift that
we recognise to be the peculiarity of those pioneers in dis-

covery and invention who are the true authors of modern progress."

Watt, who invented the steam-engine, was an artisan. It was a veterinary surgeon who invented pneumatic tyres, Browning, who invented automatic weapons, was the son of a gunsmith. At the age of thirteen he made his first gun out of the scrap-iron in his father's workshop.

De Saussure has been called with justice the father of modern geology. In the course of his mountain wanderings he must often have seen erratic boulders and moraines far beyond the limits of existing glaciers. Yet he never drew the obvious conclusions that glaciers must at one time have extended many miles beyond their present limits.

Agassiz and Charpentier, great naturalists and great observers, also missed the significance of these signposts of past glacial ages.

A chamois hunter, Perrandier by name, observed a block of granite resting on limestone in the neighbourhood of Neuchâtel. Granite cannot grow out of limestone like a mushroom, and Perrandier accordingly deduced that the granite must at one time have been carried to Neuchâtel by a glacier. From which it followed that glaciers must at one time have covered the whole of Switzerland. Perrandier was, therefore, the discoverer of the glacial epoch of the past.

Samuel Butler's criticisms of Darwin were ignored because he was an amateur but it is generally recognised to-day, even in scientific circles, that Butler's criticisms of Darwin were unusually brilliant. Professor J. A. Thomson described his book on evolution as "a keen-witted criticism of orthodox Darwinism." There are many flattering references to Butler in the centenary volume of *Darwin and Modern Science*. Professor Bateson, for instance, described Samuel Butler as "the most brilliant, and by far the most interesting of Darwin's opponents."

Again, Butler's independent re-discovery of Hering's theory of memory proves that he possessed scientific talent of no mean order. None the less, Butler's criticisms were ignored, and Butler himself was completely boycotted by the scientific world. And not only by the scientific world. His later books were virtually ignored in that lay press which took its opinions in scientific matters from the recognised leaders of orthodox science.

It is only since Butler's death that his real merit has been recognised. Sir Francis Darwin, Charles Darwin's son, paid him a generous, chivalrous tribute in his address to the British Association in 1908. Professor Marcus Hartog, in the introduction which he wrote for Butler's book, *Unconscious Memory*, gives an impressive list of scientists who have been influenced by Butler's views, and concludes with the following tribute:

". . . Butler failed to impress the biologists of his day, even those on whom, like Romanes, he might have reasonably counted for understanding and for support. But he kept alive Hering's work when it bade fair to sink into the limbo of obsolete hypothesis. To use Oliver Wendell Holmes's phrase, he 'depolarised' evolutionary thought. We quote the words of a young biologist, who, when an ardent and dogmatic Weismannist of the most pronounced type, was induced to read *Life and Habit:* 'The book was to me a transformation and an inspiration.' Such learned writings as Semon's or Hering's could never produce such an effect: they do not penetrate to the heart of man; they cannot carry conviction to the intellect already filled full with rival theories, and with the unreasoned faith that to-morrow or next day a new discovery will obliterate all distinction between Man and his makings. The mind must needs be open for the reception of truth, for the rejection of prejudice; and the violence of a Samuel Butler may in the future, as in the past, be needed to shatter the coat of mail forged by too exclusively professional a training."

Butler insisted that the fact co-ordinator had the right to make use of the facts which the fact collectors had collected. An architect, he explained, does not quarry his own bricks. "If the facts are sound," he wrote, "how can it matter whether A. or B. collected them? If Professor Huxley, for example, has made a series of original observations (not that I know of his having done so), why am I to make them over again? What are fact collectors worth if the fact co-ordinators may not rely upon them?"

Commander Acworth provides a more recent example of a writer whose brilliant criticisms were ignored because he was an amateur. He was one of the first to enunciate, and certainly the first fully to appreciate, the importance of the law which he describes as the first law of currents. "No bird and no machine can experience any pressure from the movement of the medium in which it is supported and operating."

He quotes many passages from distinguished scientists who fall into the error of supposing that a bird in flight *feels* the wind. A bird in flight is, of course, *affected* by the wind, delayed by a head wind and helped by a following wind, but in so far as its sensations are concerned, storm and calm are much the same thing. From this law Commander Acworth had deduced a fascinating theory of bird migration.

The book was virtually boycotted by the scientific Press, but enjoyed a magnificent reception in the lay Press. Competent laymen pointed out that Commander Acworth's premises appeared to be unassailable, and assumed that the conclusions which he deduced from those premises would either be accepted or refuted by scientists. The scientists, however, adopted much the same tactics as those which enjoyed temporary success in the case of Samuel Butler.

There were honourable exceptions. Mr. T. A. Coward, one of the leading ornithologists of the world, reviewed the book in *The Manchester Guardian*, and described it as "a really remarkable book—a direct challenge soundly reasoned, to generally accepted ideas about flight, especially migratory flight of birds, insects, and indeed anything, including aircraft, which moves in a single moving medium."

Nature, on the other hand, dismissed the book described by an acknowledged expert as "a direct challenge soundly reasoned, to generally accepted ideas about flight" with a few silly sneers, and thereby failed in its duty to the layman who has the right to expect a paper of this standing to provide him with the necessary data for pronouncing opinion on original theories which challenge existing orthodoxies. *Nature's* treatment of Acworth may be compared with the treatment which Dewar received when he sent the results of his investigations about the fossil record to the Editor of *The Proceedings of the Zoological Society* (see p. 128). Though many articles on palaeontology have appeared in this publication, Dewar's article, which was as important a challenge to orthodoxy as Acworth's book, was returned to him by the Secretary with the following remarks: "I am sorry, but the Publication Committee cannot accept your paper. We got the opinion of a first-rate palaeontologist and geologist about it, and he told us that although it must have taken a very long time to compile it, he thought this kind of evidence led to no valuable conclusion."

Please note that the palaeontologist in question did not challenge the accuracy of the evidence. He merely *disliked* the conclusion to which it seemed to point.

There is a disconcerting similarity between the reactions of the scientians and Marxists to unorthodox views. There are still some civilised reviewers who will give warm praise to a well-written statement of a case which they reject, but there is an increasing tendency for scientians to imitate the Marxists by praising books which conform to and by damning (or worse still ignoring) books which run counter to accepted orthodoxies.

(VI)

In this chapter I have tried to summarise the principle varieties of scientian propaganda. These are:—

(1) A glorification of scientists as such which is based on a false doctrine of man, on the illusion that a scientist as such is inoculated against the human tendency to welcome evidence which conforms with what he wishes to be true and to reject evidence which conflicts with his desires.

(2) A false doctrine of bias leading to the false conclusion that scientians are always unbiased and Christians always biased.

(3) An attempt to rule the amateur out of court and to impose upon the man in the street a dictatorship of specialists.

The scientific expert has his value, but it is unhealthy for the expert and demoralising for the public for his authority to be accepted with uncritical respect. Organised science is gradually usurping the position which was once held by the Church. Scientists are beginning to assume that their pronouncements on religious or political or social problems deserve a respect greater than that accorded to the view of the non-scientific. "I do not think," said Lord Rayleigh in his Presidential Address to the British Association, "that the scientific worker has a claim superior to that of other people to assume the attitude of a prophet. In his heart he knows that underneath the theories he constructs there lie contradictions which he cannot reconcile."

(VII)

The prophesies of the nineteenth century "Dawnists" who predicted that science would take the place of religion have been falsified by history. Science, let me repeat, is morally neutral and serves the purpose of a Himmler no less than of a Pasteur. The scientist whose life is consecrated to the service of God ranks among the benefactors of mankind, but the scientist who is infected by the heresy of Scientism is in danger of losing the common touch, for science tends to create an aristocratic attitude of contempt for the common man. The doctrine of man's immortal soul is man's only protection against the secular humanitarian, impatient of misfits and dysgenic types who retard the evolution of man into superman.

"This world and its future," writes Mr. H. G. Wells, "is not for feeble folk any more than it is for selfish folk. It is not for the multitude but for the best. The best of to-day will be the commonplace of to-morrow" (a view, by the way, for which there is no scientific evidence whatever). "If I am something of a social leveller it is not because I want to give silly people a good time, but because I want to make opportunity universal, and not miss out one single being who is worth while."

All the inhumanity of the secular humanitarian emerges in this grim confession of faith. We have travelled a long way from St. Francis' "Let the Lord God be praised in *all* his creatures," and from the Christ who died not only for Mr. H. G. Wells but also for the "feeble folk" whom Mr. Wells despised and for the "silly folk" who have as much right to eternal beatitude as the great "Dawnist" who could offer them no hope of "a good time" in the utopia of the secular scientian.

CHAPTER XV

"SIT DOWN BEFORE FACT"

(1)

NO LETTER which Huxley wrote has been more often quoted than his letter to Charles Kingsley in which he stated his conception of the scientific code.

"Science seems to me to teach in the highest and strongest manner the great truth which is embodied in the Christian conception of entire surrender to the will of God. Sit down before fact as a little child, be prepared to give up every preconceived notion, follow humbly wherever and to whatever abysses nature leads, or you shall learn nothing. I have only begun to learn content and peace of mind since I have resolved at all risks to do this."

A fine ideal, but unfortunately the scientist finds it no easier to live up to the scientific ideal than the theologian to the Christian ideal. The reactions of Huxley, a scientist of undoubted integrity, to unwelcome facts, were much the same as the reactions of the more simple-minded believers to the fossils which appeared to throw doubt on Genesis.

The sincerity of Huxley's determination to "sit down before fact" was subjected to a severe test by the invitation which he received to examine the mediumship of Daniel Douglas Home.

Home was the most famous of all psychical mediums. He was never detected in fraud, and to this day no sceptic has been able to put forward a plausible explanation of the phenomena which he produced.

"A highly desirable characteristic of Home's mediumship", wrote that eminent scientist Lord Rayleigh, "was the unusual opportunity allowed to the sense of sight. Home always objected to darkness at his séances."

Home's mediumship created such a sensation that a committee was appointed by the Dialectical Society of London to investigate the phenomena which he was alleged to produce.

Thirty-four gentlemen of standing were appointed, including well-known physicians, surgeons, barristers, and two fellows of scientific societies. The Dialectical Society fully expected and hoped that the committee would receive evidence establishing the fraudulent basis of the alleged phenomena. Most of those who agreed to serve on the committee did so in the determination to unmask what they believed to be an imposture. The committee met on forty occasions, and the report which they finally presented caused amazement and dismay among the Dialectical Society, who refused point-blank to publish it. The committee, fortunately, were spirited enough to publish the report at their own expense, though it was the exact opposite from that for which they had confidently hoped. The report concludes with the following observation:

"In presenting their report, your committee, taking into consideration the high character and great intelligence of many of the witnesses to the more extraordinary facts, the extent to which their testimony is supported by the reports of the sub-committees, and the absence of any proof of imposture or delusion as regards a large portion of the phenomena . . . deem it incumbent upon them to state their conviction that the subject is worthy of more serious attention and careful investigation than it has hitherto received."

Here are some extracts from the report:

"Thirteen witnesses state that they have seen heavy bodies— in some instances men—rise slowly in the air and remain there for some time without visible or tangible support."

"Five witnesses state that they have seen red-hot coals applied to the hands or heads of several persons without producing pain or scorching, and three witnesses state that they have had the same experiment made upon themselves with the like immunity."

Huxley was invited by the Dialectical Society to join their committee, and he replied, much as a cardinal might reply if he was invited to examine the case for Anglo-Israelism:

"I regret that I am unable to accept the invitation of the committee of the Dialectical Society to co-operate with a committee for the investigation of 'spiritualism'; and for two reasons. In the first place, I have not time for such an enquiry, which would involve much trouble and (unless it were unlike all inquiries of that kind I have known) much annoyance. In the second place, I take no interest in the subject. The only case of 'spiritualism' I have had the opportunity of examining into myself, was as gross an imposture as ever came under my notice. But supposing the phenomena to be genuine—they do not interest me. If anybody would endow me with the faculty of listening to the chatter of old women and curates in the nearest cathedral town, I should decline the privilege, having better things to do. And if the folk in the spiritual world do not talk more wisely and sensibly than their friends report them to do, I put them in the same category. The only good that I can see in the demonstration of the truth of 'spiritualism' is to furnish an additional argument against suicide. Better live a crossing-sweeper than die and be made to talk twaddle by a 'medium' hired at a guinea a séance."

Huxley failed to realise that the question at issue was not whether the life of a crossing-sweeper was richer and more varied than the life of a spirit, but whether the fact of spirit communications had been proved. The spiritualist might well have rejoined, "Sit down before fact as a little child, be prepared to give up every preconceived notion, follow humbly wherever and to whatever abysses Nature shall lead . . . even to the abyss of the spiritualistic heaven."

"The odd point," as William James so justly remarks, "is that so few of those who talk in this way realise that they and the spiritists are using the same major premise and differing only in the minor. The major premise is: 'Any spirit-revelation must be romantic'. The minor of the spiritist is: 'This *is* romantic'; that of the Huxleyan is: 'This is dingy twaddle', whence their opposite conclusions!"

Is there any reason why discarnate spirits should not display the same range of intelligence as incarnate spirits, those for instance with whom we come into contact in our every day life? In this world the most intelligent spirits are not those who are in general the most accessible. The conversation of incarnate spirits is, as we know, only too often trivial, dull and unintelligent. Why then should we be surprised by the trivial chatter of the séance room?

Huxley's reluctance to examine the phenomena was inspired not by scientific and rational considerations but by aesthetic prejudices similar to those which biased Kepler against the possibility that planets might move not in "perfect" circles but in "imperfect" ellipses.

L

(II)

The attitude of the Victorian scientians to psychical phenomena was a breach of the code which Huxley had formulated in his letter to Kingsley, first because a *prima facie* case had been established for the genuineness of these phenomena, secondly the phenomena, if genuine, constituted a formidable challenge to orthodox science. If the phenomenon of "levitation" could be proved one of two things would follow. *Either* discarnate spirits were responsible for the levitation *or* orthodox dynamics would need to be radically revised. Either alternative is a challenge to scientists.

My statement that a *prima facie* case for investigation has been established is based on many facts of which the most important are the following. I shall content myself with a brief summary, giving page references to my earlier book *The Flight from Reason*, in which the points that follow have been elaborated.

1. Thirty-four members of the Dialectical Society met on forty occasions. Their testimony to the supranatural phenomena which they witnessed constituted an *a priori* case for scientific investigation. The case for investigation, which was overwhelming when Huxley was invited to join the committee, has been progressively reinforced ever since.

"To imagine," writes Professor Richet, "that all metaphysics are but illusion: to suppose that William Crookes, A. R. Wallace, Lombroso, Zölln, F. W. H. Myers, Oliver Lodge, Aksakoff, J. Ochorowicz, J. Maxwell Boutleroff, Du Prel, William James, Morselli, Botazzi, Bozzano, Flammarion, A. de Rochas, A. de Gramont, Shrenk-Notzing, and William Barrett were all, without exception, liars or imbeciles, is to suppose that two hundred distinguished observers, less eminent, perhaps, but persons of high and acute intelligence, were also liars or imbeciles."

2. Mass hypnotism is no explanation for these phenomena have been recorded not only by human witnesses but also by scientific instruments. If a group of people sit together in a confined space, the temperature will normally rise. It is, however, an established fact that there is a sharp drop in temperature immediately preceding the manifestation of supernormal phenomena. Dr. Tyllyard, an Australian scientist, introduced into the séance room a thermograph which was synchronised

with a watch by means of which he recorded the precise moment at which the phenomena took place. The thermograph recorded a steady rise in temperature between phenomena, and a sharp drop immediately preceding the manifestations.

These experiments were recorded in *Nature* (July 31st, 1926), and the paper describing them was among the first articles on psychical phenomena to appear in that very conservative periodical.

3. Even more remarkable were the paraffin glove tests, in the description of which I shall use the word "spirit" as a convenient abbreviation for "the alleged materialisation which was alleged to be caused by a discarnate spirit."

It was at the *Institut Metapsychique* that the famous paraffin glove test was employed for the first time. This test was made by Professor Richet and Dr. Geley, and the first experiments took place with the Polish medium Kluski.

Dr. Geley, before the sitting began, prepared a bath of paraffin wax.

During the séance the "spirit" was requested to immerse his hands into the paraffin bath. The spirit obeyed, and the spirit hand emerged covered with a thin coating of paraffin, a fragile shell about the sixteenth of an inch in thickness.

It would, of course, be impossible for a human being to withdraw his hand from such a delicate paraffin shell without breaking it; for the hand could not pass through the narrow opening where the shell had solidified around the wrist.

The spirit then dematerialised its hand in the paraffin shell which was, therefore, left intact.

The thin paraffin shells were preserved and made permanent by filling them with plaster. The paraffin gloves have been submitted to professional moulders who declared that they could not reproduce these gloves by any process known to them. A professional moulder who wished to obtain a mould of a hand with bent fingers would make this mould in two sections, joining the sections together. The paraffin gloves show no trace of a join.

In many of these paraffin gloves the hands are closed, the thumbs bent and the finger-tips joined to the palm. A well-known scientist, who disbelieved in psychical phenomena, attempted to produce these paraffin gloves in his laboratory. The contrast is very striking between the swollen, shapeless shells which he produced and the delicate paraffin shells produced at the séance, shells which clearly show all the lines in the hand and which are perfect in their moulding.

The lines on the hands and the finger-prints on these paraffin moulds have been shown to be entirely distinct from the finger-prints either of the medium or of any of the sitters present at the séance. In order to prove that the paraffin shells were not manufactured outside and introduced surreptitiously into the séance room, Dr. Geley took the precaution of mixing cholesterin in the paraffin bath which he himself brought into the séance room. After the séance concluded, he tested the paraffin gloves and satisfied himself that they had been formed from the paraffin which had been treated with cholesterin.

4. It is difficult to believe that mediums untrained in legerdemain could beat the best conjurors at their own game, but no conjuror has reproduced these phenomena under identical conditions. Archdeacon Colley offered a thousand pounds to any conjuror who could reproduce materialisations under the conditions which had been imposed by him on the mediums who had produced materialisation in his presence. Maskelyne claimed to have satisfied these conditions and went to court to secure the thousand pounds. The jury decided against him.

In November 1929 Mr. Harry Price challenged Mr. Noel Maskelyne to reproduce in the National Laboratory of Psychical Research phenomena which he claimed had been produced by the Austrian medium Rudi Schneider and to reproduce these under the conditions imposed on Schneider. Mr. Maskelyne declined the challenge. (See *The Flight from Reason*, p. 207.)

(III)

Ninety-five per cent of alleged psychical phenomena are no doubt due to natural causes, such as fraud or hallucination or coincidence, but there remains a small residue of supranatural phenomena, the reality of which must be admitted unless we take refuge in complete scepticism as to the possibility of proving unusual facts by human testimony. The evidence for phenomena such as levitation is so overwhelming that a scientian who rejects such facts, and who accepts evolution is self-convicted of choosing his beliefs on much the same principle as a lady chooses a hat, to suit his mental complexion.

The evidence for evolution is largely based on inferences from a record which is admittedly fragmentary, a record of changes which took place, if they took place at all, millions of years ago. The case for supranatural phenomena is based on the evidence of contemporary scientists whose examination of the phenomena has been conducted with all the resources of modern science.

It is of course possible to accept the phenomena without accepting the spiritist explanation, but the *prima facie* case for a systematic investigation is even stronger on this hypothesis than on the spiritist hypothesis. If, for instance, levitation takes place without the intervention of discarnate or incarnate spirits, orthodox dynamics are exposed as inadequate and levitation is a fact far more revolutionary in its implications than the discovery of a new planet such as Neptune, whose movements conform to the requirements of orthodox astronomy. The refusal of the overwhelming majority of Victorian scientists to investigate phenomena which constituted a direct challenge to orthodox dynamics would only have been justified had there been no evidence, accepted by reputable scientists, for the genuineness of these phenomena.

I have never believed that communication with the dead has been proved but it is not easy to reject the possibility that some of these phenomena are due to discarnate intelligences. It is possible for those who accept certain of these phenomena as genuine to insist that though our limited knowledge does not enable us to explain these phenomena, we have every reason to hope that the better informed scientists of the future will be able to prove that these so-called supranatural phenomena are explicable within the framework of natural law. Naturally the Scientian who appeals with confidence to the missing links in his argument which have vanished from the strata of the remote past has no diffidence about predicting that other missing links will turn up in the remote future, but such an appeal necessarily sterilises all true research, for the essence of research is the open mind—readiness to "sit down before fact as a little child."

When Leverriere discovered that the movements of planets cannot be accounted for by the non-planetary agencies he might have taken refuge in the formula that these puzzling "perturbations" would be explained by the better informed astronomers of the remote future without invoking the hypothesis of a new planet. But Leverriere was a scientist and not a fideist. He was prepared to admit the possibility of other agencies than those of which the orthodox astronomers of his day were aware. And consequently he discovered Neptune.

Our problem is not dissimilar. Can these allegedly supranatural phenomena be explained in terms of known agencies or are the perturbations (popularly known as miracles) due to supernatural or supra-natural agencies? If we rule out in advance the possibility that such agencies may exist, we enter on our research with a closed mind, but in this event we shall have the honesty to admit that the method of science only appeals to us when it leads to conclusions which conform to our fideistic prejudices.

"Sit down before fact as a little child, be prepared to give up every preconceived notion, follow humbly wherever and to whatever abysses nature leads, or you shall learn nothing."

This humble following of fact led Huxley to no abysses. On the contrary, it conducted him gently to the Presidency of the Royal Society, to a Privy Councillorship, and to a pension from a grateful nation.

On the other hand Sir Oliver Lodge who really practised what Huxley only preached and who "gave up every preconceived notion" in his search for truth, ruined thereby his chances of becoming President of the Royal Society.

(IV)

Thanks to Oliver Lodge and Conan Doyle I enjoyed unusual opportunities of attending séances at which the greatest mediums of their period demonstrated their powers. I was never able to accept the spiritualistic explanation of the many extraordinary phenomena which I witnessed. I found it easier to believe that low grade discarnate intelligences were masquerading as the spirits of the departed than that communication had been established with the dead, and I expressed these views in books published long before I became a Catholic.

My experiences however convinced me that it would be very difficult to study these phenomena with a mind unhampered by any dogmatic assumptions as to the nature, existence or non-existence of discarnate spirits without coming to the conclusion that non-human intelligences exist and produce manifestations in this world. It is, for instance, almost impossible to explain the phenomena recorded by Mr. Harry Price during his prolonged investigation of Borley Rectory except on the hypothesis that mischievous spirits, known as poltergeists, have been proved to exist. These phenomena, though trivial and unedifying, are none the less important. We may regret that Mr. Harry Price never entertained an angel unawares and that archangels do not appear in response to the invitation of psychical researchers, but let us at least be grateful that the humble poltergeists are more obliging. So far as the refutation of materialism is concerned it is the existence and not the intelligence of discarnate spirits which is decisive. The scientific proof that poltergeists exist is all that we need to destroy the imposing edifice of scientific materialism.

Moreover the horrors of nazism and communism have made it easier for man to believe in Satanic manifestations. Our Victorian forefathers looked forward to the day when the belief in such things would vanish under the influence of science, but most Victorians had not come into contact with satanism in action. To-day there are many people who find it easier to believe in Satanic than in angelic manifestations, in ghosts than in the Holy Ghost, in poltergeists than in God. The first step in the conversion of the muddled modern mind is to prove that a spirit world exists. No matter whether these spirits be good or evil. Once that step has been taken, it is less difficult to win a hearing for theistic arguments, but it is a waste of time to begin with the Aquinate proofs.

The dominant superstition of the nineteenth century was the belief that materialism was the only creed consistent with the scientific outlook. Only a minority of old-fashioned scientists out of touch with modern thought remain loyal to this outlook. This change of mental climate is largely due to the cumulative results of psychical research in many fields, from materialisations to telepathy. It is becoming increasingly difficult to reconcile the assured results of psychical research with the materialistic creed. Let us therefore do honour to the small company of nineteenth-century scientists who braved the ridicule of their obscurantist and conventional colleagues by exploring these bye-ways of knowledge. They may have failed to demonstrate the immortality of the soul, but at least they succeeded in refuting the argument which draws its strength from a materialistic conception of the relation between the mind and the body of man. They may have failed to prove spiritualism, but they contributed to the disproof of materialism.

(v)

Huxley justified his refusal to examine the mediumship of Home by his dislike of the "twaddle talked by mediums". No such pretext could be advanced to explain the neglect of scientists to investigate the miracles of Lourdes. The most remarkable of modern miracles did not, however, take place at Lourdes but in the shrine of our Lady of Lourdes at Oostacker near Antwerp in 1873. Peter de Rudder was a Belgian farm labourer whose left leg was shattered by the fall of a tree. Seven years passed and the bones were not united. He made a pilgrimage to Oostaker, entered the grotto, prayed and felt a sudden sensation. Forgetting his crutches, he rose, knelt before the statue of our Lady and walked out of the grotto completely cured. The testimony of the doctor who examined his leg before he went to Oostaker and bore witness to the sudden closing up of the wounds and the sudden reunion of the bones is given in a small pamphlet published by the Catholic Truth Society under the title of "A Modern Miracle".

I submitted the evidence to Haldane in our published controversy. After pointing out some minor discrepancies in the pamphlet he wrote: "I think the odds are that the bones were united, and the septic wounds healed, in a few hours, the most probable alternative being a pious fraud enacted by a large number of people."

The miracles alleged to have been observed at Lourdes differ from other faith cures in respect of the scientific scrutiny to which they are subjected. These cures are submitted to the examination of the Medical Bureau at Lourdes which welcomes to its investigations any visiting doctor irrespective of his nationality or religion. Lourdes was visited before the war by an average of about 500 doctors annually. It is unusual for a miracle to be entered in the records unless the patient has returned in the following year and established the permanence of the cure. Blindness, ulcers, cancer and various other organic diseases have been instantly cured at Lourdes.

(VI)

All I hope to establish in this chapter is that there is a *prima facie* case for the investigation of the miracles at Lourdes, for if this be established, the conclusion is inevitable that the scientific world has neglected a field of research concerned with questions of ultimate importance.

That there is a case for investigation was admitted by J. B. S. Haldane in our published correspondence. He claims, it is true, that "most of the Lourdes miracles could, I think, be paralleled in ordinary medical practice," but adds, "Still, one or two of the more surprising Lourdes miracles, such as the immediate healing of a suppurating fracture of eight years' standing, seem to me to be possibly true, and, if so, very remarkable and *worth investigating*, although if they were shown to be true, they would not prove the particular theory of their origin current at Lourdes" (italics mine).

The most impressive tribute to the reality of the Lourdes miracles comes from the pen of Dr. Alexis Carrel, who writes:

". . . To-day any physician can observe the patients brought to Lourdes, and examine the records sent to the Medical Bureau. . . . Our present conception of the influence of prayer upon pathological lesions is based upon the observation of patients who have been cured almost instantaneously of various affections, such as peritoneal tuberculosis, cold abscesses, osteitis, suppurating wounds, lupus, cancer, etc. . . . The miracle is chiefly characterised by an extreme acceleration of the processes of organic repair. There is no doubt that the rate of cicatrisation of the anatomical defects is much greater than the normal one. The only condition indispensable to the occurrence of the phenomenon is prayer. *But there is no need for the patient himself to pray, or even to have any religious faith*"—this excludes auto-suggestion as a cause—"It is sufficient that some one around him be in a state of prayer. Such facts are of profound significance. They show the reality of certain relations, of still unknown nature, between psychological and organic processes. *They prove the objective importance of the spiritual activities, which hygienists, physicians, educators, and sociologists have almost always neglected to study*. They open to man a new world" (italics mine).

The fideism of the true scientian is not easily eroded. Zola visited Lourdes, and wrote a novel about his experiences. The "La Grivotte" of his novel was Mlle Lebranchu and Zola accurately describes her condition as he saw her on the way to Lourdes. "It was", writes Zola of "La Grivotte" and the description is accurate of Mlle Lebranchu, "a case of lupus which had preyed upon the unhappy woman's nose and mouth. Ulceration had spread and was hourly spreading and devouring the membrane in its progress. The cartilage of the nose was almost eaten away, the mouth was drawn all on one side by the swollen condition of the upper lip, the whole was a frightful distorted mass of matter and oozing blood." So far Zola's description of "La Grivotte" tallies exactly with the medical record of Marie Lemarchand, but his account is incomplete. The apices of both lungs were affected and she had sores on her leg. Dr. d'Hombres saw her immediately before and immediately after she entered the bath. "Both her cheeks, the lower part of her nose, and her upper lip were covered with a tuberculous ulcer and secreted matter abundantly. On her return from the baths I at once followed her to the hospital. I recognised her quite well although her face was entirely changed. Instead of the horrible sore I had lately seen, the surface was red, it is true, but dry and covered with a new skin. The other sores had also dried up in the piscina." The doctors who had examined her could find nothing the matter with the lungs, and testified to the presence of the new skin on her face. Zola was there. He had said, "I only want to see a cut finger dipped in water, and come out healed." "Behold the case of your dreams, M. Zola," said the President, presenting the girl whose hideous disease had made such an impression on the novelist before the cure. "Ah no!" said Zola, "I do not want to look at her. She is still too ugly", alluding to the red colour of her skin.

Before he left Lourdes he summed up the credo of the true scientian in a memorable confession of faith. To the President of the Medical Bureau he said: "Were I to see all the sick at Lourdes cured, I would not believe in a miracle."

(VII)

Familiar though I am with the literature of materialism, I have yet to discover a serious attempt to meet the case against materialism.

That case may be summarised as follows: Science requires theism for its justification, for materialism deprives scientific research of its rational basis. If materialism be true "our conclusions are the inevitable product of forces which are quite alien to reason." Now the inspiration of scientific research is the belief that the disinterested search for truth is one of the noblest activities of the human mind, but truth on the materialistic hypothesis is unascertainable, for thought is nothing but an epiphenomenon. "Thought and feeling," as Professor Huxley suggested, "have nothing to do with determining action; they are merely by-products of cerebration, the indices of changes which are going on in the brain."

If this be true, objective knowledge including scientific knowledge is unobtainable, for the processes of thought in the mind of the scientist bear "the same ineffectual relation to the activity of a brain as a steam whistle bears to the activity of a locomotive." Therefore if materialism be true scientific research is a farce. Science, in fact, as Lord Balfour insisted, requires theism for its completion.

Now the universe may be a play without author, plot or coherence. The pattern which science tries to discover in natural phenomena may not exist. The mental processes of the scientist may be nothing more than the by-product of material and irrational forces, and scientific research may be a futile farce. But no scientist worthy of the name has ever acted on this assumption. Men like Huxley were inspired by their implicit fideism rather than by their explicit materialism. Thomas Huxley might write as if he were a materialist. He may have yielded academic assent to the possibility that his own mental processes were nothing more than "by-products of cerebration," but the faith which sustained him, the faith which he never explicitly avowed was a faith in the reality of spiritual values. The scientians were saved by their unavowed and implicit faith in spiritual values. Had they been rationalists they would either have abandoned scientism or committed suicide.

(VIII)

Does the universe make sense, or is unreason the lord of all?
Is our planet the stage for a drama with a plot, or the setting
for the meaningless dance of unrelated atoms? Is life a spiritual
adventure or a brief and brutish flicker of ephemeral consciousness? *These* are the ultimate problems, compared to which the
secular problems with which scientists are concerned are
relatively unimportant.

How then can we explain the fact that most scientists have
declined to admit that science is concerned with these problems,
in spite of the fact that the scientist can and should help us to
determine whether a particular phenomenon is or is not explicable within the framework of natural law? What defence can
scientists offer for the fact that the minority of courageous
scientists who acted on Alexis Carrel's principle, "Science has
to explore the entire realm of reality," risked their professional
careers as the result of their fidelity to scientific ideals?

Leverriere was honoured by the entire scientific world
because he discovered the planet Neptune, but derision was the
penalty to which scientists were exposed who investigated the
evidence for the reality of a spiritual realm. No human being is
richer or healthier because Leverriere discovered Neptune. The
material and spiritual welfare of humanity is unaffected by this
discovery. There are no worshippers of Neptune, no sect of
Neptunians who disarm criticism by remarking "If you knew
what Neptune means to me I think you would understand." No
man has ever visited and perhaps no man will ever visit Neptune.

There are, however, people who believe not only that a realm
exists to which man passes at death but also that there is irre-
futable scientific evidence for the existence of this realm. The
proof that Neptune exists has not had the slightest influence on
human history, but if this other realm could be proved to exist,
the effect would be momentous. It is indeed difficult to estimate
the consequences which would follow from the scientific demonstration of immortality. To take one example out of many: No
intelligent person denies that among the many factors which
have contributed to the sharp decline in moral standards during
recent years the decline of religious belief is not the least important. Renan was a sceptic but he was an intelligent sceptic. "It
seems possible," he wrote, "that the collapse of supernatural

belief will be followed by the collapse of moral convictions, and that the moment when humanity sees the reality of things will mark a real moral decline."

"The truth is that civilisations collapse," as Mr. Monk Gibbon rightly observes, "without that essential reverence for absolute values which religion gives. Rome had discovered this in the days of her decadence. Men live on the accumulated faith of the past as well as its accumulated self-discipline. Overthrow these and nothing seems missing at first, a few sexual taboos, a little of the prejudice of a Cato, a few rhapsodical impulses, comprehensible we are told only in the literature of folk-lore—these have gone by the board. But something has gone as well, the mortar which held society together, the integrity of the individual soul; then the rats come out of their holes and begin burrowing under the foundations and there is nothing to withstand them."

Professor William McDougall believes that the dogmas of the different religions are, in the main, the product of emotion and irrationalism, but he insists that "the strength of the social sanctions derived from the belief in the supernatural powers was a main condition of the strength and stability of society and that no society had been able to survive in any severe and prolonged conflict of societies without some effective system of such sanctions. . . . In the main those societies which had been most stable and capable of enduring had been least tolerant of the spirit of enquiry; on the other hand the flourishing of scepticism had been too often the forerunner of social decay as in ancient Rome. . . ."

(IX)

Now it would be difficult for the most obscurantist of scientians to deny that a *prima facie* case has been established for the reality of supranatural phenomena, and nobody, not even a scientian, could deny that the scientific proof of a spiritual realm would be infinitely more important than any discovery in the history of science. Furthermore, it is becoming increasingly difficult to deny that the cumulative effect of the evidence for supernatural phenomena such as the miracles at Lourdes, and psychical phenomena such as telepathy provide a decisive refutation of materialism. Now materialism, as we have seen, not only deprives man of all dignity and his thought of all claim to consideration, but also deprives science of its *raison d'être*. If scientists, therefore, were governed by rational considerations they would have regarded all forms of research which provided evidence against materialism as supremely important, and would have honoured those who devoted their lives to this type of research.

It is perhaps fortunate that organised science in the twentieth century has fewer means at its disposal for harassing the heretic than the organised theologians of the sixteenth century. The Inquisition was a detestable institution, but Inquisitors were at least defending a spiritual philosophy which gives dignity to human life and which, little as they realised the fact, was to provide science with a *raison d'être*. The scientians who disapproved of all investigations which tended to establish the spiritual nature of man and *therefore* the rationality of their own scientific investigations, had no such excuse. The failure of modern scientists to put first things first and to give due honour to men who were investigating the evidence for a spiritual interpretation of life remains one of the most perplexing chapters in the history of science, a glaring example of *trahison des clercs*, that treason of the intellectuals which is responsible for most of the miseries of the contemporary world.

CHAPTER XVI

THE INCONSISTENCIES OF SCIENTISM

(1)

THE repudiation of the supernatural, which is the essence of scientism, leads to materialism and the most logical form of materialism is behaviourism. It was in his Rede lecture of 1885 that Professor Huxley sowed the seeds of the last and most lunatic variant of materialism.

"Professor Huxley," said Mr. Romanes, "in his Rede Lecture of 1885, argues by way of perfectly logical deduction from this statement, that thought and feeling have nothing to do with determining action; they are merely the by-products of cerebration, or, as he expresses it, the indices of changes which are going on in the brain. Under this view we are all what he terms conscious automata, or machines which happen, as it were by chance, to be conscious of some of their own movements. But the consciousness is altogether adventitious, and bears the same ineffectual relation to the activity of the brain as a steam-whistle bears to the activity of a locomotive, or the striking of a clock to the time-keeping adjustments of the clockwork. . . . Now this theory of conscious automatism is not merely a legitimate outcome of the theory that nervous changes are the causes of mental changes, but it is logically the only possible outcome. Nor do I see any way in which this theory can be fought on grounds of physiology."

This view also met with the approval of Professor Clifford and Mr. Spalding who, in the course of an article which he contributed to *Nature* on August 2nd, 1877, wrote as follows:

"We assert not only that no evidence can be given that feeling ever does guide or prompt action, but that the process of its doing so is inconceivable."

Samuel Butler quotes other passages from contemporary scientists in favour of the theory that mental processes have no effect on physical processes, from which, as he remarks, it is obvious that they must have supposed "that physical processes would go on just as well if there were no accompaniment of feeling and consciousness at all."

Men and animals are permitted, according to this theory, to think and to feel and even to reflect, but everything would go on exactly the same even if the consciousness which is a mere by-product of the physical movement in their brains did not exist. Juliet would set up precisely the same physical movements in the brain of Romeo even if Romeo and Juliet were both automata. The clues left by an unconscious murderer would produce just the same physical effect on the brain of an unconscious detective, and the unconscious witness in the witness-box would set up exactly the same physical reaction as the brains of an unconscious jury and of an unconscious judge. And finally an unconscious hangman would then proceed to hang an unconscious murderer.

Most materialists would resent being described as behaviourists but would find it impossible to prove that behaviourism was not a logical deduction from the materialistic premise. The behaviourist in fact is an honest but tactless member of the materialist family, who insists on exhibiting the family skeleton under the impression that it is a handsome family portrait. The saner materialists realise that behaviourism belongs to the lunatic fringe of human thinking and that materialism itself will inevitably be repudiated by all save the insane unless it can be dissociated from behaviourism. But though the materialist would like to believe that behaviourism is nothing more than a parody of a tenable philosophy, he is beginning to suspect that behaviourism does no more than reveal, in all their repellant absurdity, doctrines which are an integral element of materialistic philosophy.

If however we are prepared to maintain that thought and will are nothing more than epiphenomena with no influence on events, we have no rational basis for intellectual, moral or aesthetic judgments. Of course criminals could still be judged and condemned. To a murderer who pleaded that the murder which he had committed was the result of forces over which he had no control, a behaviourist judge could reply: "I have no control over the forces which compel me to condemn you to death. You are not responsible for the murder which you committed and I am not responsible for the sentence of death which

I now propose to pass. Console yourself with the reflection that the execution which will take place in four weeks' time will be the result, to quote Huxley, of 'a mutual inter-reaction according to definite laws of the forces possessed by the molecules of the primitive nebulosity of which the universe consisted'."

Society will always find means for dealing with crimes against life and against property, and a prudent fear of punishment will always be a powerful social factor even in a materialistic state. But conscience, a far subtler social factor, would disappear in a social state where the citizens were saturated with the doctrines of materialism.

Conscience and moral judgment are out of place in a world of machines. If a dishonest and plausible salesman palms off on you a second-hand car which breaks down on its first hill, you will be disappointed with the car and indignant with the salesman. You will reserve your moral judgment for the salesman. If, however, you are a consistent determinist you will be forced to admit that the salesman was no more responsible for his moral defects than the car for its mechanical defects. You will have no right to discriminate between moral and material defects.

Whatever may be the case with the moral indignation provoked by the failings of other people, there is, at least, something to be said for the social value of the moral indignation provoked by one's own misdoings. "It may be," as Lord Balfour remarked, "a small matter that determinism should render it thoroughly irrational to feel righteous indignation at the misconduct of other people. It cannot be wholly without importance that it should render it equally irrational to feel righteous indignation at our own. Self-condemnation, repentance, remorse, and the whole train of cognate emotions, are really so useful for the promotion of virtue that it is a pity to find them at a stroke thus deprived of all reasonable foundation, and reduced, if they are to survive at all, to the position of amiable but unintelligent weaknesses."

The fact that moral indignation is "deprived of all reasonable foundation" by the philosophy of materialism does not rob materialists of the pleasures of moral indignation. Oscar Wilde once suggested as a suitable theme for an essay "Moral Indignation, its Cause and Cure." Clearly materialism was not the cure for which Wilde was seeking. Mr. Cohen, the Editor of the

Freethinker is a materialist and no doubt the moral indignation which is the dominant note in his editorials is the result of "a mutual inter-reaction according to definite laws of the forces possessed by the molecules of the primitive nebulosity of which the universe consisted." Mr. Cohen, if he were consistent, would not differentiate between a Christian erupting superstition and a volcano erupting lava, but Mr. Cohen is not consistent. As a rigid determinist he rejects the whole concept of freedom. Our actions and our thoughts are pre-determined by inexorable law. There is, he believes, no such thing as *free* will and no such thing as *free* thought, and yet the paper in which this gospel is proclaimed is called *The Freethinker*.

(II)

No less inconsistent is the scientian attitude to truth.

The consistent materialist (or naturalist, using the word in its philosophical sense) must admit that truth is unobtainable.

"Some naturalists," writes Mr. C. F. Lewis, "whom I have met attempt to escape by saying that there is no ground for believing our thoughts to be valid and that this does not worry them in the least. 'We find that they work,' it is said, 'and we admit that we cannot argue from this that they give us a true account of any external reality. But we don't mind. We are not interested in truth. Our habits of thought seem to enable humanity to keep alive and that is all we care about.' One is tempted to reply that every free man wants truth as well as life, that a mere life-addict is no more respectable than a cocaine-addict. . . . I feel also that the surrender of the claim to truth has all the air of an expedient adopted at the last moment. If the naturalists do not claim to know any truths, ought they not to have warned us rather earlier of the fact? For really from the books they have written in which the behaviour of the remotest nebula, the shyest photon and the most prehistoric man are described, one would have got the idea that they were claiming to give a true account of real things. The fact surely is that they are nearly always claiming to do so. The claim is surrendered only when the question discussed in this chapter is pressed; and when the crisis is over the claim is tacitly resumed."

And not only the claim to no truth, but also the claim that the distinguishing mark of the scientist is the disinterested passion for truth. Could any inconsistency be greater than the contrast between "We are not interested in truth but only in helping to keep humanity alive" and the religiosity of scientism proclaiming through a thousand tracts addressed to the un-educated that scientists are not as other men, such as this publican of a Christian who is only interested in truth in so far as truth can be prostituted in the service of dogma.

(III)

Mr. Bertrand Russell is one of the few sceptics who face the logical consequences of naturalism.

"That man is the product of causes which had no prevision of the end they were achieving; that his origin, his growth, his hopes and fears, his loves and his beliefs, are but the outcome of accidental collocations of atoms; that no fire, no heroism, no intensity of thought and feeling, can preserve an individual beyond the grave; that all the labours of the ages, all the devotion, all the inspiration, all the noonday brightness of human genius, are destined to extinction in the vast death of the solar system, and that the whole temple of man's achieve-ment must inevitably be buried beneath the debris of a universe in ruins—all these things, if not quite beyond dispute, are yet so nearly certain, that no philosophy which rejects them can hope to stand. Only within the scaffolding of these truths, only on the firm foundation of unyielding despair, can the soul's habitation henceforth be safely built."

It is not surprising that most scientians prefer to evade the grim conclusions of their creed. Many of them profess a lordly indifference to the question of survival. Preoccupied as they are with questions of universal interest, they are serenely remote from the petty problem of individual personality. In a series of broadcast addresses, published under the title *Points of View*, Mr. Wells provided a listening world with a new criterion of intelligence.

"Our individuality," he wrote, "is so to speak an inborn obsession from which we should escape as we become more *intelligent* . . . personality, individuality, is a biological device which has served its end in evolution and will decline. A con-sciousness of something greater than ourselves, the immortal soul of the race, is taking control of the direction of our lives."

What did Mr. Wells mean by "the immortal soul of the race"? Did he mean anything or was he merely evading the grim implications of naturalism? Man was created to worship God. When the instinct for worship is denied its natural outlet, it finds expression in the personification of abstractions such as "truth" or "life". In *The Outline of History* Mr. Wells wrote:

"The life to which I belong uses me and will pass on beyond me and I am content."

And here by way of contrast is Aristotle on the same theme: "For death it is a dreadful thing. It is the end." The old Greek, one feels, faces the inexorable fact of death like a man, whereas the modern scientian escaped from reality into the cloudland of misleading metaphor. And in point of fact Mr. Wells was far from "content" when the "life" which had used him was on the point of passing on beyond him. *Mind at the end of its Tether* was his final testament to the world, and how did the world look to this great utopian when he knew himself to be at the end of *his* tether. "A frightful queerness," he wrote, "has come into life. . . . There is no way out of or round or through the impasse. It is the end . . . the attempt to trace a pattern of any sort is absolutely futile. . . . The present writer has no compelling argument to convince the reader that he should not be cruel or mean or cowardly."

Professor J. B. S. Haldane in his contribution to *Points of View* remarks: "I shall last out my time and then finish. This prospect does not worry me, because many of my works will not die when I do." I do not question Haldane's sincerity when he claims to be unworried by the prospect of death. A fellow officer of his in the first world war recalled with a mixture of admiration and irritation Haldane's contempt for danger. He has proved his courage not only in war but also in peace, for he subjected his body to experiments dangerous not only to health but also to life, notably in connection with posion gas experiments. His courage, however, is more admirable than his logic, for it is illogical to equate death and extinction, and frivolous to dismiss what is important as unimportant. It was of frivolity such as this that Pascal was thinking in a famous passage of his *Pensées*.

"Prétendent-ils nous avoir bien réjoui, de nous dire qu'ils tiennent que notre âme n'est qu'un peu de vent et de fumée, et

encore de nous le dire d'un ton de voix fier et content? Est-donc
une chose à dire gaîment?"

Again I doubt whether any man who has enjoyed, as Haldane
has enjoyed, the great adventure of life can draw much consolation from the thought that posterity may continue to profit by
his solution to the equation $\Delta n_n = k\varphi(n_n)$, even if this consolation were not inconsistent with that concern for the common
man which the *Daily Worker*, of which he is a director, continues
to profess, for it is only an élite insignificant in numbers which
can hope to bequeath anything of value to posterity.

Christians are sometimes reprimanded for their egoistic
interest in the survival of their petty personalities. But is it more
laudable to desire the perpetuation of one's petty achievements
than one's petty personality? Haldane devoted the first part of
his talk to the unimportance of death, and the second part of
his talk to the importance of increasing the expectation of life.

"I am," he writes, "a citizen of the British Empire which includes the great Dominions. Our highbrow friends complain
that the Dominions have produced little great art or literature,
and I answer that at least they have done something unique.
Before the war, the average expectation of life of a baby born in
New Zealand was sixty years, in Australia fifty-seven years, in
Denmark, the next healthiest country, fifty-six years. England
also ran. I am proud to belong to a Commonwealth which has
won the first and second places in the great race against death."

I cannot follow this reasoning. He tells us that it is a matter
of great importance that Mr. Jones shall exist for sixty years
rather than fifty years, but that it is a matter of no importance
if he ceases to exist at sixty years instead of continuing to exist
for all eternity. If we increase our expectation of life by ten per
cent we need not worry about our contribution to literature and
art, but it is a matter of indifference whether we succeed in
proving that our expectation of life is eternal.

(IV)

The bad golfer is not accused of inconsistency because he fails
to go round the course in Bogey, and the bad Christian should
not be accused of inconsistency merely because he does not live
like a saint. Few Christians live up to, and few materialists live
down to their creed, but the materialist can fairly be charged

with inconsistency, for the moral principles by which the good materialist regulates his life have no place in a creed which provides us with no criterion for distinguishing between a St. Francis and a Himmler. The behaviour of the noblest saint and of the vilest sinner are alike the result of "a mutual inter-reaction according to definite laws of the forces possessed by the molecules of the primitive nebulosity of which the universe consisted."

The only consistent materialist is the man who *behaves* as if moral restraints were irrational. Fortunately most materialists are not consistent. materialists preach the gospel of determinism, and insist that man is as much the prey of circumstance as the beasts, and as incapable as they are of free choice between good and evil. And after doing all in their power to blunt the distinction between man and beast, they are horrified when men begin to behave like beasts.

"Many a scientist," writes Professor Whitehead, "has patiently designed experiments for the purpose of substantiating his belief that animal operations are motivated by no *purposes*. He has spent his spare time in writing articles to prove that human beings are as other animals so that 'purpose' is a category irrelevant for the explanation of their bodily activities, his own activity included. Scientists animated by the purpose of proving that they are purposeless constitute an interesting subject for study."

However conscientiously the materialist (or scientian) may try to be consistent, he finds it impossible to avoid using phrases which are meaningless in his philosophy, phrases and words such as "purpose", "ought", "cruel", "tyranny", "liberty". He will demand "academic freedom" on one platform, and deny the possibility of freedom on the next. He may dismiss Christian morality as a behaviouristic by-product of material forces, but he forgets his philosophy where he himself, or the class or race to which he belongs, is the victim of injustice. He may deny the objective existence of moral values, but he has no doubt that it was wicked of the church to persecute Galileo and infamous of Hitler to expel Einstein.

At the end of the war I read a paper on evolution to an Oxford club. A refugee who was present twitted me with my old-fashioned approach to the problem. The modern scientist, he remarked, had abandoned the Baconian induction from facts. He was an artist, accepting a theory such as evolution for personal reasons, using such facts as fitted his predilections and discarding those which did not. The speaker was a member of that gifted race which has produced the greatest of religious mystics and the most thorough of nihilists, and I have never heard a more blatant defence of nihilistic irrationalism than he proceeded to develop. "There is no past and no future and no present and no time. Things just are. It's silly to try to prove relations between them. All facts are isolated and meaningless." I asked him if he maintained that there were no values, such as truth or beauty or goodness in the universe. "Of course there aren't" he replied. "And no basis for moral judgments?" "Certainly not." "Then you can't condemn Hitler for driving you out of Germany?" He looked as if he would have liked notice of that question.

There is always some moral judgment which the moral nihilist refuses to forego. The crimes of which other people are the victims may be transformed in his vocabulary into behaviouristic reactions to which it would be absurd to apply such outworn categories as "sinful" or "wicked" but the crime of which he himself is the victim can only fitly be described in old-fashioned Biblical terms. There is always some dogma to which the sceptic clings, some standard of absolute behaviour uninfected by his relativity. A reviewer who signs himself "T. L. S." summed up the essential inconsistency of modern scepticisms in his criticisms of Bertrand Russell's Philosophy and Politics. "T. L. S." quotes Bertrand Russell's remark, "The genuine Liberal does not say 'This is true'; he says 'I am inclined to think that in present circumstances this opinion is probably the best,' " and adds "Forgetting himself slightly in his eloquent peroration Russell demands that 'Liberal beliefs should be wholehearted and profound, not apologetic towards dogmatism of the Right or the Left, but persuaded of the value of liberty, scientific freedom, and mutual forbearance' . . . We can scarcely be satisfied with an appeal to be wholehearted in being half-hearted."

The truth is that the scientian can only escape inconsistency, if he repudiates all morality and surrenders the right to condemn any action however vile. But scientians are never consistent. "A scientific realism," writes Professor Whitehead, "based on mechanism, is conjoined with an unwavering belief in the world of men and of the higher animals as being composed of self-determining organisms. This radical inconsistency at the basis of modern thought accounts for much that is half-hearted and wavering in our civilisation. It would be going too far to say that it distracts thought. It enfeebles it, by reason of the inconsistency lurking in the background. After all the men of the Middle Ages were in pursuit of an excellency of which we have forgotten the existence. They set before themselves the ideal of the attainment of a harmony of the understanding. We are content with superficial orderings from diverse starting points."

CHAPTER XVII

THE SUICIDE OF THOUGHT

(I)

THE Logosoclasm which attacks reason is akin to the iconoclasm which attacked religious art, for reason and beauty are aspects of the divine. Surrealism, the claim to be above reality, is a by-product of Logosoclasm. In the beginning was the Logos and the Logos was with God and the modern attack upon the Logos is perhaps the beginning of the end, the opening of the last phase of a civilisation which has revolted against reason.

The Logosoclast is the ultimate sceptic, the man who despairs of truth, believing that objective truth is unobtainable. The logosoclast insists that the "reasons" with which men defend their particular brand of error are mere "rationalisations" of beliefs which are imposed upon them by their environment or their hereditary.

There is nothing anti-rational in the belief that there are truths which are perceived through other channels than the processes of reason. Kant, for instance, recognised the validity of reason in its own sphere, and maintained the supremacy of pure reason over sense and experience, but he also insisted that the existence of God and the immortality of the soul are "postulates of the moral law," and that they are objects of faith and not of direct intuition. It is arguable that Kant believed that if there is a "knowledge" of God as distinct from faith (in the sense in which he uses the word "faith"), then this knowledge must be by means of intellectual intuition, since the principles of the *Critique of Pure Reason* do not admit the possibility of proving God's existence metaphysically, but there is nothing anti-rational in the contention that there are truths which the unaided human reason could never discover.

Again, an uncompromising rationalist might agree with Carrel that "intelligence is almost useless to those who possess nothing else. The pure intellectual is an incomplete human being". Similarly Spengler cannot be convicted of Logosoclasm

merely because he goes far beyond Alexis Carrel in his contempt
for doctrinaires and pure intellectuals. Spengler ranks "all that
one has and does not learn" far above the knowledge which is
consciously acquired from books, and, as instances of this higher
intuition he cites social and diplomatic tact, the collector's eye
for works of art, and the subtle insight of the judge of men. Instinctive knowledge has "cosmic and dreamlike sureness" which
we see in the circlings of a flock of birds or in the movements of
a thoroughbred horse. An individual or an institution or an age
is "in form" when it possesses this cosmic sureness. When an
athlete is "in form" the riskiest shots come off. When an army
is "in form" as was the German army that overran France in
1940 or the Eighth Army in North Africa, nothing can arrest
its forward march. Field Marshal Montgomery's predictions
which alarmed so many people by their note of cocksure confidence were inspired by the conviction that the Eighth army
was "in form". An art period is "in form" when its tradition is
second nature. Now, according to Spengler, the typical intellectual is never "in form", and therefore the place for men of
theory is not at the head of, but in the train of great events.
"Real history passes judgment on the theorist not by refuting
him but by ignoring him." The theorists may *write* history but
it is the destiny men, guided by supra-rational intuition, who
make history.

Keyserling, a Baltic German by birth, carries the deification
of intuition a stage further than did Spengler. In his *America
Set Free* he writes: "During my travels about the country, I
guarded myself with almost old-maidish precautions against
information. I looked at none of the obvious sights if I could
help it. I asked few questions. I succeeded in meeting none of
those men who are called great because they happen to be, as
they say in America, on the map. I went out little; I read hardly
any papers. . . . I used exclusively the faculty of intuition. . . .
I stayed in the United States too long—fully four months. Intuition works instantaneously and a protracted experience does
not improve its processes."

From which it would seem that Keyserling's interpretation of America would have been even more profound had
he been detained in Ellis Island, and sent home by the next
boat.

Keyserling, it is clear, had travelled a long way along the road which was to lead from Luther's "Reason, the Devil's greatest whore" to Hitler's scream "I think with my blood".

"Thou shalt love the Lord thy God with all thy heart and with all thy soul and with all thy mind and with all thy strength."

Four ways of love, all necessary if religion is to conform to the pattern which Christ desired. A religion which is only of the mind is a dessicated and sterile faith, which bears much the same relation to a living faith as a Continental Railway Guide to the ecstasy of a journey to the Alps or to Italy. Equally if God is not loved "with all thy mind" and if reason be dethroned, the first milestone is passed on the road which leads from the religion of the mind to the religion of the blood. "My great religion", wrote D. H. Lawrence, "is a belief in the blood, the flesh, as being wiser than the intellect. We can go wrong with our minds, but what our blood feels and believes and says is always true. The intellect is only a bit and a bridle. What do I care about knowledge? . . . the real way of living is to answer to one's wants. Not 'I want to light up my intelligence with as many things as possible' but 'For the living of my full flame I want that liberty, I want that woman. . . . I want to insult that man.'"

"Here is the last ditch of materialism", writes Hugh Kingsmill, "in which in every age a few desperate persons sick of society and the world, but still tied to the will, fight to promulgate the idea that happiness depends on the absence of ideas."

(II)

Nobody would suspect Professor Harold Laski of a Catholic bias, and his tribute to the influence of Catholicism on economics is not only impressive but, for reasons which will shortly become apparent, relevant to the theme of this chapter.

"The Middle Ages," he writes, "are permeated by the idea of a supreme end beyond this life to which all earthly conduct must conform. The pursuit of wealth for its own sake is deemed incompatible with that idea. Wealth was regarded as a fund of social significance and not of individual possession. The wealthy man did not enjoy it for its own sake; he was a steward on behalf of the community. He was therefore limited both in what he might acquire and in the means whereby he might acquire it.

The whole social morality of the Middle Ages is built upon this doctrine. It is enforced both by the rules of the church and by the civil law. . . . By the end of the fifteenth century the capitalist spirit began to attain a predominant hold over men's minds. What does this imply? That the pursuit of wealth for its own sake became the chief motive of human activity . . . the Liberal doctrine is the philosophic justification of the new practices."

In the age of reason men tried to adapt economics to what they believed to be revealed truth. In the beginning was the Logos, and of that Logos a just social system will be the reflection. Because selfishness is inherent in human nature, they failed to practice what they preached, but they did not preach what they practised. Now just as the revolt against reason and the objective standards which reason imposes manifested itself in Luther's revolt against objective morality, so also it manifested itself in the revolt against objective economics. "The Liberal doctrine" as Professor Laski rightly observes, "is the philosophic justification of the new *practices*" (italics mine). Mediaeval Catholics continued to preach what they had the greatest difficulty in practising. The Liberals started from current practice, and adapted their preaching to those practices. Mediaeval economics were influenced, as Laski points out, by Catholic doctrine, but the Marxist, of course, cannot admit this. He assumes that mediaeval Catholicism (and mediaeval sociology) were the by-products of mediaeval economics. Now if philosophy be the by-product of economics, it is clear that *no* philosophy can give us a true picture of objective reality. Marxism, which was a by-product of the industrial revolution, has therefore no more claim to permanent validity than the *Summa Theologica* which the Marxist no doubt regards as a product of mediaeval economics. If, then, the Marxist is correct no philosophy can be true. If Marx was right, Marx must be wrong.

(III)

The Christian is prepared to defend his faith in the deity of Christ by methods which would be approved in a court of law. He submits the documents in the case, the four Gospels, to the most exacting scrutiny and endeavours to show that every alternative explanation for the empty tomb is inconsistent with the evidence. In his refutation of rival philosophies he begins by a careful study of the evidence and arguments advanced by those whom he is seeking to refute. A good controversialist, as Chesterton rightly remarked, must be a good listener.

Now the scientians and the Logosoclasts are not good listeners. It is only the exceptional secularist who has even an elementary knowledge of Christian apologetics. If I were spending a few weeks in India or China or Japan I should be ashamed to know as little, at the end of my stay, about the religions of those countries as the average secularist knows about what is still nominally the religion of England. The scientians lacked scientific curiosity so far as Christianity was concerned, but it was left to the prophets of the new psychology to repudiate the last pretence of scientific method, either in the rejection of rival philosophies or in the establishment of their own philosophy. St. Peter urged Christians "to be ready always to give an answer to every man that asketh you a reason of the hope that is in you". The Freudians are unprepared to give a reason either for the Freudian hope, or for the anti-Christian hate that is in them. Freud, the greatest of modern Logosoclasts, offers us nothing which a lawyer or historian would recognise as evidence in support of his own explanation of the origin of religion.

Religion, according to Freud, is derived from the attempt of the son to put himself in his father's place—the Oedipus complex. Jung, who is in general far wiser than Freud in his approach to religion, develops the same theme. "The religious instinct feeds upon the incestuous libido of the infantile period."

The Freudian theory is based on a series of assumptions, for which there is no evidence. He begins by building from the bricks of fancy an imaginary picture of primitive men. Primitive men, Freud *assumes*, lived in hordes, which Freud *assumes* consisted of one male (the "old man"), and of a number of females and children. As the children grew up the "old man" begins to fear for his position, and to suspect that his sons might make advances to the females of his tribe. He therefore decides to expel these dangerous rivals from the herd.

"This primal state of society", Freud naively admits, "has nowhere been observed", in which it differs from the "primal state of Christianity" which has been recorded by observers, in documents whose accuracy has emerged triumphant from hostile examination.

The young males react against the "old man's" designs by murdering him. They then eat him in order to absorb those of his qualities which they most admire, courage, strength and so forth. (No evidence is offered for this Freudian flight of fancy.) The half-brothers who have killed the "old man" are consumed with remorse once the old man is dead—and eaten. To quiet their consciences they found an institution, partly social, partly religious, in which the "old man" is personified by a totem animal which no individual member of the group is allowed to kill but which is solemnly sacrificed by the group as a whole, who thus share the common guilt. Realising that their solidarity is threatened by sexual jealousies, they forbid sexual intercourse with a woman of the horde. A man who wants a wife must seek one in another horde. Hence the horror of incest.

Now there are tribes which have a totem animal which is sacrificed by the tribe as a whole, and in these tribes no man may marry a member of his own totem group. But there is not a single fact in support of the Freudian explanation of the origin of totemism, and not the slightest justification for the fantasy which associates the origin of religion with the origin of totemism. This whole structure of bogus anthropology rests on nothing more substantial than Freudian fideism.

As an antidote to the Freudian attempt to interpret religion in terms of sex, I commend William James's diagnosis of the Freudian fallacy.

"It is true," writes James, "that in the vast collection of religious phenomena some are undisguisedly amatory—e.g. sex deities and obscene rites in polytheism, and ecstatic feelings of union with the Saviour in a few Christian mystics. But then why not equally call religion an aberration of the digestive functions and prove one's point by the worship of Bacchus and Ceres, or by the ecstatic feelings of some other saint about the Eucharist? Religious language clothes itself in such poor symbols as our life affords, and the whole organism gives overtones of comment whenever the mind is strongly stirred to expression. Language drawn from eating and drinking is probably as common in religious literature as is language drawn from the sexual life. We 'hunger and thirst after righteousness'; we 'find the Lord a sweet savour'; we 'taste and see that he is good'."

William James then discusses the argument that religious melancholy and conversion are essentially phenomena of adolescence and therefore synchronous with the development of sexual life. "Even were the asserted synchrony unrestrictedly true as a fact (which it is not), it is not only the sexual life but the entire mental life which awakens during adolescence. One might then as well set up the thesis that the interest in mechanics, physics, chemistry, logic, philosophy, and sociology, which springs up during the adolescent years along with that in poetry and religion, is also a perversion of the sexual instinct . . . the religious life depends just as much upon the spleen, the pancreas and the kidneys as on the sexual apparatus and the whole theory has lost its point in evaporating into a vague general assertion of the dependance, *somehow* of the mind upon the body."

(IV)

The basic assumption of the new psychology is the belief that the function of reason is to invent arguments in favour of beliefs which are, in point of fact, imposed upon us by irrational forces, our instincts, or sexual complexes, lust for power, etc.

"Rationalisation" is defined by psychologists as the practice of producing reasons for a belief or an action which bears no relation to the motives and reasons really responsible for the beliefs or actions in question. A bad workman finds fault with his tools, thereby "rationalising" the real reason for bad work, his incompetence or laziness.

"The rationalisation of religious beliefs," writes Mr. A. G. Tansley, "that are to all appearances contradicted by the experience of life constitutes a regular system which is called Christian apologetics."

It would be far truer to say that the rationalisation of *irreligious* beliefs that are contradicted by the experience of life constitutes a regular system which is called Freudian apologetics. Again, the "reasons" with which men justify their revolt against traditional morality are "rationalisations" of human weakness in face of temptation. If all reasoning be only "rationalisation", if the only interesting thing about a man's beliefs are not the beliefs themselves, still less the reasons whereby he defends them, but the unconscious complexes and instincts which are responsible for his particular brand of error, objective truth is clearly unobtainable. If this be so, *if* all that is worth learning about religion can be discovered by psycho-analysing the religious, then clearly the truth about the new psychology is only ascertainable by psycho-analysing the psycho-analysts. It is indeed not improbable that Freudianism might help to explain Freud. His hatred of Christianity is not surprising, for the Austrian universities were notoriously anti-semite, and Freud himself describes a dream provoked by his fear of being deprived of academic honours because of his Jewish race.

Again, it would be interesting to psycho-analyse all those who maintain that sexual desires, normal or perverted, are the chief factors in the choice of creed and in the formation of character. The sexual records of those who attribute everything to sex might provide useful evidence in support of the theory that beliefs are mainly determined by personal desires.

We have seen that if the Marxist interpretation of history be valid, Marxism has no claim to be considered valid. It is equally true that if Freudianism be true, Freudianism has no claim to be regarded as objectively true. Every Logosoclast is busily engaged in sawing away the branch on which he is sitting. Philosophers who spend their time demonstrating that all philosophies, including by implication their own, are invalid have a natural affinity with the scientists, "animated by the purpose of proving that they are purposeless."

One of the results of psycho-analysis is, as Dr. Joad has pointed out, a refusal to discuss any view on its merits. "If X expresses an opinion Y, the question discussed is not whether Y is true or at least reasonable, but the considerations which led X to believe it to be true. Objective truth being regarded as unobtainable, what alone is thought interesting are the reasons which lead people to formulate their particular brands of error. . . . If it is impossible to reach objective truth on *any* question, objective truth will also be unobtainable in regard to the question why X holds opinion Y. For the views of Z on the subject will not, in fact, tell us anything about the hidden motives of X. They will merely reflect the hidden motives of Z in adopting his particular view of X's motives."

Señor Salvador de Madariaga in the preface to his book on Spain attributes to the flight from objectivity to popular misconception of the doctrine of Relativity. He writes:—

"The last twenty years or so have seen such a deterioration of the standards of objectivity and the last five years such an orgy of passionately held half-truths that it sounds almost old-fashioned to claim to base one's conclusions on an implicit belief in an objective reality independent of our mental whims and our unruly emotions. When Einstein, perhaps unwisely, described as the theory of Relativity his mighty step forward on the road towards that immutable reality around us, every hasty aesthetic thinker too lazy to hammer on to the stubborn block of the unknown, every political zealot too shaky as to the mental basis of his particular 'ism', hailed relativity as salvation; so that argue as honestly as one may, and as carefully as one's mental integrity dictates, there will always be a polite shelving of one's arguments with a seemingly open-minded, 'Mr. So-and-so speaks from the point of view of the middle-class Liberal' or some such meaningless device for refusing to think, or more generally for refusing to give up what one has held as thought."

Einstein has helped to undermine our faith in the objectivity of pure mathematics. Applied mathematics may well be only relatively true, but pure mathematics is the science of timeless and unchanging truths.

Only mathematicians can understand the complications of Einstein's theories, and it is not surprising that the man in the street should be bemused by the word "relativity", and doubt the existence of any absolute truths such as the truths of pure mathematics. It is indeed unfortunate that people who should know better often write as if Euclidean geometry had been invalidated by Einstein's discoveries, whereas the fact is that the propositions of Euclid remain absolutely true for the only form of space with which Euclid was concerned. The point may be illustrated by an analogy. Many years have passed since an anonymous author wrote an entertaining book on the subject of "Flatland". The inhabitants of Flatland were only conscious of two dimensions, and could not conceive the existence of three-dimensional space. Let us asume that the universe inhabited by the Flatlanders was only flat in appearance, and was in reality the surface of a vast sphere. If the imagination of the Flatlanders

N

was limited to two dimensions they might remain completely
unconscious of the fact that their space was curved, and that
what they assumed to be a plane surface was in fact a curved
surface. If we credit them with mathematical ability they would
soon discover that the sum of the three angles of a triangle in
their space deviated slightly from two right-angles, and that
Euclidean two-dimensional geometry was not wholly valid in
their universe. From this they might deduce the fact that their
universe was in fact three-dimensional. Similarly, there are
many facts which indicate that our own space is fourth-dimen-
sional space to which Euclidean three-dimensional geometry
may not apply without modification. But to write as if Euclid
had been superseded or invalidated is nonsense, for his propositions are still true for the only kind of space with which he was
concerned. It is therefore rubbish to write, as Spengler writes,
that "there is no mathematic, only mathematics." Every new
mathematical discovery adds something which is eternally true
to our stock of knowledge.

It is forty years since Mr. Chesterton foretold the ultimate
scepticism in which even mathematical truths would be doubted.
"Thomas Huxley", he wrote, "displayed a humility so simple
that he was content to learn from Nature, but the new sceptic
is so humble that he doubts if he can ever learn. . . . The new
humility which makes a man doubtful about his aims, will make
him stop working altogether. . . . We are on the road to produce a race of men too mentally modest to believe in the
multiplication table."

The most improbable of Chesterton's predictions are coming
true. Thus Professor Haldane, in his controversy with me, remarks that a disbelief in the multiplication table "would be a
salutary phase", and though he thought it was true that
$2 \times 3 = 6$ he was "willing to consider the possibility of exceptions to it".

All this parade of humility and reluctance to dogmatise
vanishes when we cross the frontiers of fideistic faith. The
Scientian is prepared to consider the possibility that twice two
does not equal six, but is not prepared to entertain the hypothesis
that the different families in nature were separately created.
He is dogmatic about things which are more than doubtful
but ostentatiously diffident about things which are certain.

(v)

The flight from objectivity is mainly due to the great Logosoclasts, to men like Marx and Freud, and to Einstein whose influence was logosoclastic whatever may have been his private convictions. These men were giants but even pygmies have a certain importance as factors in the disintegration of thought. The mere fact that Dr. Watson, for instance, could have exercised a considerable influence on American thought, is a symptom of intellectual decay, for in saner ages Dr. Watson would never have found a publisher, much less a professorial appointment at a great American university. Dr. Watson, a major prophet of the philosophy of behaviourism, knows no philosophy and boasted of his ignorance. "I don't think I've missed anything." The quality of his thought and the clarity of his style may be judged by two characteristic extracts.

"It is advisable for the time being to allay your natural antagonism and accept the behaviouristic platform at least until you get more deeply into it. . . . Later we shall take up the procedure by means of which we can get stimuli which do not ordinarily call out responses to call them out."

The subtlety of his metaphysical approach is evident in the following passages.

"Behaviourism holds that the subject matter of human psychology is the behaviour of the human being. Behaviourism claims that consciousness is neither a definite nor a usable concept. The behaviourist who has been trained as an experimentalist, holds, further, that belief in the existence of consciousness goes back to the ancient days of superstitition and magic. . . .

"No one has ever touched a soul, or seen one in a test tube, or had in any way come into relationship with it as he has with the other objects of his daily experience. The behaviourist cannot find consciousness in the test tube of his science. . . . Consciousness has never been seen, touched, smelled, tasted or moved."

Upon which Mr. Julius Mark commented: "The world would not get very far if the physicist, instead of assuming the existence of energy, and making use of it in his experiments, would drop all his work because his five senses do not reveal it."

"The behaviourist," Dr. Watson continues, "makes no

mystery of thinking. He holds that thinking is behaviour, is motor organisation, just like tennis playing or golf or any other form of muscular activity. But what kind of muscular activity? The muscular activity that he uses in talking. Thinking is merely talking, but talking with concealed musculature."

Professor William McDougall conceded that Dr. Watson's book "goes far to justify Dr. Watson's contention that his thinking processes are nothing more than the mechanical play of his speech organs."

Once again we find the Logosoclast sawing away the branch on which he is sitting. If thinking processes are merely the mechanical by-products of muscular activity, why should we accept Behaviourism, or treat with respect the "reasons" whereby Dr. Watson defends behaviourism?

If consciousness does not exist, why should we expect to find anything in a test tube? To "find" is to become conscious of, and Dr. Watson admits by implication the existence of consciousness when he contrasts the things which he expects to find in a test tube and the things which he does not expect to find.

The behaviourist, Dr. Watson assures us, has "dropped from his scientific vocabulary all subjective terms such as sensation, perception, image, desire, purpose, and even thinking and emotion as they were subjectively defined."

Elsewhere he asserts that behaviourism "ought to make men and women eager to rearrange their own lives". "Ought" implies a free choice, "eager" and "rearrange" imply "desire" and "purpose", words which Dr. Watson dismisses as "mediaeval conceptions". But why should we expect to discover consistency or meaning or reason in a philosophy whose prophets repudiate reason and meaning?

"The premises of the behaviourist," writes Dr. Watson, "contain no propositions about meaning."

Dr. Watson's success in deceiving "hosts of young Babbits" is easy to understand. Behaviourism is welcomed not as the solution of an intellectual problem, but as a solvent of objective codes, the moral restraints of which are regarded as irksome. The essence of the revolt against reason is, as I have insisted throughout this book, a revolt against objectivity in general, in morals no less than in thought.

The disciples of Dr. Watson, as Dr. Morse observed in his

Preface to the *Symposium on Behaviourism*, were delighted "to hear that the old gods are dead and the old beliefs with their checks and balances and controls are without validity and foundation in fact; that man is merely a two-legged goat who has been absurdly and unnaturally conditioned by the psycho-social environment projected from the far-distant and ignorant past; that the time has come for them to recondition themselves and strike off the antiquated shackles—to give man full rein to their impulses, instincts, and tendencies, or, as the college flappers say, to liberate their libido and 'can' their complexes. Though why a Robot should advise other Robots what to do is another of the mysteries behaviourism has not solved."

CHAPTER XVIII

THE CONFLICT BETWEEN SCIENCE AND ATHEISM

(1)

EVERY good scientian believes first that the Church has always been hostile to science, and secondly that the repudiation of religion would accelerate the tempo of scientific progress. The first of these misstatements is based on the *unique* error which the Church committed in her relations with scientists, the case of Galileo. The truth is that the Church has a magnificent record in the realm of scientific achievement. Here are a few names of eminent Catholic scientists which have passed into common speech: Copernicus, Pope Gregory, Galvani, Ampère, Volta, Couloumb, Mendel, Pasteur, Röntgen and Marconi.

Modern astronomy is Copernican, our calendar is Gregorian; iron is galvanised; electricity is measured by amps, volts and couloumbs; cattle breeding is conducted on Mendelian principles; milk is pasteurised; scientists make use of the Röntgen rays for their experiments; and Marconi has provided scientians with the chance of informing hundreds of thousands of unseen listeners that the Church to which the inventor of this new medium of communication belongs is an enemy of science.

Dr. Coulton once quoted a foolish remark to the effect that "a Jesuit scientist can never freely publish his real opinions on scientific questions." There is no scientific question on which there is the remotest possibility of conflict between Catholic and scientific teaching. Haldane and Joad when challenged, in my controversies with them, to name a single doctrine of the Church which had been disproved by science had to concede by implication that there were no such doctrines. If Dr. Coulton had been interested in Jesuit scientific achievements he would have discovered that they are famous for their contributions to astronomy. More than a dozen Jesuits have their names printed on the map of the moon. One of these, Clavius, was the mathematician whose calculations justified the new Gregorian calendar, though it was not accepted in Protestant England until over a hundred years later; another, Secchi, may be called a founder of the modern science of astrophysics; while a third, Boscovich (1711–87) anticipated in his published works some of our modern physical theories including that of Relativity.

The first of these popular misrepresentations, the alleged hostility of the Church to science is disproved by past history, the second that the repudiation of religion accelerates the tempo of scientific achievement is disproved by the contemporary history of Soviet Russia.

(II)

Soviet Russia is the first state to adopt scientism as its state philosophy, for Marxism is merely one of the more irrational variants of scientism. Few men occupy a loftier position than Darwin in the Marxist pantheon, and nowhere is the repudiation of the supernatural more whole-hearted than in the philosophy of communism.

If the scientian premises be correct, both science and scientists should flourish in the Soviet Union. What are the achievements of Soviet science? If there be any names to set beside Copernicus, Galvani, Mendel, Pasteur and other eminent Catholic scientists, it would be interesting to know whether their achievements have been concealed for security reasons. The inflated claims made for Soviet science were subjected to a devastating analysis by Professor A. V. Hill in. *The New Statesman* (June 27th, 1940).

What is the status of Soviet scientists? In that new society which once promised to abolish privilege, Soviet scientists proudly proclaim that they are a privileged class. Professor S. I. Vavilov, President of the Moscow Academy of Sciences, makes this point in his book *Soviet Science in its New Phase* (1946).

"From the start," he writes, "the Soviet regime took steps to improve the conditions of life of our scientists, putting them on a preferential footing in respect of food, housing, clothing, and remuneration. This continued even during the worst years of the war when other sections of the population had to suffer great privations. . . ."

In 1944 I was often puzzled by what seemed to me the un-scientific attitude of certain scientists among my friends whose uncritical enthusiasm for the Soviet government puzzled me. And then one day I understood. "In Soviet Russia," I said to a friend of mine, "you would have the status and emoluments of a general if not of a field marshal. We all tend to think well of social systems which bring our class or our professional group to the top."

"I admit," said my friend, "that I cannot help being biased in favour of a government which knows how to treat scientists properly."

But does Russia treat scientists properly? The Soviet scientists may be enviable so far as material status and material rewards are concerned, but man does not live by bread alone. Intellectual freedom is at least as important to the true scientist as material rewards. He must be free "to sit down before the fact like a little child." The autonomy of science is indispensable to her well-being.

Now the Catholic scientist is free. As a scientist he approaches a scientific problem with far greater detachment than the atheist, for whereas a Catholic scientist examining the evidence for an alleged miracle would be perfectly free to consider all possible explanations, Natural and supernatural, the atheist's explanation would have to conform not to the evidence but to his ideological preconceptions.

In Soviet Russia as in Nazi Germany science is enchained. In this as in most other things there is nothing to choose between the national communism of Russia and the national socialism of Germany.

Is there for instance any difference of principle between:

"We serve the German way in mathematics. . . ."

" 'German physics?' one asks; I might rather have said Aryan physics. . . . But I shall be answered: 'Science is and remains international. It is false. We renounce international science. We renounce the international republic of learning. We renounce research for its own sake'."

and the following passages from *Soviet Science in its New Phase* by Professor S. I. Vavilov, President of the Moscow Academy of Sciences:

"*Soviet science is not merely a branch of world science operating on the territory of the U.S.S.R. No, it is a distinct science, different in character, in scope.*"

"*The fundamental feature of Soviet science is that it alone possesses a clear philosophical basis. Such a basis is essential in scientific enquiry. For our science dialectical materialism of Marx—Engels—Lenin—Stalin is that basis.*"

"*Our aim is to enter the arena of world science on a wide front, armed with the irresistible arguments of dialectical materialism, and (in that world arena of science) we shall combat all foreign concepts antagonistic to ours.*"

(III)

Nowhere has the persecution of intellectuals in general, and of scientists in particular, been more thorough than in Soviet Russia. "I have seen educated men coming out of Russia," said Leo Pasvolsky, "their general appearance, and particularly the crushed hopelessness of their mental processes is a nightmare that haunts me. . . . Such an exodus of the intelligent and the educated as there has been out of Russia no country has ever seen."

In a letter to *The Times* (April 24th, 1933) Sir Bernard Pares mentions the case of a distinguished ichthyologist Professor Tchernavin. "Of the fifty-one in his own branch of science, twenty-five have been shot and twenty-six deported in three years (1930–32).

"Among those whom he knew personally or met in prison his list includes six academicians and thirty-six professors in various fields or custodians of museums."

Now it may well be the case that most of these scientists were persecuted not for their scientific views but for their political heresies, and that they should therefore be classified with Bruno rather than with Galileo (see page 81). But whereas Bruno was a rare exception, the Brunos who have been murdered by the Bolsheviks can be counted in their hundreds. Moreover, there have been many cases of scientists who have been persecuted because their scientific opinions did not conform to ideological orthodoxy.

Mr. W. H. Chamberlin in *Russia's Iron Age* cites a journal entitled *For Marxist-Leninest Natural Science* which campaigned enthusiastically for "party spirit in mathematics" and "for purity of Marxist-Leninist theory in surgery."

Victor Serge, who faced death fighting for communism in the front line trenches during the attack on Petrograd, devotes a chapter of his book *Russia Twenty Years After* to a description of "Managed Science".

"Geologists," he writes, "have been imprisoned for having interpreted subsoil qualities differently from what was wanted in high places. . . . The subsidies generously allotted to the physiologist Pavlov for his researches into conditional reflexes did not prevent the arrest of his collaborators and friends. The encouragement given to the academician Yoffe for his researches into the structure of the atom did not prevent the deportation of his collaborators. The physicist Lazarev, after having been in the very front rank of Soviet science, was imprisoned, deported and then amnestied."

Eugene Lyons, whose enthusiasm for Russia did not survive his experiences as a foreign correspondent in that country, describes the "revolt against intelligence" that is, the revolt against reason, in his striking book *Assignment in Utopia*.

"The roster of scientists, historians, academicians, famous engineers, technical administrators, statisticians arrested at this time reads like an encyclopaedia of contemporary Russian culture."

He supports by detailed evidence his assertion that history, psychology and science are forced to "goose step the party line." "Even in the natural sciences there was plenty of grotesquery about 'Leninist surgery' and 'Stalinist mathematics' and ideological deviations in biology."

I cannot conclude this chapter better than by a quotation from "Critic" in *The New Statesman* (August 21st, 1948):

"That William Jennings Bryan of the U.S.S.R., Vice-President Lysenko, is trying to stage a Russian 'monkey-trial'. The issue is not that ape-into-man is an affront to the Book of Genesis but that Abbé Mendel's peas are an affront to Karl Marx. This Marxist fundamentalist has impeached his fellow-geneticists for observing the experimental proofs of hereditary transmission, as propounded by that bourgeois, clerical, premature Fascist, Abbé Mendel, over a century ago. At his instigation, the Academy of Agriculture has accused the Soviet biologists, Schmalhausen, Zavadovsky, Zherbak, Dubinin and others, of 'servility to the bourgeois, reactionary biologists' (the geneticists of the rest of the world). The Academy invokes Stalin, the 'luminary of advanced science', and Darwin, whom it dare not denounce as 'bourgeois' because he has a niche in the Marxist pantheon, against the heretics who dare to believe the evidence of their own experiments. It would be ludicrous if it were not sinister.

"The Royal Society elected the famous Russian, N. I. Varilov, a foreign Fellow, only to find that two years before he had died in prison on the *lettre de cachet* of his triumphant rival Lysenko ... Lysenko talks to the peasants about the 'souls' of plants and 'love-marriages', disdains experimental 'sophistries' and scorns absolutely statistical genetics, which he does not even pretend to understand and damns by bell, Marx and candle. It must be rather embarrassing for J. B. S. Haldane, who in his excellent science articles in the *Daily Worker* religiously gives each its proper Marxist interpretation, to be confronted with this Marxist interpretation of his own work. He is, after all, one of the world's greatest statistical geneticists."

(IV)

The consternation which this persecution has provoked is evidence of the fact that the modern world is losing the power to face the inevitable consequences of a false philosophy. Nobody who has been taught to think straight, as mediaeval students were taught to think straight, would be naive enough to register surprise at the Marxist attack on science. Any competent philosopher must realise that a system of thought which attacks objectivity must inevitably, in the final analysis, attack science, the essence of which is objectivity.

Mr. E. F. Carritt, for instance, has never, so far as I know, taken a sympathetic interest in Catholic rationalism, and has declared himself to be "in sympathy with the objectives of communism," but he is too good a philosopher not to perceive that Marxism is essentially anti-rational. Mr. Carritt, who is a Fellow of University College, Oxford, and a lecturer in philosophy, points out that "if a man's economic situation only in the last resort determines his beliefs about other matters, then clearly different men must in different situations have different beliefs about the same facts mathematical, historical, economic, but all of these cannot certainly be true; nor is it easy to see how any of them should be."

If, then, as the Marxist believes, a man's economic situation determines his views about science, the persecution of scientists in Russia is consistent with Marxism, for unless a Russian scientist is a convinced Marxist, his scientific outlook must inevitably be unsound; not necessarily untrue, for Marxism is not concerned with objective truth, but unsound because nothing which does not contribute to the advance of the Marxist revolution can be sound.

Science is objective, and the revolt against reason, which is a revolt against objectivity, must inevitably lead to an attack on the objectivity of science.

Reason is the censor which forbids us to adapt objective truth to the exigencies of political opportunism or sexual desire. Objective ethics are formally repudiated in the Marxist creed.

"What coincides with the interests of the Proletarian Revolution is ethical," writes E. Yaroslavsky.

"We say that our morality," writes Lenin, "is wholly subordinated to the interests of the class-struggle of the proletariat."

The Marxists are, so far as I know, the first Logosoclasts to use the word "objective" as an explicit term of abuse.

The circumstances in which objectivity was pronounced heretical are worth recalling. A certain Professor G. F. Alexandrov had written *A History of Western Philosophy* which was published by the Institute of Philosophy in Moscow in 1946. It was sponsored by his fellow-philosophers, approved by the Academy and selected as a text-book for University students. It was well reviewed in *Pravda* and *Isvestia*. Subsequently it was deleted for heresy, and Stalin "directed" (to quote *Pravda*) that a public "discussion" should be held on it.

The nature of "discussion" in a logosoclastic state is significant. Zhdanov, Secretary General of the Communist Party, appeared in the rôle of prosecutor and eighty-four academicians, professors, and would-be professors entered their names as wishing to take part in the "discussion". All of them, including those who had first praised the book, expressed their detestation of its heresies.

In civilised countries a scholar is expected to be *dispassionate* and *calm* when discussing views with which he disagrees. Not so in the topsy turvy world of Russia where all values are reversed. Zhdanov denounced the Professor on the ground that "he dispassionately and calmly describes the various pre-Marxist systems of philosophy. . . . Such flabby, toothless, vegetarian approach to the history of philosophy, such backboneless *objectivism* cannot be tolerated by Marxism" (italics ours).

In civilised countries "educational" is not a term of abuse, but Zhdanov attacks Professor Alexandrov's book on the ground that it is "too educational".

"By discussing *objectively and dispassionately* the various bourgeois philosophical theories he, by implication, pays tribute to the academic traditions of bourgeois philosophers. . . ." He does, indeed, and thereby separates himself from those who have relegated dispassioned objectivity to the dust heap of discarded habits. Professor Alexandrov's sin was a sin of omission, his failure to describe the Western philosophers as "Fascist beasts" or "Fascist Cannibals", thereby establishing his solidarity with those who have not forgotten what Zhdanov describes as "one of the most fundamental postulates of Marxism to wage a merciless war against its opponents of whatever school."

CHAPTER XIX

THE NEW ICONOCLASTS

For poets like Dryden and Pope, for painters like Michel Angelo and Poussin, we can only have an angry and in no sense patronising pity.

Herbert Read

(1)

ON THE façade of the little church at Campione there is engraved a tribute to the masons of Milan Cathedral which may be rendered thus:

By what remote parentage, by what silent preparation, by what vast agreements is nourished the eternal dream of art.

The Bolshevik and the Parlour Bolshevik are in revolt against the "remote parentage" of European culture, against the "silent preparation" which is as necessary in social reconstruction as in art, and against the "vast agreements" which are the foundation of European culture.

Now the revolt against Reason finds expression in the revolt against difficulty. Chastity is difficult and consequently the rationalisers of self-indulgence are at work explaining that men commit adultery from the highest of motives. It is difficult to paint well. Let us therefore popularise a new "school" in which the incompetent and the idle and the untalented will be able to compete on equal terms with the competent, the industrious and the talented. Fashion forces even those who have served the apprenticeship of "silent preparation" to disguise the technique which they have mastered and to conceal their native skill. It is difficult, for instance, not to suspect Hodler of deliberately painting badly in order not to lose the suffrages of progressive critics. He could, when he wished, paint the human body with a mastery of tactile values which reminds one of Masaccio, but he could also placate the Herbert Reads with mis-shapen, badly drawn, and crudely coloured forms.

Mr. Herbert Read who edits and who writes an introduction to *Surrealism* rightly insists on its relationship to Marxism. He tells us that it was "his ambition to do for the realm of art on the basis of Hegel's dialectic something analogous to what Marx, on the same basis, did for the realm of economics. With such a philosophy of art one could then proceed to a complete re-assessment of aesthetic values." After a laudatory reference to the Marxist dialectics he continues, "What I wish to stress now is that surrealism is an application of the same logical method to the realm of art." And again surrealism, like Marxism, "implies a monism or identity of matter."

Herbert Read is as ingenious as Marx in evading exact definition where exact definition would be embarrassing. "It would be absurd," he writes, "to call the surrealist anything but a *dialectical* materialist," but he does not tell us why it would be absurd or why surrealists who accept, so Mr. Read tells us, "monism or identity of matter," differ from all other materialistic monists.

"Surrealism," writes Herbert Read, "is anti-rational". The Surrealists in their various manifestos boldly proclaim their revolt against reason. "The surrealists," writes Mr. Priestley, "stand for violence and neurotic unreason." "Surrealism," to quote Palinurus, "is a typical city delirium movement, a violent explosion of urban claustrophobia; one cannot imagine surrealists except in vast cities. . . . The nihilism of Céline and Henry Miller is another product, and so are those main movers, Marx with his carbuncles, Hitler with his Beer-Hall."

Surrealism, in fact, is related to the irrationalism of Marxism much as Chartres is related to the rationality of Christianity.

Surrealism is the expression in art not only of the revolt against reason, but also of that ultimate despair which we call nihilism. Picasso's art for instance is, as Dr. Kurt Badt rightly insists, "one of the most luxuriant blooms of the flower of nihilism. That this bloom through its luxuriance has a definite fascination, nobody would deny but it is the fascination of the 'Nihil', the 'Nihil' nourished from the soil of 'everything is allowed'. (Es ist jedoch der Reiz des 'nihil', des Nihil genährt von dem Boden des 'Alles ist erlaubt') . . . Here we find nothing but ruins, disintegration of values and cynicism, and it is these that he expresses in his painting. Of authentic tragedy no trace, and no trace of authentic humanity. For if everything is allowed, freedom is transformed into hate and sadism. Defeat is transformed into degeneration. . . . Picasso's philosophy is nothing but the restless cynicism of the nihilist. Hence the frequent changes of style."

In the final phase of nihilistic art, painting is abandoned, and the artist merely collects random objects and exhibits the results. I remember an exhibition of modern art at Venice in the late thirties. One of the exhibits was a slate, such as school children use, on to which the following objects had been glued, a cigarette end, a bit of sea-weed, a lock of grey hair, and a small section of rubber tubing. That exhibit was a reflection on the integrity of modern critics, for if sincerity had not been the first casualty in the modern revolt against the Logos, nobody who was not certifiable would tolerate such absurdities.

Mr. Herbert Read, potentially a gifted critic, might have purged modern art of much of its absurdity, and yet Mr. Herbert Read invites our admiration for a study by Hans Arp, which consists of a newspaper, not the painting of a newspaper but the newspaper itself, folded into a bowl-like shape, and revealing one of the headlines, *Mutilé et apatridé*. Children make paper boats out of newspapers, but they do not expect their creations to be the subject of serious criticism. But on the whole Hans Arp would be well advised to confine himself to playing about with bits of newspaper, to judge by the specimen of his sculpture reproduced by Mr. Read, *Concrétion humaine*, two stony tumours separated by something which looks like the butt-end of a shell case.

You can't argue with critics who would have us swoon with delight when confronted with this kind of charlatanism, because it is useless to argue with people whose sincerity one doubts. "Everyone in his heart knows that these things are bad," writes that distinguished hellenist Professor Gilbert Norwood, "but dare not say so." Precisely. Nine-tenths of modern art criticism is due to a failure of nerve, the timid conformity to a foolish fashion. "People mumble phrases about 'keeping an open mind' or 'conventions kill art.' The real reason is that they have no standards. Conventions do not kill art; on the contrary they make it possible. And it is just as fatal to 'keep an open mind' about everything as to keep it about nothing. . . . Tradition need not be a chain; it may be a life-line. That cubist group of cog-wheels which its maker called 'statue of a soldier'—what are we to say to it? It makes us ashamed, but we cannot say why, and we are a prey to shibboleths in its favour which sound as convincing as shibboleths directed against it. . . . You can best put the thing in its proper place by comparing it with the Venus of Milo in the Louvre or the Delphian Charioteer in the British Museum. . . . Those Greek statues give you peace, not only calm of soul, but mere comfort in dealing with matters of taste. . . ."

(II)

Those who are determined to conform to artistic and literary fashions are equally ready to admire compositions consisting of bits of rubber tubing and cigarette ends or literary gibberish. Gertrude Stein, for instance, cashed in very cleverly on the aesthetic "progress" which coincided with a regress from reason. Here is a sample of her contribution to literary Surrealism:

"Rules are not what are not sometimes and always with feathers and parallelograms are longer and not warmer when exceptions are there. A cucumber can be its own father if wanted and not wanted and are not wanted and a father can be its own cucumber if feathers are wanted and not exceptions."

This sort of thing was much admired by advanced critics. But *was* it admired? "Everybody in his heart knows that these things are bad but dare not say so." Why not? What is the key to this "Treason of the clerks," this tragic dereliction of those who should guide the literary and artistic taste of their generation. The principal explanation is not the wickedness of man but the weakness of man. Not vice but snobbery accounts for the insincerity of those who affect to experience aesthetic ecstacy when confronted with a cigarette end and a piece of rubber tubing glued to a slate. You cannot repudiate reason, as the surrealists repudiate reason, without repudiating truth, and insincerity is merely one of the many forms of falsehood.

(III)

"In a world of competing tyrannies," writes Mr. Herbert Read, "the artist can have only one allegiance: to the dictatorship which claims to end all forms of dictatorship, and promises, however indefinitely, the complete liberation of man, the dictatorship of the proletariat."

o

Has Mr. Read one point of sympathetic contact with the proletariat whose dictatorship he yearns for? Is or is it not a fact that whereas the average working man has a natural admiration for and sympathy with a sporting peer, he has a hearty dislike for left-wing intellectuals? It would be difficult to decide whether Marxist intellectuals dislike the proletariat more than the proletariat dislike Marxist intellectuals. Marx and Engels never bothered to conceal from each other their detestation of the proletariat. "What is the rabble good for if it forgets to fight?" writes Engels to Marx. And again, "the people are of no importance whatever."

Would Mr. Read thrill with pleasure if his aesthetic tasts coincided with those of the proletariat. Is not surrealism a recoil from the criteria of the ordinary man?

The works of genius have a universal appeal. The connoisseur and the ordinary man can both enjoy a masterpiece by Michael Angelo, for whom Mr. Read has "an angry and in no sense patronising pity", but the surrealists have nothing to offer to the man in the street, and in this at least they are consistent Marxists.

It is, of course, the greatest rubbish for these anarchic individualists to pose as supporters of Marxist socialism. They are anarchists in rebellion against every form of control, including the control of the state. Perhaps of all political systems the *laissez-faire* Liberalism of the eighteen-thirties provided the most congenial environment for the artist. For the true artist resents every encroachment by the state on his liberty and his purse. He must be free to travel where he wills, to settle down where he wishes, to stay abroad as long as he wishes, to paint what he wishes, and above all he requires a large number of rich men who are prepared to pay good prices for his work. A hundred years ago all these conditions could be found in capitalistic England. None of them can be found in modern England, still less in Soviet Russia. Even Mr. Herbert Read knows that. "Even communism," he wrote in 1933, "the creed of liberty and fraternity has made the exigencies of a transitional epoch the excuse of an unnecessary and stupid form of aesthetic intolerance." It would be an understatement to describe this as an understatement.

Mr. Kurt London, who described himself as a friend of the

Soviet Union writes thus of the artists in Soviet Russia: "On the one hand a carefree, pleasant and full life beckons them, if they are willing to sing the tune called by Stalin. On the other hand, they would be outlawed, and become not only artistic but also social outcasts, if they follow the bent of their personality. What is more they lose the economic base of their existence. The only course left open to them is either to give up their profession or their conscience. Art like science must conform."

Shostakovich's popular opera *And Quiet Flows the Don* was widely praised by musical critics in Soviet Russia until *Pravda* sniffed out ideological heresy in operatic formalism, whereupon the critics came to heel. Yuri Olesha who had been an ardent admirer of Shostakovich's opera, promptly recanted. "If I do not agree with the articles in *Pravda* about art, I have no right to experience patriotic pleasure. . . . If I do not agree with the party in a single point, the whole of life must be dimmed for me."

On April 10th, 1935, the artist Nikritin was summoned before an Art Commission which had discovered the clear evidence of a class-attack "inimical to Soviet power" in a painting of Venus, a young man and a young girl, and workers in the Metro building. Examples such as these could be multiplied indefinitely.

One of the more nauseating aspects of the Marxists is their lack of class solidarity. The supreme *trahison des clercs* is the servile praise by intellectuals in countries which are till free of the Russian tyranny which transforms intellectuals into mental prostitutes. . . . "The artist can have only one allegiance, to the dictatorship of the proletariat" . . . I am sure that Mr. Read no longer adheres to this *confessio fidei*.

(IV)

In the ages of great art men were proud to carry on the tradition of a school. The modern craze for innovation at all costs is the consequence of that inflated egoism which is concerned not with the interpretation of a vision but with the advertisement of an ego. Many of the greatest artists were so little interested in self-advertisement that they frequently omitted to sign their works.

Why are most modern critics either indifferent to or actively hostile to beauty? Because most modern critics are in revolt against the Creator of all beauty. Reason, holiness, beauty are all aspects of the divine and the revolt against reason entails the revolt against holiness and the revolt against beauty.

"Great art," writes Geoffrey Scott, "will be distinguished from that which is merely aesthetically clever by a nobility that, in its final analysis, is moral, or rather the nobility which in life we call moral is itself aesthetic. . . . There is, in fact, a true not a false analogy between ethical and aesthetic value: the correspondence between them may even amount to an identity. The 'dignity' of architecture is the same 'dignity' that we recognise in character."

Let the verdict of the most brilliant aesthetic critic of the years between the wars be reinforced by the verdict of a distinguished scientist.

"In modern civilisation," writes Alexis Carrel, "individuals whose conduct is inspired by a moral ideal are very seldom encountered. However, such individuals still exist. We cannot help noticing their aspect when we meet them. Moral beauty is an exceptional and very striking phenomenon. He who has contemplated it but once never forgets its aspect. This form of beauty is far more impressive than the beauty of nature and of science. It gives to those who possess its divine gifts, a strange, an inexplicable power. It increases the strength of intellect. It establishes peace among men. Much more than science, art and religious rites, moral beauty is the basis of civilisation."

It is as exceptional for a modern intellectual to praise moral beauty as to praise aesthetic beauty. The cult of ugliness in art is closely associated with the cult of ugliness in behaviour. Mr. Read, for instance, admires the surrealists and he also admires the Marquis de Sade and Byron "because they prove that the most deeply rooted of taboos such as incest can be thwarted by the individual will."

Mr. Read reproduces in his work some examples of Salvator Dali's art. Dali was a characteristic surrealist not only in art but also in life. "While crossing the hall," he writes, "I caught sight of my little three-year-old sister crawling unobtrusively through a doorway. I stopped, hesitated a second, then gave her a terrible kick in the head as though it had been a ball, and continued running, carried away with a 'delirious joy' induced by this savage act."

George Orwell, a socialist who has never compromised his integrity or conformed to fashion, quotes this passage and continues: "Several other incidents of the same kind are recorded, including (this was when he was twenty-nine years old) knocking down and trampling on a girl 'until they had to tear her bleeding out of my reach'," writes Orwell, "there is always one escape: *into wickedness.*" Orwell is not a snob, he does not mind using the unfashionable word "wicked". "Always do the thing that will shock and wound people. At five throw a little boy off a bridge, strike an old doctor across the face with a whip and break his spectacles, or, at any rate, dream of doing such things. Twenty years later gouge the eyes out of dead donkeys with a pair of scissors. . . . And after all it pays! It is much less dangerous than crime. If you throw a dead donkey at people, they throw money back. . . ." Or, for that matter, a live donkey.

Some little time before the first world war, a paint brush was tied to a donkey's tail, and the result of tail lashing against a canvas was sent to a Paris exhibition labelled, if I remember aright, "Sunset". Some of the advanced critics were much impressed. Then there was the Cambridge hoax when, once again, advanced critics paid solemn tribute to paintings exhibited at Cambridge by two undergraduates, whose sole object was to test the gullibility of modern critics.

Then there was the superb hoax perpetrated by George Edinger on academic prophets of advanced cults. Duly disguised as a Viennese Professor, he delivered a lecture on the new psychology, which contained among other contributions to advanced thought the dictum, "Consciousness is a chunk of space-time happenings." The academic disciples of Freud and Jung nodded solemnly and drank in every word.

The most successful of these hoaxes was perpetrated in Australia. "Ern Malley," writes *Janus* in the *Spectator* for June 30th, 1944, "said to have died in 1943, was the *dernier cri* among esoteric poets in Australia. He was lauded to heaven by Max Harris, Editor of Adelaide high-brow review, *Angry Penguins*, and by one of the University lecturers in literature. The vogue indeed reached America. But Ern Malley, it turns out, never was. Two former members of Sydney University, now in the forces, who evidently share my views on certain types of modern poetry, have claimed paternity for the eulogised verses. Their technique was simple. They opened various books, took out sentences at random, and strung them together in accordance with one over-ruling principle that in no circumstances must they make sense. The first three lines of one poem 'Culture as Exhibit' came straight from a report on mosquito breeding grounds.''

(v)

Snobbery is the key to the praise of gibberish and incompetence in literature and in art. These timid appeasers of incompetence and charlatanism have not the courage to denounce the apostasy in literature and in art which is the direct consequence of theological apostasy, the direct consequence because the cult of ugliness in life as in art is a manifestation of the revolt against the Creator of all beauty. And because these men have repudiated all objective standards, and are solely concerned to conform to a debased and ever-changing fashion, they are terrified of being out of step, and their reluctance to condemn anything which a rival critic might praise makes them the victim of every practical joker tempted by legs of infinite elasticity.

There is no charge which these Logosoclasts more bitterly resent than this charge of insincerity which they bring so freely against theological and political conservatives, but I have too great a respect for Mr. Read's talents as a critic to believe in his sincerity when he praises gibberish in paint, and for his humanity to believe him sincere when he praises the most brutal tyranny of all recorded history, and for his character to credit him with sincerity when he writes rubbish about the Marquis de Sade. I can pay him no higher compliment as a man than to assert that I am quite sure that he does not practice what he preaches.

(vi)

Shortly before freedom and democracy had been destroyed in Poland I tuned in by accident to Moscow, and the voice of the English announcer came through: ". . . Stalin's determination to assist all freedom-loving Poles to establish a free, democratic and independent Poland. . . ." Few things are more irritating than an elusive memory which refuses to come into focus. There was something perplexingly familiar about the lunacy of Soviet propaganda, a lunacy subject to the laws of a pananoic logic . . . *"free, democratic and independent"* which of course is basic Russian for *"enslaved, communist, satellite"*. . . . *Where* have I come across this sort of thing before? . . . Of course . . . How stupid of me to forget the originator of basic Russian. I took down *Alice Through the Looking Glass* from my shelves and began to read . . .

" *'When I use a word,'* Humpty Dumpty said in a rather scornful *tone,* 'it means just what I choose it to mean—neither more nor less.'

" 'The question is,' said Alice, 'whether you can make words mean different things.'

" 'The question is,' said Humpty Dumpty, 'which is to be master—that's all.' "

And where the Marxists are masters, a word means just what the Marxists "choose it to mean—neither more nor less."

The shy clerical Don who wrote his fantasia to give delight to a little girl, the original of "Alice", was an unconscious prophet. *Alice Through the Looking Glass* reflected the shape of silliness to come. The dialectics of the Mad Hatter are slightly saner than the dialectics of the Marxist in Blunderland. The revolt against reason was nothing more than an underground movement when Lewis Carroll was writing, and the social order was still informed by the values of Christian rationalism. Even those who describe themselves as "rationalists" still had some respect for reason. The lunatic fringe of humanity were still in mental homes and not yet in control of great states. The protagonists of Christianity and secularism still observed the traditional rules of rational controversy. Huxley did not maintain that his only concern was to promote Anglicanism and to encourage clericalism. Gladstone did not retort that he would not rest until he had converted the Bishops to Darwinism and liberated the Church from all dogmas, for neither Huxley nor Gladstone had been initiated into the secrets of Surrealist controversy.

The dialectic of irrationalism has its own conventions, as is apparent in the argument between that sturdy rationalist Alice and the Surrealist Humpty Dumpty. Nothing, as Humpty Dumpty was one of the first to discover, must ever be called by its proper name. A democrat, for instance, must be attacked as

a Fascist, the Red Nazism of Russia must be described as democratic and Satellites must be referred to as "free and independent".

The second principle of surrealist controversy is not to defend
yourself against a charge but to repeat the charge as if the
prosecutor were in the dock. Thus Russia's routine reply to
unavailing protests against her camouflaged annexation of one
satellite country after another is solemnly to rebuke the Western
Allies for intervention in the domestic affairs of "free and independent" Rumania, Bulgaria, Hungary, or Czechoslovakia as
the case may be. No wonder that Mr. Read insists on the relationship between surrealism in art and Marxism, for Marxism
is surrealism in the realm of politics. Europe through the Looking Glass has its own logic, for even a lunatic will often argue
logically from his own premises, and draw quite consistent conclusions from the hypothesis that he is the true King of England
and that the doctors have conspired to certify him.

And what could be more Humpty Dumptyish than the im-
passioned apologetics for the kind of art that Alice would no
doubt have been called upon to admire had she visited an art
exhibition in Looking Glass World.

It is not in the least surprising that Mr. Herbert Read speaks
of Carroll with the greatest respect, for the Alice books are
masterpieces of surrealism, but surrealism with a difference.
Alice is the heroine of these books and her sturdy sanity is a
perfect foil to the surrealist lunacy of the characters. Carroll's
standards are the standards of Christendom, and that is why his
humour enchants us, for there is nothing funny about a world
in which *everybody* is mad.

For whereas Lewis Carroll's sympathies are with Alice, Mr.
Herbert Read defends not only surrealist art but also surrealist
ethics. He quotes with approval one of the silliest remarks ever
made by a clever man: "The least repressed of people are
generally the most moral," or as Huysmans puts it, "au fond
. . . il n'y a de réellement obscènes que les gens chastes." St.
Teresa of Lisieux was obscene and the Marquis de Sade, who
was certainly "the least repressed", was the "most moral".
"When I use the word 'moral'," said Humpty Dumpty in a
rather scornful tone, "it means just what I choose it to mean—
neither more nor less."

In the crazy Europe through the Looking Glass in which we are living, the amoralists have stolen the parsons' pulpit manner and immoral uplift finds expression in lay sermons such as this by Mr. Herbert Read:

"Byron is the only European poet who might conceivably occupy in our hierarchy the position held in France by the Marquis de Sade. The function of such figures is to be so positive in their immorality that morality becomes negative by comparison. They show, by the more than human energy of their evil, that evil too, as Milton was compelled to admit, has its divinity. In short they realise the conventionality of all systems of morality. They prove that the most deeply rooted of taboos such as incest can be thwarted by the individual will; and the courage they manifest in such defiance is so absolute that a figure like Byron becomes the unconfessed hero of humanity. The dilemma that faces all moralists is that the repression of instincts is apt to breed a worse disease than their free expression; incidentally it entails a feebler art."

By way of contrast to surrealistic rubbish, let me quote the realistic verdict of a scientist.

"It is well known," writes Dr. Alexis Carrel, "that sexual excesses impede intellectual activity . . . while the weak, the nervous and the unbalanced become more abnormal when their sexual appetites are repressed, the strong are rendered still stronger by practising such forms of asceticism."

The "defiance so absolute" of conventional codes which moves Mr. Read to such ecstatic praise is often tempered by uneasy doubts. Emancipation from "deeply rooted taboos" is achieved with difficulty for it is remarkable how frequently those who defiantly proclaim their contempt for conventional morality bitterly resent their idols being accused of conventional immorality.

Mr. Herbert Read, for instance, bridles with indignation when Mr. Priestley draws attention to the fact that the surrealists included an undue proportion of perverts. "They stand for violence and neurotic unreason," writes Mr. Priestley. "They are truly decadent. You catch a glimpse behind them of the deepening twilight of barbarism that may soon blot out the sky until at last humanity finds itself in another long night . . . there are too many effeminate or epicene young men lisping

and undulating . . . frequently they have strong sexual impulses that they soon contrive to misuse or pervert."

Mr. Herbert Read was much distressed by this "insult". But
why "insult"? If de Sade and Byron are praised for their perversions, Mr. Read should welcome what he ought, if he were
consistent, to regard as a tribute to the surrealists. Instead, after
quoting Mr. Priestley's indictment, he continues:

"The kind of insult that Mr. Priestley hurls at the surrealists
is the kind of insult that used to be insinuated about the Bolsheviks until the purity and disinterestedness of their lives could
no longer be disguised," excepting of course from Stalin who
liquidated every member of the old guard of pure disinterested
Bolsheviks other than those who escaped into exile. . . . "As
a matter of fact the surrealists are no less aware than Mr.
Priestley of undesirable elements in their midst; but they are
not themselves to be identified with such elements. It is true
that they cannot protest against the perversions of a moral code
for which they have no respect. But they despise the people who
indulge in perversion."

If one has no respect for a code, one should respect those who
defy it, but it would be idle to expect consistency in a surrealist.
At one moment he will be lauding the Marquis de Sade to the
skies, at the next bridling indignantly because somebody is rash
enough to assume that he means what he says. The convention-
ally unconventional are always liable to react to conventional
conventionalism. At one moment they demand for the artist the
most complete liberty for sexual self-expression. At the next
moment they are indignant when some critic calls attention to
the unpleasant habits of some of their most lauded idols.

Professor Thomas Bodkin evoked shrill cries of protest from
advanced intellectuals when he contrasted in the pages of *The
New English Review* "the serene dignity and moral worth" of the
great painters of the past with the "deplorable characters who
infest the ranks of 'modern painters'." The passage in question
was reprinted in his book *The Approach to Painting* (page 181).
Professor Bodkin describes the exact technique of launching the
latest exponent of the latest lunatic style. A venal author writes
a laudatory introduction to a catalogue. "Honest dupes and
venal critics" puff the paintings in the press. A strictly limited
edition of reproductions of the paintings is published, limited

"because it would be unwise to risk it coming to the notice of independent reviewers" and by these means a few score paintings are unloaded on fools on the tacit understanding that the painter will be dropped in a year or two when the time has come to foist another brand of rubbish on the public.

CHAPTER XX

THE REVOLT AGAINST MEANING

(1)

THIS book is not a study of contemporary errors with which I am only concerned in so far as they are the by-products of the revolt against reason. It would, for instance, be impossible briefly to discuss Existentialism, quite apart from the fact that Existentialism is a label which covers several sects ranging from Theists on the one hand to an atheist such as Sartre on the other hand. Again, I have no space for a detailed discussion of logical positivism, but I welcome this, the latest mental mode at Oxford, because logical positivism provides valuable evidence in support of my contention that the revolt against reason ultimately leads to a revolt against meaning.

Logical positivism began in Vienna after the first world war and was introduced into this country by an Austrian who settled in England, Ludwig Wittgenstein, but the main discredit for popularising this new mode of irrationalism must be conceded to Professor A. J. Ayer of London University, whose qook, *Language, Truth and Logic*, has acquired at Oxford, according to a correspondent of *The New Statesman* (June 26th, 1948), almost "the effect of a philosophic Bible."

The main effect of this book has been to transform the flight from reason into a flight from *reasoning*. The Victorians who described themselves as "rationalists" made some attempt to refute what they imagined to be the arguments whereby Christtians defend their faith. The modern fashion of evading dialectical battle by psycho-analysing rather than refuting the Christian has been carried one stage further by Professor Ayer. He neither answers the arguments of the Christian nor analyses his complexes. He proposes a criterion for rational discussion which, if adopted, will dispense him from all obligation to engage in rational discussion with a Christian.

His primary interest in a proposition is not whether it is true or false, but whether it is "meaningful". The old type of atheist who still believed in reason tried to prove either that a particular philosophical system was false or that its truth could not be established. The logical positivist is content to maintain that all metaphysical systems are *meaningless*. Others may have been content to maintain that Plato or Plotinus or St. Thomas Aquinas or Kant or Hegel or Whitehead were mistaken. Professor Ayer maintains that their systems of thought are not thoughts in the true sense of the term and can be dismissed as unworthy of study. Plato, Plotinus, St. Thomas Aquinas and Kant were not merely mistaken. They talked pure twaddle.

According to Ayer there are two and only two types of statement that have meaning and that convey real knowledge about things.

First there are *"analytical propositions"*, such as logical and mathematical expressions. The proposition $2 \times 3 = 6$ merely says the same thing in two ways, 6 being merely a different expression for 2×3. This type of proposition is a *tautology*, a linguistic statement of something which is already implicit in the original statement. Every mathematical and logical proposition is in the final analysis tautological, being nothing more than the translation into another mode of expression of axioms or postulates which were already implicit in the original statement.

Secondly propositions have meaning when they affirm or deny facts. Such propositions are only "meaningful" when they are verifiable.

"The meaning of a proposition," says Schlick, "lies in the method of its verification."

What does the logical positivist understand by "verification?" A statement according to Ayer is verifiable if "some possible *sense-experience* is relevant to the determination of their truth or falsehood."

Professor Ayer is prepared to admit as "meaningful" certain historical statements such as "The Battle of Waterloo was fought in 1815" because he considers that we can conceive the kind of sense-experience which would verify this statement, but the practical effect of this criterion is to eliminate metaphysical thought and to deny validity to any form of thought other than that of science on the one hand or "tautological" propositions on the other hand.

(II)

The overwhelming majority of philosophers, important enough to be mentioned in histories of philosophy, are agreed on one point, at least, however much they may disagree on all others. They distinguish between the temporal order which includes the familiar world, and the eternal order which contains "values" such as truth, goodness and beauty.

The theist believes that these values are aspects of the divine, and are the source respectively of metaphysics, ethics and aesthetics. "In other words," as Dr. Joad puts it with his customary succinctness, "it is because the universe contains a moral order that some things are right and wrong; because it contains an aesthetic order that some things are beautiful and some ugly, and because there is such a thing as truth that some judgments are true and some false."

Professor Ayer parts company with all those who have believed in an order of reality beyond the reach of "sense-experience", and therefore denies the validity of ethical, aesthetic or metaphysical thinking.

Aesthetic judgments, for instance, tell us nothing about the object (painting or sculpture) and not very much about the aesthetic critic other than the fact that the critic has certain feelings. As no aesthetic judgment is "meaningful", arguments about aesthetics are pointless. It is not "meaningful" to say that a painting by Titian is greater art than a painting by Landseer. In short, aesthetic criticism is twaddle.

Ethical judgments have no more claim to be "meaningful" than aesthetic judgments. They are mere "pseudo-concepts", in other words mere fictions. "Hence also there can be no ethical propositions" is Wittgenstein's simple solution to the ethical problems which have been debated by man since man began. All twaddle.

"If I now generalise," says Professor Ayer, ". . . and say, 'stealing is wrong', I produce a sentence which has no factual meaning—that is expresses no proposition which can be either true or false. It is as if I had written 'Stealing money!' " "Stealing is wrong" tells no more about stealing than "This painting is beautiful" tells us about painting. All we learn from these statements is that certain things produce certain feelings in the speaker. The only difference between "I revere St. Francis"

and "I am horrified by the cruelty of Himmler" is the difference
between an approving and a shocked noise.

"The question," writes Ayer, "how a man ought to live is one
to which there is no authoritative answer. It has to be decided
by each man for himself," and if Himmler decides that his way
of life involves massacring millions of Jews in gas chambers,
there is no criterion by which we pronounce this way of life to
be inferior to that of St. Francis.

Metaphysical propositions are as meaningless as ethical and
aesthetic judgments.

"It is characteristic of an agnostic," writes Ayer, "to hold
that the existence of a god is a possibility in which there is no
good reason either to believe or disbelieve; and it is characteristic of an atheist to hold that it is at least probable that no god
exists. And our view that all utterances about the nature of God
are nonsensical, so far from being identical with, or even lending
support to, either of these familiar contentions, is actually incompatible with them. For if the assertion that there is a god is
nonsensical, then the atheist's assertion that there is no god is
equally nonsensical, since it is only a significant proposition
that can be significantly contradicted."

(III)

Logical positivism is a pretentious name for a new variant of
the scientism which in its less camouflaged form is becoming
increasingly discredited. The thesis that reality is coterminous
with the phenomena which are the subject of scientific investigation is a lingering prejudice, a survival of nineteenth-century
fashion.

There is, admittedly, nothing inherently irrational in the assertion that the evidence for the supernatural is *inadequate*. One
may criticise the judgment of those who adopt this agnostic
position, but not their logic, but to maintain that the evidence
for the supernatural is not even worth *examining*, and that no
proposition about the supernatural can possibly be "meaningful" is nothing more than inverted fundamentalism. It is, in
effect, a refusal to accept the principles of scientific investigation, a declaration in advance that no facts will be considered
which conflict with *a priori* prejudices.

If there be a supernatural realm, and even Ayer would concede that the existence of such a realm cannot be *disproved*, Ayer's criterion would effectively prevent him discovering it. He is in much the same position as Columbus would have been had he asserted at the outset of his voyage that no proposition about lands as yet undiscovered could be deemed to be "meaningful".

This refusal to examine the evidence for the supernatural, and the attempt to dismiss any propositions about the existence of God as "nonsensical" is an interesting symptom of the decline of scientific materialism. The case for the supernatural has been so strongly reinforced in the last fifty years that the modern sceptic avoids the arena, and rationalises his failure of nerve by pretentious circumlocutions.

Logical positivism should more correctly be described as illogical negativism.

It is illogical because, as Dr. Eric Junger has pointed out in a brilliant article, "the fundamental doctrine of logical positivism, its principle of verifiability and meaning is untenable on its own ground. The decisive argument against its validity is that the very thesis that ascribes meaning only to propositions which express either facts or logical procedure itself neither states an empirical fact nor represents a logical procedure. It is thus on its own showing a pseudo-Proposition and therefore meaningless."

A proposition is only meaningful if it be tautologous or verifiable by Sense Experience.

This, the basic doctrine of logical positivism, is (a) not tautologous and (b) cannot be verified by sense experience. It is therefore on the Ayer thesis "nonsensical". It should be clear even to a logical positivist that you cannot verify by sense experience the non-existence of a realm which is asserted by Ayer to be imperceptible to sense experience.

The thesis "A realm of reality exists which is not perceptible to our senses" is not refuted by *repeating* the thesis in slightly different words.

Logical positivism like other varieties of modern irrationalism is inherently self-destructive. Just as the logical conclusion from Marxist or Freudian philosophy is that no philosophy (including Marxism and Freudianism) can possibly be true, so the basic premise of logical positivism refutes logical positivism.

Logical positivism is as vulnerable in detail as in substance. Consider for instance the hypothesis that if an assertion be nonsensical, its contradiction is equally nonsensical, a hypothesis which Ayer applies to the hypothesis of God. A characteristic specimen of pseudo-logic, which equates as equally nonsensical the illusions of a mental patient and the contradictions of his doctor who is trying to cure him.

Professor Ayer is prepared, as we have seen, to classify as "meaningful" historical statements such as the fact that the Battle of Waterloo was fought in 1815. He accepts such statements because he believes that we can conceive the kind of sense-experience whereby they could be verified. Now he also maintains that the existence of God cannot be proved or even shown to be probable. He may therefore be presumed to accept the only alternative explanation for the origin of species, some form of mechanistic evolution, including the belief in spontaneous generation. Is this belief "verifiable by sense experience?"

Again, what is the sense experience which verifies the belief that the whale is descended from land mammals? Not only are there no intermediates in the fossil record, but nobody has produced a plausible hypothetical series of links connecting whale and land quadrupeds. Whatever foundation there may be for this belief it is not of the type which conforms to Professor Ayer's criterion of significance. Therefore the assertion that evolution has occurred "is nonsensical, and the assertion that it has not occurred is equally nonsensical."

Finally even if we accept the logical positivist criterion, Ayer's conclusion that no significant proposition can be formulated on the subject of God does not follow.

The theist claims that there are many facts verified by sense experience which point towards a theistic conclusion. Nobody would suspect Professor J. B. S. Haldane of any bias in favour of theism in general or of Catholicism in particular, yet he conceded, as I have shown, that certain Lourdes miracles are "possibly true" though even in that case he was not prepared to "accept the particular theory of their origin current at Lourdes" (see page 167).

Be that as it may, these surprising phenomena at least deserve, as Haldane concedes, to be invesitgated. The cure of a suppurating wound is certainly a "sense experience". It is claimed that these facts have been verified by competent scientific observers. The evidence for them is certainly infinitely stronger than the evidence for the evolution of a land mammal into a whale.

You may or may not accept the hypothesis that these phenomena are due to the direct agency of God, but the proposition that they are cannot be dismissed as meaningless by a *logical* "logical positivist" for the evidence in support of that proposition is based on sense experience in the familiar world.

Again the Christian thesis that national apostasy always entails tragic consequences is a proposition which has been verified by the terrible "sense experiences" of those who have had the misfortune to live in countries dominated by dictators who are atheistic or, as in the case of Hitler, implicitly atheistic. Russia is the first European country formally to adopt an atheistic philosophy as the state philosophy, and the Christian explanation of the consequences of that apostasy are certainly "meaningful".

(IV)

"The only way to get rid of temptations," said Oscar Wilde, "is to yield to them", and those who are anxious to anaesthetise their consciences will welcome the assistance of logical positivism, a congenial philosophy for those who wish to "rationalise" their repudiation of the traditional morality of the west. I agree with Dr. Unger that Professor Ayer's originality consists in the fact that no philosopher has been more "outspoken in his denial of the possibility of any moral knowledge."

According to him all moral concepts, such as good, bad, virtuous, wicked, reliable, treacherous, etc., in so far as they imply that one ought or ought not to behave in a certain way, are pseudo-concepts. The practice of virtue is difficult even if one believes in Kant's categorical imperative, still more difficult if one holds that it is nonsensical to say that one way of life is morally better than another, or that there is any moral obligation to prefer self-discipline to self-indulgence. It is indeed "meaningful" that such a doctrine should be preached by a man holding a chair of philosophy at a leading university.

The late Professor Collingwood of Oxford clarified the implications of logical positivism in a memorable passage. "Since," he writes, "one must not seek it (guidance) from thinkers or from thinking, from ideals or from principles, one must look to people who were not thinkers (but fools), to processes that were not thinking (but passion), to aims that were not ideals (but caprices), and to rules that were not principles (but rules of expediency). If philosophers had wanted to train up a generation of Englishmen and Englishwomen expressly as the potential dupes of every adventurer in morals or politics, commerce or religion, who should appeal to their emotions and promise them private gains which he neither could procure them nor even meant to procure them, no better way of doing it could have been discovered."

Perhaps the only significant thing about these modern attacks on significance is the light-hearted fashion with which people accept and positively welcome these philosophies which undermine all standards of value and which rob the universe of all meaning. Even if the universe were meaningless why should people be so pleased about its absence of meaning. Why this "ton de voix fier et content" to quote Pascal's query about the proud and happy voice in which contemporary anti-rationalists announced that "the soul is nothing but a puff of wind and smoke."

Among the prophets and disciples of logical positivism there may be men of the most austere and ascetic lives, but the anti-rationalists certainly make many recruits from those who are too weak to support the exacting demands of reason. If the only *meaning* of life is to be found in self-discipline and self-conquest the denial of meaning is a consolation of sorts for those who have failed to give significance to their own lives.

CHAPTER XXI

POSTSCRIPT

AMONG the many causes of the present distress not the least important is the lack of interest in philosophy.

Had the statesmen of Europe realised the importance of philosophy they would have recognised the inevitable consequences of nazi nihilism and would have taken the necessary steps which would have averted the second World War. Had the representatives of the west understood the implications of Marxism they would at least have avoided the supreme folly of failing to secure a land access to Berlin.

The pre-occupation of secular sociologists with political considerations is the principle cause of the catastrophic blunders which gave Hitler and Stalin opportunities for evil of which they availed themselves to the full. The destruction of democracy in Germany by the Nazis and of Kerensky's experiment in democracy by the Bolsheviks is not the primary cause of European distress. The horrors of Marxism and communism are the consequences not so much of political but of philosophic errors. Lenin substituted the worship of the proletariat for the worship of God, Hitler the worship of the German race for the worship of Christ. In no country is the proletariat more enslaved than in Russia and no race has suffered a more tragic humiliation than the German. The Babylonian captivity was God's punishment for the apostacy of Israelites but the sufferings of the Israelites were less than those endured by the Germans and the Russians under the yoke of atheistic Marxists.

I grew up in that climate of Victorian England in which it was assumed that men would continue to behave like Christians long after they had ceased to believe like Christians. Religion was useful as an instrument of personal sanctification, but the prosperity of the state depended not on the philosophy dominant among her rulers but on their attitude to secular issues such as Free Trade or compulsory education. Even among convinced and devout Christians it was only a minority who, like Newman,

yielded a real and not a purely notional assent to the belief that
the gradual dechristianisation of England would inevitably
bring in its train disasters in the temporal sphere. Few of Newman's contemporaries really believed that the prosperity of
Victorian England was an ephemeral phenomenon. Nothing
could look more secure than the Empire on which the sun never
set. Fewer still realised that the revolt against God would find
expression in a revolt against reason, a revolt against holiness
and a revolt against beauty.

History bears witness to the fact that the transition from a
religious to a sceptical philosophy has never yet failed to spell
disaster, but there is no lesson which mankind seems more
reluctant to learn from the past. Even to-day when the consequences of apostasy in Germany and in Russia are patent to
all but mental defectives, our political physicians are, in the
main, pre-occupied with secular remedies. More socialism, or
more private enterprise, Western Union, and so forth. I do not
wish to belittle the importance of politics or the usefulness of
some of the proposed remedies for what is primarily a spiritual
malady. In Germany to-day far more effort should be made to
enlist the active support of the Catholic and Protestant leaders
whereas in point of fact we are acting on the assumption that the
only people really worth backing are the Socialists who would
be transformed overnight into National Socialists if a new Hitler
arose.

Even those political commentators, who are beginning to
realise that Europe cannot be saved by secular remedies alone,
often write as if Christianity were on trial, and as if Christianity
would be judged by the degree to which it conforms to the
policy of a particular political party, and not as if political
parties should be judged by the degree to which their policy
conforms to Christian principles.

"I am a keen supporter of the Labour Party," a gifted Anglican parson recently remarked to me, "but it is not only for
political reasons that I was delighted by their victory in 1945.
So long as the Tories were in control the Tories were a useful
scapegoat. They could be blamed for all our troubles. Now that
Labour has come into power even Trade Unionists are beginning to suspect that socialism is not the final cure for our
troubles." An unconscious echo perhaps of Aristotle's "The

evils of which men complain are not due to the rejection of communism but to the wickedness of man."

The great Victorian sceptics were living on the declining capital of the creed which they rejected.

> There was an old man of Moldavia
> Who did not believe in his Saviour
> But erected instead
> With himself as the head
> The religion of decorous behaviour.

That particular religion is certainly declining. In the final analysis the irrational does not survive. If "decorous behaviour" is robbed of all rational foundation, decorous behaviour will disappear, and the creed of the moral agnostic is replaced by the creed of the logical positivist for whom "stealing is wrong" is a statement as meaningless as "stealing is money".

"The highwaymen," said Horace Walpole, "have become so tame that they even come into our houses". Their successors are displaying a similar tameness to-day.

Is there any hope of arresting the dechristianisation of England and the consequences of that dechristianisation which are already becoming only too apparent? The sentence which I have quoted from Walpole was written in the trough of a religious decline from which England was rescued by Methodism and the Oxford Movement. Are there any signs of similar revival to-day? Is there any evidence of a return to reason? The best that can be said is that the intellectual movement of our times is preparing the ground for such a revival. It takes about twenty years for a philosophic revolution to make a great impression on the educated classes and three score years and ten for its influence to reach the uneducated. The man in the street to-day has heard of Darwin but will not hear of Eddington and Noüy for another half century. Scientific materialism is still powerfully entrenched among those scientists who have had no training in abstract thought, but among scientists with some understanding of metaphysics, scientism is a spent force. The results of this revolution, however, will probably not reach the uneducated until the end of the century. Meanwhile the more thoughtful of the younger generation are aware of the fact that materialism is bankrupt and that atheistic Marxism has proved to be the most tragic experiment in the history of mankind.

Those who once found in Marxism a substitute for religion are disillusioned and unanchored. The collapse of scientism and Marxism has therefore created a vacuum, and this vacuum provides Christians with a magnificent opportunity. If the past be any guide to the future it is an opportunity which Christians will fail to take and if so, the pattern of Israel will be reproduced in modern Europe and something worse than a Babylonian captivity will be our fate, for I doubt if a secularised Europe can indefinitely hold at bay the forward march of Asia which Christian Europe arrested again and again. Kierkegaard said that one day Christianity would be taken away from Europe as the only method of forcing Europeans to understand the magnitude of their debt to Christianity. But I am sanguine enough to hope that Hilaire Belloc may prove to be the better prophet, and with his prediction I am inclined to agree.

"Our Europe cannot perish. Her religion which is also mine has within it victorious energies of defence which are the prime condition of her establishment. . . . The soul of her is a certain spirit at once reasonable and chivalrous and against that spirit the gales of hell will not prevail."

Whether Kierkegaard's prediction comes true depends both on spiritual and material factors. Europe in the past has been saved not only by the prayers but also by the swords of Christian men. In the material sphere it is American support which alone prevents Russia overrunning Europe, but in the final analysis Europe cannot be saved by material factors alone. Europe must recover her soul and not only her soul but her mind. If the anti-rationalists are not dethroned Europe will be lost. Europe must return to the Logos or perish, and the return to reason implies a return to God, for as Pascal insists there are only two sorts of people whom one can call reasonable: those who serve God with all their heart because they know him, and those who search for him with all their heart because they know him not.

IL N'Y QUE DEUX SORTES DE PERSONNE QU'ON PUISSE APPELER RAISONNABLES, OU CEUX QUI SERVENT DIEU DE TOUT LEUR COEUR, PARCE QU'ILS LE CONNAISSENT OU CEUX QUI LE CHERCHENT DE TOUT LEUR COEUR, PARCE QUI'LS NE LE CONNAISSENT PAS.

NOTES

Chapter V

ANGELS ON A NEEDLE-POINT

Many years ago the great positivist, Frederic Harrison, wrote:
"Of all the epochs of effort after a new life, that of the age of
Aquinas, Roger Bacon, St. Francis, St. Louis, Giotto, and Dante, is
the most purely spiritual, the most really constructive and, indeed,
the most truly philosophic."

The proportion of educated people who would agree with Mr.
Harrison is far greater to-day than it was when he was alive, for the
prestige of mediaeval thought has increased in recent years. But there
are still people whose interest in the culture of Europe ends with
Virgil and only picks up the dropped threads again somewhere about
the Renaissance.

My friend Cyril Joad, for instance, took a First in that school of
"more humane letters" at Oxford which is called "more humane"
because it ignored mediaeval philosophy. And it is therefore not surprising that, though Joad has written one of the best guides to
modern philosophy, he cheerfully announced on the Brains Trust in
1941 that:

"In the Middle Ages, most people believed, indeed it was an
article of faith, that a certain number of angels could dance on the
point of a pin, and the great question was as to how many there
should be. That was faith in the Middle Ages."

The first person to attribute this thesis to St. Thomas Aquinas was
Isaac D'Israeli, father of the great Prime Minister, in his *Curiosities
of Literature*. Brewer, of *Phrase and Fable* fame, contributed his own
variety of "phrase and fable" by deriving St. Thomas' title of *Angelic
Doctor* from the fact that he had "*discussed the knotty point of how many
angels can dance on the point of a needle*." On the other hand, Brewer, as
Father Brodrick points out, had scruples which did not trouble
D'Israeli. He did at least have the grace to add that what St.
Thomas in fact discussed was "*more strictly speaking, Utrum angelus
possit moveri de extremo ad extremum non transeundo per medium?*" "Now
the 'more strictly speaking' of this emendation," adds Father Brodrick, "is a joyful thing, for it is as though one were to say: 'The man
had red hair, or, more strictly speaking, his wife was wearing a new
hat'."

W. S. Scott, the distinguished Shelley scholar, in the introduction
to his excellent selection from Donne is guilty of the same attribution.

As the last two books which were sent to me for review contained
references to the needle-dancing angels, I felt that the time had come
to track this rubbish to its source. None of the learned Dominicans at
Blackfriars, where I was spending the weekend, could give me any

precise reference to scholastic writings in which this thesis, in however different a form, had been discussed. The Bellarmine Society, which specialises in this type of research, referred me to an excellent article by Father James Brodrick, s.j., in *The Tablet* of October 10th, 1942. He writes:

"In 1890, *Notes and Queries*, that national chastener of all who Talk at Random, resumed earlier inquiries into the history of the conceit, and managed to trace angels and needles back to the year 1638, when William Chillingworth published his famous *Religion of Protestants*. A Jesuit had cast aspersions on the learning of the Anglican divines, which rankled with William because he was of that fraternity himself, though somewhat shaky on the point of Sabbatical worship. He retorted scornfully that men might be learned even though they 'dispute not eternally . . . whether a million of angels may not sit upon a needle's point.' Despite the new position of the angels, this is plainly the same old story. Chillingworth links it with the really clever and amusing *Chimera bombinans in vacuo*, and certainly the two conceits had a similar origin, not in the speculations of any Catholic theologian, but in the brain of some smart humanist or reformer who wanted to make scholasticism look ridiculous. It was the same ingenious propagandists who succeeded in converting the venerated name of Duns Scotus, 'of reality the rarest-veined unraveller,' into a synonym for a blockhead."

The angel-needle thesis, if in fact it was ever debated, was almost certainly a debating exercise to sharpen the wits of pupils. Angels, it was believed, were pure intelligences not material, but limited, so that they could have location in space but not extension; rather like a point which in theory has position but no magnitude. Thus an angel could not *occupy* space—i.e. a needle point—but could be *located on* a needle point.

Miss Dorothy Sayers, in a brilliant article ("The Lost Tools of Learning," *Hibbert Journal*, October 1947), remarks that Dr. Joad's answer reduced the late Charles Williams to "helpless rage" and illustrates this mediaeval thesis by a useful analogy. An unlimited amount of people might concentrate their thoughts on the point of a needle and their thoughts would be *"there"* in the sense that they would be nowhere else, but though *"there"* their thoughts would occupy no space and therefore an unlimited number of thoughts might dance upon the point of a needle. The practical lesson to be drawn from what she writes is not to use words like "there" in a loose and unscientific way without specifying whether you mean "located there" or "occupying space there". She adds, "Scorn in plenty has been poured upon the mediaeval passion for hair-splitting, but when we look at the shameless abuse made in print and on the platform of controversial experiences with shifting and ambiguous connotation, we may feel it in our hearts to wish that every reader and hearer had been so defensively armoured by his education as to be able to cry *Distinguo*."

Miss Sayers writes to me that she has never been able to find any authoritative source for this problem about the angels and the needle. She states: "I have always heard it referred to as a problem debated in the schools; but I should not be surprised to find that the precise terms of it were formulated by some scoffer who wanted to put across a nasty crack at the Schoolmen. But, regarded as a problem about locality and space and the nature of angelic substance, it is a perfectly sensible debating subject."

Chapter VII

THE INEXPLICABLE BLASPHEMY

This is to be found in Luther's *Table-Talk* (Weimar edition, vol. ii, page 107). Pierre Bayle in the seventeenth century regretted that they had been published, for this eminent Huguenot was disgusted by the coarser passages, but he never dreamt of denying their authenticity. The reporters had taken them down, practically under the dictation of the Reformer, and in all cases while he was speaking. Sometimes we have the same words reported by two or three different reporters, and where this is the case the wordings agree.

Wiener quoted a passage from the *Table-Talk* in which Luther states that Christ committed adultery three times, first with the woman at the well, secondly with Mary Magdalene, and thirdly with the woman taken in adultery, "whom he let off so lightly. Thus even Christ who was so holy had to commit adultery before he died."

The Weimar edition which I consulted had been in the London Library for forty years. The second volume, in which this passage is to be found, was *uncut*. Here is the original:—

"*Christus adulter. Christus ist am ersten ein ebrecher worden Joh. 4, bei dem brunn cum muliere, quia illi dicebant: Nemo significat, quid facit cum ea? Item cum Magdalena, item cum adultera Joan. 8, die er so leicht dauon lies. Also mus der from Christus auch am ersten ein ebrecher werden ehe er starb.*"

This terrible passage raises many problems.

First. Can these words be interpreted mystically? Did Luther only *mean* that Christ takes our sins upon him? This is certainly not what he *said*. There is a whole universe separating the conception of a Christ who *suffers for* our sins and a Christ who *commits* our sins. Moreover, the mystical interpretation is quite inconsistent with the filthy suggestion that the disciples did not ask indiscreet questions when they found Christ with the loose woman at the well, or with the implication that Christ spared the woman taken in adultery because he was her partner in this sin.

Secondly. Was Luther correctly reported? Probably, for no editor who was not mentally defective could include such a passage unless he was convinced that it was genuine.

Thirdly. Did this represent Luther's considered opinion? Certainly not. It may be that he made this statement when he was excited by wine. The rather incoherent mixture of Latin and German would be explicable on this theory.

Fourthly. Why was this passage not suppressed by the editor? I have no clue to this mystery. The fact that it was not suppressed is clear evidence of the collapse of standards under the influence of Luther. You have only to ask yourself whether such a horror could have been included in the table-talk of a devout Catholic such as St. Thomas More to realise the effect of the Lutheran "Reformation".

Fifthly. Why have so few people ever heard of this passage? Neither Catholics nor Lutherans minced their words in the controversies which divided Germany, but even Denifle seems to have felt that this passage was too terrible to quote. And it is for this reason that I have relegated it to an appendix. I could not omit it altogether for it has great relevance to the theme of this book, that the revolt against Reason leads to a collapse of all standards, standards of taste no less than standards of truth and standards of morality.

Luther's coarseness. "Was soll man sagen, wenn Luther schon in Jahre 1521 die Ehe ein 'besch . . . Sakrament nenn'." "What can one say when Luther already in the year 1521 describes marriage as a '—— Sacrament'?" (The word which Denifle indicates without printing in full belongs to the vocabulary of the lavatory.) Denifle, i, 819.

Here are further examples of Luther's lavatory invective.

"Mit den Worten des Amsdort will er antworten: 'ich sch . . . dem Legaten and seinem Herrn in seine Dispensation Enders viii, 53, 113. Dass der Papst und Legat in A . . . wollten lecken" Enders viii, 2333. And perhaps even more revolting is the coarseness with which he speaks of the Child Jesus, "Als Kind sch . . . t und p . . . er 363" Denifle i, 819. The Lutheran cartoons reproduced by Denifle are as disgusting in their lavatory themes as the text.

TRIBUTE TO DENIFLE

Professor Kawear, a German Lutheran, in a critical review which appeared in *Theol. Studien und Kritiken* 1904, pays a great tribute to Denifle's unrivalled knowledge (*unvergleichlicher Kenntnis*) of mediaeval literature, and the great services which he had rendered to Lutheran research by identifying in his writings a large number of quotations from St. Augustine, Beda, Bernhard, the Breviary, etc. Another Lutheran Professor, Köhler, concedes that Denifle had some justification for his reiterated accusation that the Lutherans did not know their Middle Ages, "herein lies Denifle's strength and the weakness of the Lutheran research so far."

Chapter X

THE MATHEMATICAL REFUTATION OF MECHANISTIC EVOLUTION

Dr. du Noüy, an internationally known French scientist, was the first of an artistic family to be attracted to science. His original work while head of the laboratory staff of a war hospital brought him to the attention of the Rockefeller Institute in New York. Indeed, he had succeeded in solving a problem which had baffled physiologists for a long time—namely, the mathematical expression of the process of healing of wounds. Dr. du Noüy invented and devised for his work an instrument which enabled him to measure, for the first time, the three dimensions of certain molecules and to publish a direct determination of one of the fundamental constants of physical chemistry. The instrument which made this possible (Surface Tension Balance) received an award from the Franklin Institute of Philadelphia in 1923.

Dr. du Noüy has also been awarded a prize by the French Academy and by the University of Lausanne. The main argument of Dr. du Noüy's book *Human Destiny* (Longmans) is that the laws of chance are fatal to the hypothesis of materialistic evolution (Dr. du Noüy accepts evolution though he is aware of the immense difficulties of this theory). Dr. du Noüy does not write as the apologist of any particular communion and his remarks on institutional religion are neither as profound nor as original as he seems to suppose. Indeed, his book illustrates the peril of taking one's analogies from activities of which the writer has no personal experience, mountaineering for instance.

"No matter what our religion," he writes, "we are all like people at the bottom of a valley who seek to climb a snowy peak that dominates all others. We all have our eyes fixed on the same goal, and we agree that there is but one summit to reach. Unfortunately, we differ on what road to take. But all these different parties," he adds, "know that some day provided that they never stop ascending they must all meet at the top of the mountain and that the road to reach it matters little."

It is not true that mountaineers invariably reach the summit provided that they do not stop ascending or that the route chosen is a matter of indifference. A climber who is well guided stands a thousand-to-one chance of reaching the summit of the Eiger and returning safely provided that he follows the normal route, but more than half the guideless climbers who attempted the North face, the most difficult and dangerous ascent in the Alps did not reach the summit and perished on the mountain. The convinced supporter of any form of institutional religion could turn du Noüy's analogy against him and reply: "Climbers who are naturally expert do not need guides and can try fancy routes. Men who are naturally good will reach heaven however odd and dangerous the route they follow, but ordinary folk would perhaps do best to choose a good guide and stick to the safest route."

The main thesis of this remarkable book is that the laws of chance are fatal to the materialistic hypothesis. The main argument is based on the index of dissymmetry. If ten white and ten black balls were placed in a tube which could only admit one ball at a time, and if the white and black balls alternated, the degree of dissymmetry would be said to be be 0.5. If on the other hand the ten white balls were altogether in the bottom of the tube and the ten black balls altogether in the top of the tubes the degree of dissymmetry would be expressed by number 1. 1 corresponds to maximum dissymmetry and 0.5 to perfect homogenity. A universe large enough to render it probable that a single living molecule should appear possessing the degree of dissymmetry found in *all* living molecules would be one sextillion, sextillion, sextillion times greater than Einstein's estimate of our universe. The chances are, therefore, one followed by 321 noughts to one against the appearance of a single molecule with the degree of dissymmetry found in all living molecules. That is the odds against the spontaneous generation of life in the form of one living molecule but one such molecule would be of no use. Hundreds of millions of identical ones would be necessary.

REFERENCES

THE reader should have no difficulty in tracing a reference in this book if he will note the following:—

1. *Italicised words* mark the *beginning* of a reference, and phrases which would normally be italicised, i.e. op. cit. are *not* italicised. Confining italics to the key word which places a quotation facilitates reference. This key word is usually the name of the author quoted, but sometimes the first words of the quotation are italicised.

2. Where the *title* of the book is given in the text, only the author's name is given in the key word reference.

3. *Book titles* are indicated by single quotation marks, quotations proper by double quotation marks.

4. Where an author is quoted more than once in the same *section* of a chapter, all the references are grouped together. Otherwise references are given in the order in which they appear in the text.

5. General Abbreviations:—Q.B.=quoted by. Op. cit. refers to a book quoted in the text or in an earlier chapter.

6. *Missing references.* References are given for about 90% of the passages quoted in this book. Twenty years ago I did not realise as I do now the importance of references, and some of the passages which I quoted in earlier books and now requote were not identified by references and I have had to read so many new books to bring the subject up to date that I could not afford the time to re-read the books quoted without references in *The Flight from Reason.*

CHAPTER I (In Search of Definitions)
(1) *Trench:* 'England Past and Present'. *Whewall* Q.B. Trench.
(2) *St. Augustine:* 'Confessions' I. 1. *Hughes:* 'History of the Church' III. 113. *Gerson* Q.B. Hughes op. cit. "*Where there is* . . ." Q.B. Hughes.

CHAPTER II (The Birth of Rationalism)
"*Come now*" Isaiah I. 18. "*Nihil quod* "Cicero quoting Zeno: 'De Natura Deorum' II. 8, II. 37. *Dawson:* 'Rationalism and Intellectualism' in the book 'Enquiries'.

CHAPTER III (The Uncertain Frontier)
(1) *Brunner:* 'Revelation and Reason'. *Kierkegaard* Q.B. Brunner.
(3) *Illa Ipsa:* Apol. 50. *Et ipse statim:* Ad Scap., 5. *Harnack:* 'Dogmengeschichte' III. 97. *St. Augustine:* Letter to Consentius, n. 3, 8, etc. *Portalié:* 'Catholic Encyclopaedia' II. 104.
(4) *Gilson:* 'Etudes de Philsophie Médiévale' 79, 96, 29.

237

CHAPTER IV (The Ultimate Heresy)

Aquinas: 'De unit. intell.' c. VII. *Luther:* 'Disputationen' 487. Disputatiorem a.a. o. Thesen 1–3. *Tyrell:* 'Lex Orandi' 161. *Inge:* 'Outspoken Essays' 109.

CHAPTER V (The Age of Reason)

(1) *Taylor:* 'The Medieval Mind'. *Aquinas:* 'Sum. Theol.' I. 32, i. ad Resp. *Gilson:* op. cit. 114, 119, 124.

(2) *D'Arcy:* 'St. Thomas Aquinas'. *Adams:* 'Mont St. Michel and Chartres' 287. *Whitehead:* 'Science and the Modern World'. *Hughes:* 'History of the Church' III. 15.

(3) *"I could not bear"* quoted in the 'Life of Dr. Arnold'. *Whitehead* op. cit.

CHAPTER VI (Reason Dethroned)

(1) *Rupp:* 'Martin Luther—Hitler's Cause or Cure?' 15, 32. *Wiener:* op. cit. 37.

(2) *"Ratio est"* Disp. 814. *"Man is especially . . ."* Comment. on John I. 4. W.A. 46, 532. Weinar XL P.I. 363, 25. *"Does Reason shed"* Q.B. Maritain in 'Three Reformers' 32. *"God only gave"* Erl 49, 229 (1538). *"But in spiritual"* Ebdf. 45, 336; 47, 128 ff., 51, 400 f. *"Reason is the Devil's whore"* Ebdf. 29, 241, 16, 142, 144, Erl 16, 145, 148. *"It pertains"* Disp. Ed. Drews 42. *"It is impossible"* Erl 44, 158 (1537–1540). *"Reason is contrary"* Disp. Ed. Drews 42. Erl.

(3) *"The Sorbonne"* Disp. 487. *"Impossible and absurd in philosophy"* Disp. a.a., O. Thesen 1–3. *Tyrell:* 'Lex Orandi' 161.

(4) *"Nothing can cure"* Opp. exeg. lat., I, 212, 26–27, 29–30 (1536) Weim XLII 8–10. *"God condemns us all"* Weim XVI von Nov. 5, 1525. *"There is only one moment"* De Wette II. 640. *"Blessed robber"* Weim XI. 394 f. *Rupp* 22. *Denifle:* 'Luther und Lutherthuum. Zweite, durchgearbeite Auflage. Ergänzt und herausgegeben von P. Albert Maria Weiss. O.F. Mainz, 1906. ii, 18, 19, 20, 22, 23, 94, *"One may find"* Erl 20, 72. *St. Thomas More:* 'Dialogue concerning Tyndale' Book IV. Chapter II. *"When were there"* Enders V. 289. *Coulton:* 'Is the Catholic Church Anti-Social?' 227.

(5) *"Si pecca"* Enders III. 208. *"Whenever the devil"* Enders VIII. 159. *"You owe God"* Weim XII. 131. *"He who believes"* Erl 11, 60, 218. *"It is not forbidden"* Weim XXIV. 305. See also Enders IV. 283, and Denifle i. 294. For *Luther on the effect of the Reformation* Enders III. 323, Erl 36, 411, Erl 1, 192, Erl 1, 14, 17, 255. *Denifle* ii 23. *Luther* Erl 8, 294. *Kettenbach:* Q.B. Denifle ii. 23) from N. Paulus, Kaspar Schatzgeyer (1898) 56, Anm I. *Günzburg.* Q.B. Denifle from Riggenbach, John. Eberlin v Günzburg (1874) p. 242. *Pirkheimer* Q.B. Denifle ii. 19. "They exchange the abuse". Luther's Sprichwörtersammlung, Q.P. Denifle i. 19. p. 24, 410.

CHAPTER VII (The Pedigree of Modern Science)

(1) *Ruskin:* 'Modern Painters' IV, 7, 6, *Sullivan:* 'The Limitations of Science'. *Singer:* 'Science, Religion and Reality'.

(2) *Aristotle:* 'Prior Analytics' I. 30. 'De Gen. et Corr.' I. 2. Q.B. Sir Edmund Whittaker: 'Space and Spirit' 27.

(3) *"incentives to piety"* 'Plea of Athenagoras for the Christians' XVI. The date of the work is about 177. Q.B. Whittaker. *"The Stoics more than . . ."* Whittaker 11. *Augustine:* 'Confessions' VII, 'City of God' X. *Whittaker:* 15.

(4) *H. O. Taylor:* 'The Medieval Mind' II. 538. *Sullivan:* 'The Limitations of Science'. *Whitehead:* 'Science and the Modern World' (Penguin edition) 23. *Spengler:* 'The Decline of the West' I. 293. *Norwood:* 'London Mercury' VII. 296. *Haldane:* 'Science and the Supernatural' 41. *Joad:* 'Is Christianity True?' 213. *Whitehead:* op. cit. 12.

CHAPTER VIII (The Age of Naive Faith)
(1) *Herschel, Spencer* Q.B. Inge: 'Outspoken Essays', second series 163. *Belloc:* 'The Cruise of the Nona'. *Balfour:* 'The Foundations of Belief'. Leo XII. Revum Novarum.

(2) *Richet:* 'Thirty Years of Psychical Research'. *Haldane:* 'Science and the Supernatural' 247, 359. *Inge:* Contribution to Symposium 'What Life has Taught Me' 68.

CHAPTER IX (Theophobia)
(1) *Broca* Q.B. R. C. Macfie in 'The Theology of Evolution'. *Sabatier* ditto.

(2) *Delage:* 'L'Heredité et les grandes problèmes de la biologie générale' 204, 322. *Weissmann:* 'The Contemporary Review' Sept. 19. 1893, 328. 'Essays' (Poulton's translation) 347. *Noüy:* op. cit. 72. *Huxley:* 'Life and Letters'. *Watson:* 'Nature' Aug. 10, 1929. *Shelton:* 'Is Evolution Proved?' 114, 122, 125.

(4) *Dwight:* 'Thoughts of a Catholic Anatomist' 20. *Osborn:* 'The Story of Earth and Man' (1898), 317. *Clark:* 'Origin and Evolution of Life', Preface, 9. *Scott:* 'Nature', Sept. 1921, 154. *Morgan:* 'Evolution and Adaptation' (1903) 43. *Spengler:* 'The Decline of the West' II. 311.

CHAPTER X (The Essence of Darwinism)
Butler Luck or Cunning. *Milum:* 'Evolution and the Spirit of Man'. The quotations at the end of the chater on taken from R. C. Macfie, "The Theory of Evolution p. 301. The quotations from T. S. Haldane are from his book 'The Philosophic Basis of Biology' p.p. 12 and 130.

CHAPTER XI (Darwinism and Evolution)
Dwight: 'Thoughts of a Catholic Anatomist' 6. *Keith:* 'Darwinism and its Critics'. *Haldane:* 'Science and the Supernatural' 132. *Noüy:* 'Human Destiny' 37, 61. *Blyton:* 'The Modern Adventure'. *Berg:* 'Nomogenesis'. *Macfie:* 'The Theology of Evolution'. *Dewar:* 'Is Evolution Proved?' 165. *Shelton:* ditto, 33. *Dewar:* 44, 241, 120, 178. *Berg:* 'Nomogenesis'. *Kellog:* 'Darwinism To-day'.

CHAPTER XII (The Case for Evolution)
Shelton: op. cit. 155. Noüy: 'Human Destiny'. Dewar: op. cit. 58.
Shelton: 140. De Beer: 'Embryology and Evolution'. Dewar: 223.
Wassman: 'The Problem of Evolution' 15.

CHAPTER XIII (Scientism the Enemy of Reason)
Chesterton: 'The Everlasting Man' 41. Shelton: op. cit. 29.
Darwin Voyage of the Adventure and Beagle iii.3 73. Butler 'Luck or Cunning' 101.

CHAPTER XIV (The Propaganda of Scientism)
(1) Lewis: op. cit. 38, 39.
(2) Dwight: op. cit. 20. Carrel: 'Man the Unknown' 144.

CHAPTER XV ("Sit down before Fact")
(2) Richet: 'Thirty Years of Psychical Research'.
(6) Haldane: 'Science and the Supernatural' 13. Carrell: 'Man the Unknown' 148, footnote 149.
    The facts are given in 'Lourdes. A History of its Apparitions and Cures' (Kegan Paul, Trench, Trubner and Co., Ltd.) by Georges Bertrin. The standard book on the medical aspect of the Lourdes cures is 'Medical Proof of the Miraculous' by E. Le Bec, Honorary Surgeon to St. Joseph's Hospital, Paris, former President of the Bureau des Constatations, Lourdes. An English translation by Dom H. E. Izard, O.S.B., was published by Harding and More, Ltd. The Catholic Truth Society publishes two booklets, 'The Miracles at Lourdes' and 'A Modern Miracle', obtainable from the C.T.S., 28, Ashley Place, London, S.W.1.

CHAPTER XVII (The Suicide of Thought)
(1) Carrel: 'Man the Unknown' 135. Spengler: 'Der Untergang des Abendlandes' first edition II. 415. II. 19. 'The Decline of the West' II. 340. II. 17. Keyserling: 20. Thou shalt love, Mark XII. 30. Lawrence Q.B. Hugh Kingsmill in 'D. H. Lawrence'.
(2) Laski: 'The Rise of European Liberalism' 20. St. Peter: I. III. 15.
(3) James: 'The Varieties of Religious Experience'. 11.
(4) A. G. Tansley: 'The New Psychology and its Relation to Life'. Joad: 'Under the Fifth Rib'. Chesterton: Orthodoxy. 53. Haldane: 'Science and the Supernatural' 34, 250.

CHAPTER XVIII (The Conflict between Science and Atheism).
(1) Coulton: 'Is the Catholic Church Anti-Social?' 79.
(2) Vavilov Q.B. Preev (see above). "We serve the German Way". These quotations are from p. 628, W. M. McGovern: 'From Hitler to Luther'.

(3) *Pasvolsky:* 'The Intelligentsia under the Soviets', 'Atlantic Monthly', Nov. 1920. *Chamberlin:* op. cit. 296. *Serge:* op. cit. 53. *Lyons:* 'Assignment in Utopia' 348, 468.

(4) *Carrit:* 'The Labour Monthly', June 1933. *Yaroslavsky:* 'Red Virtue' 125. *Lenin:* 'Third All-Russian Congress of Y.C.L.', Oct. 1920. *Alexandrov* and *Zhadov*, see above.

CHAPTER XIX (The New Iconoclasts). The Unquiet Grave. 26.
(1) *Read:* 'Surrealism' 40, 81, 37. *Palinurus:* 26. *Bader:* 'Weltwoche, Zürich'. *Norwood:* 'London Mercury' VII. 596.
(2) *Gertrude Stein:* Q.B. Lord Elton in 'St. George or the Dragon' 41.
(3) *Read* 90, 45, 90. *Engels* Q.B. by Schwarzched: 'The Red Prussian' letter, March. 2, 1852. *Kurt London* 'The Seven Soviet Arts' 361. *Olesha* Q.B. London, 81. *Nikritin* Q.B. London 228. *Stelling:* 'The Nineteenth Century' Aug. 1948, 109.
(4) *Carrel:* 130. *Read* 52. *Orwell:* 'Critical Essays' 128.
(6) *Read:* 'Surrealism' 52. *Carrel:* 'Man the Unknown' 143. *Priestley* Q.B. Read 84.

CHAPTER XX (The Revolt against Meaning)
Joad: 'The New Statesman' July 31st, 1948. *Ayer:* op. cit. 107. The Claims of Philosophy (Polemic no. 7, op. cit. (second edition 115). *Wittgenstein:* 'Tractatus Logico-Philosophicus' 6, 42. *Junger:* 'The Nineteenth Century' Aug. 1948, 85. *Collingwood:* Q.B. Joad.

INDEX

INDEX

A

Abelard, Peter, 33.
Abolition of Man, The, 144.
Acts, The, 29
Acworth, Bernard, 153–154.
Adams, Henry, 41.
Adler, Dr. Mortimer, 49.
Aesthetic criterion, 72–73, 159.
Agassiz, 152.
Age of Naive Faith, 83–93.
Albert the Great, 40, 75.
Alice in Wonderland, 213.
Amateurs versus specialists, 150–155.
Angels on pin point, 230.
Anglicanism, 11, 18, 51.
Angry Penguins, 218–225.
Antinomians, 19.
Anti-Semitism, 51.
Apologetics, development of Christian, 21–34, 40–50. See also Scholasticism.
Apriorists defined, 68.
Archaeopteryx, 126–127.
Aristotle, 23, 36, 37, 71–74, 178.
Arnold, Mathew, 49.
Arnold, Thomas, 47.
Arp, Hans, 206.
Arrival of the fittest, 113.
Artificial Selection, 129.
Assignment in Utopia, 200.
d'Autrecourt condemned, 31.
Averroes, 36.
Ayer, Professor A. J., 218–224.

B

Babylonian science, 70.
Bacon, Lord, 2.
Bacon, Roger, 75–77.

Badt, Kurt, 205.
Balfour, Lord, 86.
Barnes, Bishop, 92.
Barth, Professor Karl, 66.
Bateson, Professor, 111.
Bautain, Professor, 3.
Beauty, origin of sense, 119.
Beghards, 19–20.
Behaviourism, 173, 174–175, 193–195.
Bellarmine, Cardinal, 82.
Belloc, Hilaire, on truth, 86, on Europe, 229.
Berg, 111, 115, 122.
Bias, influence of, 148–150.
Bible, authority of, 50.
Blackfriars, 102.
Blyton, W. J., 115.
Bodkin, Thomas, 216.
Böhler, Peter, 65.
Bois, Reymond du, 98.
Braband, Siger de, 4.
Bradley, Professor, 32.
Brodrick, Father James, 231.
Brunner, Dr. Emil, 27.
Broca, P., 95.
Bruno, 18.
Buffon, 108.
Bukharin, 95.
Burton, Father, 128.
Butler, Samuel, 110, 113, 142, 150, 152, 153.

C

Cambrian period, 122.
Campione, 207.
Carrel, Dr. Alexis, on miracles, 147–148, 167. On moral beauty, 210. On sex, 215. On pure intellectuals, 183.